D1222731

大中华文库

LIBRARY

OF CHINESE CLASSICS

汉英对照

大中华文库

Library of Chinese Classics

(Chinese-English)

论 语

THE ANALECTS

韦 利 英译

杨伯峻 今译

Translated into English by Arthur Waley

Translated into Modern Chinese by Yang Bojun

湖南人民出版社

Hunan People's Publishing House

外文出版社

Foreign Languages Press

First Edition 1999

ISBN 7-5438-2088-9/B • 49

Published by

Hunan People's Publishing House

78 Yin Pen South Road, Changsha 410006, Hunan, China

Foreign Languages Press

24 Baiwanzhuang Road, Beijing 100037, China

http: // www. flp. com. cn

Printed by

Donnelley Bright Sun Printing Co., Shenzhen, China

Printed in the People's Republic of China

总　　序

《大中华文库》终于出版了。我们为之高兴，为之鼓舞，但也倍感压力。

当此之际，我们愿将郁积在我们心底的话，向读者倾诉。

一

中华民族有着悠久的历史和灿烂的文化，系统、准确地将中华民族的文化经典翻译成外文，编辑出版，介绍给全世界，是几代中国人的愿望。早在几十年前，西方一位学者翻译《红楼梦》，书名译成《一个红楼上的梦》，将林黛玉译为“黑色的玉”。我们一方面对外国学者将中国的名著介绍到世界上去表示由衷的感谢，一方面为祖国的名著还不被完全认识，甚而受到曲解，而感到深深的遗憾。还有西方学者翻译《金瓶梅》，专门摘选其中自然主义描述最为突出的篇章加以译介。一时间，西方学者好像发现了奇迹，掀起了《金瓶梅》热，说中国是“性开放的源头”，公开地在报刊上鼓吹中国要“发扬开放之传统”。还有许多资深、友善的汉学家译介中国古代的哲学著作，在把中华民族文化介绍给全世界的工作方面作出了重大贡献，但或囿于理解有误，或缘于对中国文字认识的局限，质量上乘的并不多，常常是隔靴搔痒，说不到点子上。大哲学家黑格尔曾经说过：中国有最完备的国史。但他认为中国古代没有真正意义上的哲学，还处在哲学史前状态。这么了不起的哲学家竟然作出这样大失水准的评论，何其不幸。正如任何哲学家都要受时间、地点、条件的制约一样，黑格尔也离不开这一规律。当时他也只能从上述水平的汉学家译过去的文字去分析、理解，所以，黑格尔先生对中国古代社会的认识水平是什么状态，也就不难想象了。

中国离不开世界，世界也缺少不了中国。中国文化摄取外域的新成分，丰富了自己，又以自己的新成就输送给别人，贡献于世界。从公元5世纪开始到公元15世纪，大约有一千年，中国走在世界的前列。在这一千多年的时间里，她的光辉照耀全世界。人类要前进，怎么能不全面认识中国，怎么能不认真研究中国的历史呢?

二

中华民族是伟大的，曾经辉煌过，蓝天、白云、阳光灿烂，和平而兴旺；也有过黑暗的、想起来就让人战栗的日子，但中华民族从来是充满理想，不断追求，不断学习，渴望和平与友谊的。

中国古代伟大的思想家孔子曾经说过:“三人行，必有我师焉。择其善者而从之，其不善者而改之。”孔子的话就是要人们向别人学习。这段话正是概括了整个中华民族与人交往的原则。人与人之间交往如此，在与周边的国家交往中也是如此。

秦始皇第一个统一了中国，可惜在位只有十几年，来不及作更多的事情。汉朝继秦而继续强大，便开始走出去，了解自己周边的世界。公元前138年，汉武帝派张骞出使西域。他带着一万头牛羊，总值一万万钱的金帛货物，作为礼物，开始西行，最远到过“安息”(即波斯)。公元前36年，班超又率36人出使西域。36个人按今天的话说，也只有一个排，显然是为了拜访未曾见过面的邻居，是去交朋友。到了西域，班超派遣甘英作为使者继续西行，往更远处的大秦国(即罗马)去访问，“乃抵条支而历安息，临西海以望大秦”(《后汉书·西域传》)。“条支”在“安息”以西，即今天的伊拉克、叙利亚一带，“西海”应是今天的地中海。也就是说甘英已经到达地中海边上，与罗马帝国隔海相望，“临大海欲渡”，却被人劝阻而未成行，这在历史上留下了遗恨。可以想见班超、甘英沟通友谊的无比勇气和强烈愿望。接下来是唐代的玄奘，历经千难万险，到“西天”印度取经，带回了南亚国家的古老文化。归国后，他把带回的佛教经典组织人翻译，到后来很多经典印度失传了，但中国却保存完好，以至于今天，没有玄奘的《大唐西域记》，印度人很难编写印度古代史。明代郑和“七下西洋”，把中华文化传到东南亚一带。鸦片战争以后，一代又一代先进的中国人，为了振兴中华，又前赴后继，向西方国家学习先进的科学思想和文明成果。这中间有我们的领导人朱德、周恩来、邓小平；有许许多多大科学家、文学家、艺术家，如郭沫若、李四光、钱学森、冼星海、徐悲鸿等。他们的追求、奋斗，他们的博大胸怀，兼收并蓄的精神，为人类社会增添了光彩。

中国文化的形成和发展过程，就是一个以众为师，以各国人民为师，不断学习和创造的过程。中华民族曾经向周边国家和民族学习过许多东西，假如没有这些学习，中华民族决不可能创造出昔日的辉煌。回顾历史，我们怎么能够不对伟大的古埃及文明、古希腊文明、古印度文明满怀深深的感激?怎么能够不对伟大的欧洲文明、非洲文明、美洲文明、澳洲文明，以及中国周围的亚洲文明充满温情与敬意?

中华民族为人类社会曾作出过独特的贡献。在15世纪以前，中国的科学技术一直处于世界遥遥领先的地位。英国科学家李约瑟说:“中国在公元3世纪到13世纪之间，保持着一个西方所望尘莫及的科学知识水平。”美国耶鲁大学教授、《大国的兴衰》的作者保罗·肯尼迪坦言:“在近代以前时期的所有文明中，没有一个国家的文明比中国更发达，更先进。”

世界各国的有识之士千里迢迢来中国观光、学习。在这个过程中，中国唐朝的长安城渐渐发展成为国际大都市。西方的波斯、东罗马，东亚的高丽、新罗、百济、南天竺、北天竺，频繁前来。外国的王侯、留学生，在长安供职的外国官员，商贾、乐工和舞士，总有几十个国家，几万人之多。日本派出“遣唐使”更是一批接一批。传为美谈的日本人阿部仲麻吕(晁衡)在长安留学的故事，很能说明外国人与中国的交往。晁衡学成仕于唐朝，前后历时五十余年。晁衡与中国的知识分子结下了深厚的友情。他归国时，传说在海中遇难身亡。大诗人李白作诗哭悼:“日本晁卿辞帝都，征帆一片远蓬壶。明月不归沉碧海，白云愁色满苍梧。”晁衡遇险是误传，但由此可见中外学者之间在中国长安交往的情谊。

后来，不断有外国人到中国来探寻秘密，所见所闻，常常让他们目瞪口呆。《希腊纪事》(希腊人波桑尼阿著)记载公元2世纪时，希腊人在中国的见闻。书中写道:“赛里斯人用小米和青芦喂一种类似蜘蛛的昆虫，喂到第五年，虫肚子胀裂开，便从里面取出丝来。”从这段对中国古代养蚕技术的描述，可见当时欧洲人与中国人的差距。公元9世纪中叶，阿拉伯人来到中国。一位阿拉伯作家在他所著的《中国印度闻见录》中记载了曾旅居中国的阿拉伯商人的见闻：

——一天，一个外商去拜见驻守广州的中国官吏。会见时，外商总盯着官吏的胸部，官吏很奇怪，便问："你好像总盯着我的胸，这是怎么回事?"那位外商回答说："透过你穿的丝绸衣服，我隐约看到你胸口上长着一个黑痣，这是什么丝绸，我感到十分惊奇。"官吏听后，失声大笑，伸出胳膊，说："请你数数吧，看我穿了几件衣服?"那商人数过，竟然穿了五件之多，黑痣正是透过这五层丝绸衣服显现出来的。外商惊得目瞪口呆，官吏说："我穿的丝绸还不算是最好的，总督穿的要更精美。"

——书中关于茶(他们叫干草叶子)的记载，可见阿拉伯国家当时还没有喝茶的习惯。书中记述："中国国王本人的收入主要靠盐税和泡开水喝的一种干草税。在各个城市里，这种干草叶售价都很高，中国人称这种草叶叫'茶'，这种干草叶比苜蓿的叶子还多，也略比它香，稍有苦味，用开水冲喝，治百病。"

——他们对中国的医疗条件十分羡慕，书中记载道："中国人医疗条件很好，穷人可以从国库中得到药费。"还说："城市里，很多地方立一石碑，高10肘，上面刻有各种疾病和药物，写明某种病用某种药医治。"

——关于当时中国的京城，书中作了生动的描述：中国的京城很大，人口众多，一条宽阔的长街把全城分为两半，大街右边的东区，住着皇帝、宰相、禁军及皇家的总管、奴婢。在这个区域，沿街开凿了小河，流水潺潺；路旁，葱茏的树木整然有序，一幢幢宅邸鳞次栉比。大街左边的西区，住着庶民和商人。这里有货栈和商店，每当清晨，人们可以看到，皇室的总管、宫廷的仆役，或骑马或步行，到这里来采购。

此后的史籍对西人来华的记载，渐渐多了起来。13世纪意大利旅行家马可·波罗，尽管有人对他是否真的到过中国持怀疑态度，但他留下一部记述元代事件的《马可·波罗游记》却是确凿无疑的。这部游记中的一些关于当时中国的描述使得西方人认为是“天方夜谭”。总之，从中西文化交流史来说，这以前的时期还是一个想象和臆测的时代，相互之间充满了好奇与幻想。

从16世纪末开始，由于航海技术的发展，东西方航路的开通，随着一批批传教士来华，中国与西方开始了直接的交流。沟通中西的使命在意大利传教士利玛窦那里有了充分的体现。利玛窦于1582年来华，1610年病逝于北京，在华20余年。除了传教以外，做了两件具有历史象征意义的事，一是1594年前后在韶州用拉丁文翻译《四书》，并作了注释；二是与明代学者徐光启合作，用中文翻译了《几何原本》。

西方传教士对《四书》等中国经典的粗略翻译，以及杜赫德的《中华帝国志》等书对中国的介绍，在西方读者的眼前展现了一个异域文明，在当时及稍后一段时期引起了一场“中国热”，许多西方大思想家的眼光都曾注目中国文化。有的推崇中华文明，如莱布尼兹、伏尔泰、魁奈等，有的对中华文明持批评态度，如孟德斯鸠、黑格尔等。莱布尼兹认识到中国文化的某些思想与他的观念相近，如周易的卦象与他发明的二进制相契合，对中国文化给予了热情的礼赞；黑格尔则从他整个哲学体系的推演出发，认为中国没有真正意义上的哲学，还处在哲学史前的状态。但是，不论是推崇还是批评，是吸纳还是排斥，中西文化的交流产生了巨大的影响。随着先进的中国科学技术的西传，特别是中国的造纸、火药、印刷术和指南针四大发明的问世，大大改变了世界的面貌。马克思说："中国的火药把骑士阶层炸得粉碎，指南针打开了世界市场并建立了殖民地，而印刷术则变成了新教的工具，变成对精神发展创造必要前提的最强大的杠杆。"英国的哲学家培根说：中国的四大发明"改变了全世界的面貌和一切事物的状态"。

三

大千世界，潮起潮落。云散云聚，万象更新。中国古代产生了无数伟大科学家：祖冲之、李时珍、孙思邈、张衡、沈括、毕升……，产生了无数科技成果：《齐民要术》、《九章算术》、《伤寒杂病论》、《本草纲目》……，以及保存至今的世界奇迹：浑天仪、地动仪、都江堰、敦煌石窟、大运河、万里长城……。但从 15 世纪下半叶起，风水似乎从东方转到了西方，落后的欧洲只经过 400 年便成为世界瞩目的文明中心。英国的牛顿、波兰的哥白尼、德国的伦琴、法国的居里、德国的爱因斯坦、意大利的伽利略、俄国的门捷列夫、美国的费米和爱迪生……，光芒四射，令人敬仰。

中华民族开始思考了。潮起潮落究竟是什么原因？中国人发明的火药，传到欧洲，转眼之间反成为欧洲列强轰击中国大门的炮弹，又是因为什么？

鸦片战争终于催醒了中国人沉睡的迷梦，最先"睁眼看世界"的一代精英林则徐、魏源迈出了威武雄壮的一步。曾国藩、李鸿章搞起了洋务运动。中国的知识分子喊出"民主与科学"的口号。中国是落后了，中国的志士仁人在苦苦探索。但落后中饱含着变革的动力，探索中孕育着崛起的希望。“向科学进军”，中华民族终于又迎来了科学的春天。

今天，世界毕竟来到了21世纪的门槛。分散隔绝的世界，逐渐变成联系为一体的世界。现在，全球一体化趋势日益明显，人类历史也就在愈来愈大的程度上成为全世界的历史。当今，任何一种文化的发展都离不开对其它优秀文化的汲取，都以其它优秀文化的发展为前提。在近现代，西方文化汲取中国文化，不仅是中国文化的传播，更是西方文化自身的创新和发展；正如中国文化对西方文化的汲取一样，既是西方文化在中国的传播，同时也是中国文化在近代的转型和发展。地球上所有的人类文化，都是我们共同的宝贵遗产。既然我们生活的各个大陆，在地球史上曾经是连成一气的“泛大陆”，或者说是一个完整的“地球村”，那么，我们同样可以在这个以知识和学习为特征的网络时代，走上相互学习、共同发展的大路，建设和开拓我们人类崭新的“地球村”。

西学仍在东渐，中学也将西传。各国人民的优秀文化正日益迅速地为中国文化所汲取，而无论西方和东方，也都需要从中国文化中汲取养分。正是基于这一认识，我们组织出版汉英对照版《大中华文库》，全面系统地翻译介绍中国传统文化典籍。我们试图通过《大中华文库》，向全世界展示，中华民族五千年的追求，五千年的梦想，正在新的历史时期重放光芒。中国人民就像火后的凤凰，万众一心，迎接新世纪文明的太阳。

杨牧之

1999年8月 北京

PREFACE TO THE *LIBRARY OF CHINESE CLASSICS*

The publication of the *Library of Chinese Classics* is a matter of great satisfaction to all of us who have been involved in the production of this monumental work. At the same time, we feel a weighty sense of responsibility, and take this opportunity to explain to our readers the motivation for undertaking this cross-century task.

1

The Chinese nation has a long history and a glorious culture, and it has been the aspiration of several generations of Chinese scholars to translate, edit and publish the whole corpus of the Chinese literary classics so that the nation's greatest cultural achievements can be introduced to people all over the world. There have been many translations of the Chinese classics done by foreign scholars. A few dozen years ago, a Western scholar translated the title of *A Dream of Red Mansions* into "A Dream of Red Chambers" and Lin Daiyu, the heroine in the novel, into "Black Jade." But while their endeavours have been laudable, the results of their labours have been less than satisfactory. Lack of knowledge of Chinese culture and an inadequate grasp of the Chinese written language have led the translators into many errors. As a consequence, not only are Chinese classical writings widely misunderstood in the rest of the world, in some cases their content has actually been distorted. At one time, there was a "*Jin Ping Mei* craze" among Western scholars, who thought that they had uncovered a miraculous phenomenon, and published theories claiming that China was the "fountainhead of eroticism," and that a Chinese "tradition of permissiveness" was about to be laid bare. This distorted view came about due to the translators of the *Jin Ping Mei (Plum in the Golden Vase)* putting one-sided stress on the raw elements in that novel, to the neglect of its overall literary value. Meanwhile, there have been many distinguished and well-intentioned

Sinologists who have attempted to make the culture of the Chinese nation more widely known by translating works of ancient Chinese philosophy. However, the quality of such work, in many cases, is unsatisfactory, often missing the point entirely. The great philosopher Hegel considered that ancient China had no philosophy in the real sense of the word, being stuck in philosophical "prehistory." For such an eminent authority to make such a colossal error of judgment is truly regrettable. But, of course, Hegel was just as subject to the constraints of time, space and other objective conditions as anyone else, and since he had to rely for his knowledge of Chinese philosophy on inadequate translations it is not difficult to imagine why he went so far off the mark.

China cannot be separated from the rest of the world; and the rest of the world cannot ignore China. Throughout its history, Chinese civilization has enriched itself by absorbing new elements from the outside world, and in turn has contributed to the progress of world civilization as a whole by transmitting to other peoples its own cultural achievements. From the 5th to the 15th centuries, China marched in the front ranks of world civilization. If mankind wishes to advance, how can it afford to ignore China? How can it afford not to make a thoroughgoing study of its history?

2

Despite the ups and downs in their fortunes, the Chinese people have always been idealistic, and have never ceased to forge ahead and learn from others, eager to strengthen ties of peace and friendship.

The great ancient Chinese philosopher Confucius once said, "Wherever three persons come together, one of them will surely be able to teach me something. I will pick out his good points and emulate them; his bad points I will reform." Confucius meant by this that we should always be ready to learn from others. This maxim encapsulates the principle the Chinese people have always followed in their dealings with other peoples, not only on an individual basis but also at the level of state-to-state relations.

After generations of internecine strife, China was unified by Emperor Qin Shi Huang (the First Emperor of the Qin Dynasty) in 221 B.C. The Han Dynasty, which succeeded that of the short-lived Qin, waxed powerful, and for the first time brought China into contact with the outside world. In 138 B.C., Emperor Wu dispatched Zhang Qian to the western regions, i.e. Central Asia. Zhang, who traveled as far as what is now Iran, took with him as presents for the rulers he visited on the way 10,000 head of sheep and cattle, as well as gold and silks worth a fabulous amount. In 36 B.C., Ban Chao headed a 36-man legation to the western regions. These were missions of friendship to visit neighbours the Chinese people had never met before and to learn from them. Ban Chao sent Gan Ying to explore further toward the west. According to the "Western Regions Section" in the *Book of Later Han*, Gan Ying traveled across the territories of present-day Iraq and Syria, and reached the Mediterranean Sea, an expedition which brought him within the confines of the Roman Empire. Later, during the Tang Dynasty, the monk Xuan Zang made a journey fraught with danger to reach India and seek the knowledge of that land. Upon his return, he organized a team of scholars to translate the Buddhist scriptures, which he had brought back with him. As a result, many of these scriptural classics which were later lost in India have been preserved in China. In fact, it would have been difficult for the people of India to reconstruct their own ancient history if it had not been for Xuan Zang's *A Record of a Journey to the West in the Time of the Great Tang Dynasty*. In the Ming Dynasty, Zheng He transmitted Chinese culture to Southeast Asia during his seven voyages. Following the Opium Wars in the mid-19th century, progressive Chinese, generation after generation, went to study the advanced scientific thought and cultural achievements of the Western countries. Their aim was to revive the fortunes of their own country. Among them were people who were later to become leaders of China, including Zhu De, Zhou Enlai and Deng Xiaoping. In addition, there were people who were to become leading scientists, literary figures and artists, such as Guo Moruo, Li Siguang, Qian Xuesen, Xian Xinghai and Xu Beihong. Their spirit of ambition, their struggles and their breadth of vision were an inspiration not only to the Chinese people but to people all over the world.

Indeed, it is true that if the Chinese people had not learned many things from the surrounding countries they would never have been able to produce the splendid achievements of former days. When we look back upon history, how can we not feel profoundly grateful for the legacies of the civilizations of ancient Egypt, Greece and India? How can we not feel fondness and respect for the cultures of Europe, Africa, America and Oceania?

The Chinese nation, in turn, has made unique contributions to the community of mankind. Prior to the 15th century, China led the world in science and technology. The British scientist Joseph Needham once said, "From the third century B.C. to the 13th century A.D. China was far ahead of the West in the level of its scientific knowledge." Paul Kennedy, of Yale University in the U.S., author of *The Rise and Fall of the Great Powers*, said, "Of all the civilizations of the pre-modern period, none was as well-developed or as progressive as that of China."

Foreigners who came to China were often astonished at what they saw and heard. The Greek geographer Pausanias in the second century A.D. gave the first account in the West of the technique of silk production in China: "The Chinese feed a spider-like insect with millet and reeds. After five years the insect's stomach splits open, and silk is extracted therefrom." From this extract, we can see that the Europeans at that time did not know the art of silk manufacture. In the middle of the 9th century A.D., an Arabian writer includes the following anecdote in his *Account of China and India*:

"One day, an Arabian merchant called upon the military governor of Guangzhou. Throughout the meeting, the visitor could not keep his eyes off the governor's chest. Noticing this, the latter asked the Arab merchant what he was staring at. The merchant replied, 'Through the silk robe you are wearing, I can faintly see a black mole on your chest. Your robe must be made out of very fine silk indeed!' The governor burst out laughing, and holding out his sleeve invited the merchant to count how many garments he was wearing. The merchant did so, and discovered that the governor was actually wearing five silk robes, one on top of the other, and they were made of such fine material that a tiny mole could be seen through them all! Moreover, the governor explained that the robes he was wearing were not made of the finest silk at all; silk of the highest grade was reserved for the garments worn by the provincial governor."

The references to tea in this book (the author calls it "dried grass") reveal that the custom of drinking tea was unknown in the Arab countries at that time: "The king of China's revenue comes mainly from taxes on salt and the dry leaves of a kind of grass which is drunk after boiled water is poured on it. This dried grass is sold at a high price in every city in the country. The Chinese call it 'cha.' The bush is like alfalfa, except that it bears more leaves, which are also more fragrant than alfalfa. It has a slightly bitter taste, and when it is infused in boiling water it is said to have medicinal properties."

Foreign visitors showed especial admiration for Chinese medicine. One wrote, "China has very good medical conditions. Poor people are given money to buy medicines by the government."

In this period, when Chinese culture was in full bloom, scholars flocked from all over the world to China for sightseeing and for study. Chang'an, the capital of the Tang Dynasty was host to visitors from as far away as the Byzantine Empire, not to mention the neighboring countries of Asia. Chang'an, at that time the world's greatest metropolis, was packed with thousands of foreign dignitaries, students, diplomats, merchants, artisans and entertainers. Japan especially sent contingent after contingent of envoys to the Tang court. Worthy of note are the accounts of life in Chang'an written by Abeno Nakamaro, a Japanese scholar who studied in China and had close friendships with ministers of the Tang court and many Chinese scholars in a period of over 50 years. The description throws light on the exchanges between Chinese and foreigners in this period. When Abeno was supposedly lost at sea on his way back home, the leading poet of the time, Li Bai, wrote a eulogy for him.

The following centuries saw a steady increase in the accounts of China written by Western visitors. The Italian Marco Polo described conditions in China during the Yuan Dynasty in his *Travels*. However, until advances in the science of navigation led to the opening of east-west shipping routes at the beginning of the 16th century Sino-Western cultural exchanges were coloured by fantasy and conjecture. Concrete progress was made when a contingent of religious missionaries, men well versed in Western science and technology, made their way to China, ushering in an era of direct contacts between China and the West. The experience of this era was embodied in the career of the Italian Jesuit Matteo Ricci. Arriving in

China in 1582, Ricci died in Beijing in 1610. Apart from his missionary work, Ricci accomplished two historically symbolic tasks — one was the translation into Latin of the "Four Books," together with annotations, in 1594; the other was the translation into Chinese of Euclid's *Elements*.

The rough translations of the "Four Books" and other Chinese classical works by Western missionaries, and the publication of Père du Halde's *Description Geographique, Historique, Chronologique, Politique, et Physique de l'Empire de la Chine* revealed an exotic culture to Western readers, and sparked a "China fever," during which the eyes of many Western intellectuals were fixed on China. Some of these intellectuals, including Leibniz, held China in high esteem; others, such as Hegel, nursed a critical attitude toward Chinese culture. Leibniz considered that some aspects of Chinese thought were close to his own views, such as the philosophy of the *Book of Changes* and his own binary system. Hegel, on the other hand, as mentioned above, considered that China had developed no proper philosophy of its own. Nevertheless, no matter whether the reaction was one of admiration, criticism, acceptance or rejection, Sino-Western exchanges were of great significance. The transmission of advanced Chinese science and technology to the West, especially the Chinese inventions of paper-making, gunpowder, printing and the compass, greatly changed the face of the whole world. Karl Marx said, "Chinese gunpowder blew the feudal class of knights to smithereens; the compass opened up world markets and built colonies; and printing became an implement of Protestantism and the most powerful lever and necessary precondition for intellectual development and creation." The English philosopher Roger Bacon said that China's four great inventions had "changed the face of the whole world and the state of affairs of everything."

3

Ancient China gave birth to a large number of eminent scientists, such as Zu Chongzhi, Li Shizhen, Sun Simiao, Zhang Heng, Shen Kuo and Bi Sheng. They produced numerous treatises on scientific subjects, including *The Manual of Important Arts for the People's Welfare, Nine*

Chapters on the Mathematical Art, A Treatise on Febrile Diseases and *Compendium of Materia Medica*. Their accomplishments included ones whose influence has been felt right down to modern times, such as the armillary sphere, seismograph, Dujiangyan water conservancy project, Dunhuang Grottoes, Grand Canal and Great Wall. But from the latter part of the 15th century, and for the next 400 years, Europe gradually became the cultural centre upon which the world's eyes were fixed. The world's most outstanding scientists then were England's Isaac Newton, Poland's Copernicus, France's Marie Curie, Germany's Rontgen and Einstein, Italy's Galileo, Russia's Mendelev and America's Edison.

The Chinese people then began to think: What is the cause of the rise and fall of nations? Moreover, how did it happen that gunpowder, invented in China and transmitted to the West, in no time at all made Europe powerful enough to batter down the gates of China herself?

It took the Opium War to wake China from its reverie. The first generation to make the bold step of "turning our eyes once again to the rest of the world" was represented by Lin Zexu and Wei Yuan. Zeng Guofan and Li Hongzhang started the Westernization Movement, and later intellectuals raised the slogan of "Democracy and Science." Noble-minded patriots, realizing that China had fallen behind in the race for modernization, set out on a painful quest. But in backwardness lay the motivation for change, and the quest produced the embryo of a towering hope, and the Chinese people finally gathered under a banner proclaiming a "March Toward Science."

On the threshold of the 21st century, the world is moving in the direction of becoming an integrated entity. This trend is becoming clearer by the day. In fact, the history of the various peoples of the world is also becoming the history of mankind as a whole. Today, it is impossible for any nation's culture to develop without absorbing the excellent aspects of the cultures of other peoples. When Western culture absorbs aspects of Chinese culture, this is not just because it has come into contact with Chinese culture, but also because of the active creativity and development of Western culture itself; and vice versa. The various cultures of the world's peoples are a precious heritage which we all share. Mankind no longer lives on different continents, but on one big continent, or in a "global village." And so, in this era characterized by an all-encompassing network of knowledge and information we should learn from each other and march in step along the highway of development to construct a brand-new "global village."

Western learning is still being transmitted to the East, and vice versa. China is accelerating its pace of absorption of the best parts of the cultures of other countries, and there is no doubt that both the West and the East need the nourishment of Chinese culture. Based on this recognition, we have edited and published the *Library of Chinese Classics* in a Chinese-English format as an introduction to the corpus of traditional Chinese culture in a comprehensive and systematic translation. Through this collection, our aim is to reveal to the world the aspirations and dreams of the Chinese people over the past 5,000 years and the splendour of the new historical era in China. Like a phoenix rising from the ashes, the Chinese people in unison are welcoming the cultural sunrise of the new century.

Yang Muzhi

August 1999, Beijing

前　　言

一

按传统的说法，中华文明已有五千年历史，但在当今中国，以及海外华人社区，无论是社会精英所掌握的有文字记载的所谓“大传统”,抑或是一般市民和农夫的生活所代表的所谓“小传统”，简言之，每个中国人的一举手一投足所凸现出的中国气派，无不可以从2400年前“轴心时代”的一部经典——《论语》中找到根源。

“轴心时代”是德国哲学家卡尔·雅斯贝斯(Karl Jaspers)提出的理论。他指出，在经历了史前和远古文明时代之后，在公元前500年左右，世界范围内出现了一些极不平常的事件：

> 在中国，孔子和老子非常活跃，中国所有的哲学流派，包括墨子、庄子、列子和诸子百家都出现了。和中国一样，印度出现了《奥义书》和佛陀，探究了从怀疑主义、唯物主义到诡辩派、虚无主义的全部范围的哲学可能性。伊朗的琐罗亚斯德传授一种挑战性的观点，认为人世生活就是一场善与恶的斗争。在巴勒斯坦，从以利亚经由以赛亚和耶利米到以赛亚第二，先知们纷纷涌现。希腊贤哲如云，其中有荷马、哲学家巴门尼德、赫拉克利特和柏拉图、许多悲剧作者，以及修昔底德和阿基米德。在这数世纪内，这些名字所包含的一切，几乎同时在中国、印度和西方这三个互不知晓的地区发展

起来。①

雅斯贝斯将这一时期称作世界历史的“轴心”：

> 人类一直靠轴心时代所产生的思考和创造的一切而生存，每一次新的飞跃都回顾这一时期，并被它重燃火焰。自那以后，情况就是这样，轴心期潜力的苏醒和对轴心期潜力的回归，或者说复兴，总是提供了精神的动力。②

按照帕森斯(Talcatt Parsons)的说法，在这一光辉灿烂的时期，在希腊、巴比伦、印度和中国四大文明发源地都经历了“哲学的突破”，即对人所处的宇宙的本源有了较为理性的认识,对人类所处的位置及“人之所以为人”有了新的理解。

在中国，离开了孔子和《论语》,“哲学的突破”这一命题就无从谈起。我们说，中国哲学是伦理型的，哲学体系的核心是伦理道德学说。如果说西方各种文化形态重在求真，中国的各种文化形态便是强调求善。旧时代从硕学鸿儒到武术教师，教徒弟的第一课便是如何做人，如何讲“德”。他们让学生或徒弟背诵的座右铭或警句，多出自《论语》。

中国的传统道德资源，经过几十年被弃若敝屣之后，在某些通都大邑简直成了稀罕物，讲求道德者往往被看作是傻瓜，以致有人惊呼当今是一个物欲横流、铜臭熏天的世界。但在若干“民智未开”的穷乡僻壤，我们古代典籍中蕴含的道德观念却依然留存。村夫农妇，或许他们一字不识，其言语行为中却处处体现着“仁、义、礼、智、信、忠、孝、温、良、恭、俭、让”等为人处世之道，并以此言传身教，他们的下一辈因耳濡目染而默化潜移。文革回忆录中经常有这样的描写——被整得遍体鳞伤的人们遭贬下乡，却受到亲人般的呵护——就是这种现实的反映。这类所谓“礼失求诸野”的现象说明了传统道德观念确实历久不灭，深入人心；同时也促使我们再也不能“舍弃自家无尽藏，沿街托钵效贫儿”(朱熹诗)了。我们需要重读《论语》，它是中国人的人生教科书。

《论语》究竟讲的是什么呢?

《论语》的核心思想，历来有两种看法，其一是“仁”，其一是“礼”。

历来研究《论语》的人多认为《论语》主要是讲“仁”的，认为《论语》重在讲“礼”的主要有王源、戴震、陈沣、王先谦及现代的柳诒徵、李大钊、陈独秀、侯外庐、蔡尚思、赵纪彬等。

杨伯峻先生认为《论语》的核心是“仁”。他做了一个统计：《左传》中“礼”字出现了462次，“仁”字只出现了33次；而《论语》中“礼”字出现75次(《论语词典》统计“礼”字出现了74次，见《论语译注》311页)，“仁”字出现了109次(《论语译注·试论孔子》16页)。

我们认为，《论语》的核心思想确实是“仁”。

《论语》中的“仁”一词不能一概而论。从大的方面说，它指在天下范围内行仁政；从小的方面说，它指“爱人”，指忠恕，指做人的根本——孝悌。要做一个真正的“仁人”很难，但每个人随时随地都可一点一滴地行善——践履仁德。

一、“仁”是人之所以区别于禽兽的本质所在，人活着就要践履仁德；同时，“仁”也是人生追求的最高境界与目标。志士仁人，一方面时时与“仁”同在，“不违仁”，一方面以在天下实行仁德为己任。

孔子说：“仁者人也”(《礼记·中庸》)，“富与贵，是人之所欲也。不以其道得之，不处也。贫与贱，是人之所恶也。不以其道得之，不去也。君子去仁，恶乎成名？君子无终食之间违仁，造次必于是，颠沛必于是。”(《里仁》)孔子最得意的弟子颜回“其心三月不违仁”，孔子便称赞他“贤”(《雍也》)。“仁”是毕生为之奋斗的目标：“士不可以不弘毅，任重而道远。仁以为己任，不亦重乎？死而后已，不亦远乎？”(《泰伯》)为了成全仁德，不惜献出生命：“志士仁人，无求生以害仁，有杀身以成仁。”(《卫灵公》)“仁”既是最高境界与目标，义、忠、恕、孝、悌都是广义的“仁”的子项。

二、“仁”是实践“天下为公”这一最高目标的重要步骤。

在《礼记·礼运》中，记载了孔子关于“天下大同”的设想：

> 大道之行也，天下为公。选贤与能，讲信修睦。故人不独亲其亲，不独子其子，使老有所终，壮有所用，幼有所长，矜寡孤独废疾者皆有所养，男有分，女有归。货恶其弃于地也，不必藏于己；力恶其不出于身也，不必为己。是故谋闭而不兴，盗窃乱贼而不作，故外户而不闭，是谓大同。

我认为，这一设想就是所谓“博施于民而能济众”。《雍也》：“子贡曰：‘如有博施于民而能济众，何如？可谓仁乎？’

子曰：'何事于仁！必也圣乎！尧舜其犹病诸！'"能做到"博施于民而能济众"，已不止是"仁"，而可以称为"圣"了。这一点，尧舜也未必做到了呢？这可以看出，"圣"包含了"仁"，"仁"与"圣"是一致的。

孔子认为子路、冉有、公西华、令尹子文、陈文子都没有达到"仁"的境界，即使颜渊也仅仅只是"不违仁"（《雍也》），却许管仲以仁：

> 子贡曰："管仲非仁者与？桓公杀公子纠，不能死，又相之。"子曰："管仲相桓公，霸诸侯，一匡天下，民到于今受其赐。微管仲，吾其被发左衽矣。"（《宪问》）
>
> 子路曰："桓公杀公子纠，召忽死之，管仲不死。"曰："未仁乎？"子曰："桓公九合诸侯，不以兵车，管仲之力也。如其仁，如其仁。"（《宪问》）

在孔子看来，尽管管仲既不知俭，又不知礼（《八佾》），但因为帮助齐桓公使天下有一个较长期安定的局面，从而有助于人民休养生息，那么他就是仁者。③

三、"仁"是从日常事物中一点一滴地积累起来的。"仁"是爱人。践履仁德的方法是推己及人，由近及远。

孔子不轻易许人以"仁"，"仁"是否就高不可攀呢？不是！成仁入圣，一般人难以企及；但要践履仁德，却随时可以从身边的小事做起。"为仁由己"（《颜渊》）。"仁远乎哉？我欲仁，斯仁至矣。"（《述而》）"仁者，其言也讱。"（《颜渊》）"仁者先难而后获。"（《雍也》）"刚毅木讷近仁。"（《子路》）"巧言令色，鲜矣仁。"（《学而》）"子张问仁于孔子，孔子曰：'能行五者于天下，为仁矣。''请问之。'曰：'恭、宽、信、敏、惠。恭则不侮，宽则得众，信则人任焉，敏则有功，惠则足以使人。'"(《阳货》)当然，“仁”不是琐碎的道德规范，而是“一以贯之”(《里仁》)的。具体说来,“仁”即是“爱人”(《颜渊》):“厩焚，子退朝，曰:‘伤人乎?’不问马。”(《乡党》)“仁”的本源是孝悌。“君子务本，本立而道生。孝悌也者，其为仁之本与!”(《学而》)为什么说“孝悌”是“仁”的本源呢?因为行仁的方法，其实就是将对亲人的爱加以推广扩充，所谓由近及远，由己及人。“君子笃于亲，而民兴于仁。”(《泰伯》)从消极的方面说，自己(及家人)不喜欢的，不施加于他人，这就是忠恕，“夫子之道，忠恕而已矣。”(《里仁》)“己所不欲，勿施于人。”(《颜渊》、《卫灵公》)从积极的方面说，就是自己(及家人)要站得住，也要让他人站得住；自己(及家人)要行得通，也要让他人行得通。“夫仁者，己欲立而立人，己欲达而达人。能近取譬，可谓仁之方也已。”(《雍也》)这就是孟子所谓“亲亲而仁民，仁民而爱物”。(《尽心上》)“老吾老以及人之老，幼吾幼以及人之幼。”(《梁惠王上》),亦即宋代张载所谓“民吾胞也，物吾与也”。这种将亲情之爱推广到极限的“博爱”，把人类精神提扬到了“天人合一”的境界。这种精神不但可以用以疗治当今物欲横流的人类社会，同样，可以拯救因人类过度索取而面临灭顶之灾的地球家园。

四、就“仁”与“礼”的关系来看,“仁”是本,“礼”是末；“仁”是里,“礼”是表;“仁”是内容,“礼”是形式;“仁”是终极目标，“礼”是保证这一目标得以实现的一种约束，是规范与制度。

据杨伯峻先生《论语词典》统计，《论语》中“礼”一词共出现74次，其意义为“礼意、礼仪、礼制、礼法”。我们以为，礼仪、礼制、礼法都是为“天下归仁”这一目标服务的。

子夏问曰：“‘巧笑倩兮，美目盼兮，素以为绚兮。’何谓也？”子曰：“绘事后素。”曰：“礼后乎？”子曰：“起予者商也！始可与言《诗》已矣。”（《八佾》）

“礼后”指“礼”在“仁义”之后。尽管孔子也曾借用孟僖子的话说“不学礼，无以立”（《季氏》），但他更表明“人而不仁，如礼何？人而不仁，如乐何？”（《八佾》）不学礼仪礼节，人没法在社会上立足，但只知礼节而不知“仁”，便是虚有其表的伪君子了。君子习礼的目的，是为了在天下实现仁德。“克己复礼为仁，一日克己复礼，天下归仁焉”（《颜渊》）。这是说只有克制自己，恢复礼制，普天之下才可一统于仁。孔子说的“复礼”，并不就是把“周礼”照搬回来，而是有所“损益”（《为政》）。比如，从西周以迄春秋，还时有以活人殉葬的事例，这自然是符合当时的礼制的。以贤良闻名的秦穆公就曾以“三良”殉葬，孔子去古未远，当不会一无所知。但他甚至对以陶俑殉葬都深恶痛绝：“仲尼曰：‘始作俑者，其无后乎！’为其像人而用之也。”（《孟子·梁惠王上》）“仁者爱人”，凡是不人道的行为，即使符合“礼制”，孔子也要愤怒地加以谴责。又比如，他说：“麻冕，礼也；今也纯，俭，吾从众。”（《子罕》）对麻冕可以变通，改用所费较少的丝料。这是因为孔子更看重“礼”的实质：“礼云礼云，玉帛云乎哉？乐云乐云，钟鼓云乎哉？”（《阳货》）孔子认可的“礼”的实质是什么呢?如前所述，就是仁义。孔子教导学生，始终以“仁”为终极目标，至于文学与礼仪，则是第二位的:“弟子，入则孝，出则悌，谨而信，泛爱众，而亲仁。行有余力，则以学文。”(《学而》)“君子博学于文，约之以礼，亦可以无畔矣夫。”(《雍也》)颜渊也说:“夫子循循然善诱人，博我以文，约我以礼，欲罢不能……”(《子罕》)“孝悌”是仁之本；仁者爱人，便要“泛爱众”;求仁者，自然要亲近仁人。如此修养自己以后，才去学文，才“约之以礼”。《论语》中“礼”之为用，除了“约”外，还有“节”、“齐”、“文”等:“礼之用，和为贵。先王之道，斯为美；小大由之。有所不行，知和而和，不以礼节之，亦不可行也。”(《学而》)“道之以政，齐之以刑，民免而无耻；道之以德，齐之以礼，有耻且格。”(《为政》)“若臧武仲之知，公绰之不欲，卞庄子之勇，冉求之艺，文之以礼乐，亦可以为成人矣。”(《宪问》)可见，“礼”始终是用之以约束、节制、整顿、文饰的，其终极目标始终是“仁”。“孟懿子问孝。子曰:‘无违。’……子曰:‘生，事之以礼；死，葬之以礼，祭之以礼。’”(《为政》)“慎终追远，民德归厚矣。”(《学而》)“葬之以礼，祭之以礼”即是“慎终追远”,其目的是“民德归厚”,此即“君子笃于亲，则民兴于仁”(《泰伯》)。

综上，《论语》的核心思想是“仁”,“礼”是从属于并服务于“仁”的。

二

班固的《汉书·艺文志》说："《论语》者，孔子应答弟子、时人及弟子相与言而接闻于夫子之语也。当时弟子各有所记，夫子既卒，门人相与辑而论纂，故谓之《论语》。"《文选·辩命论》李善注引《傅子》也说："昔仲尼既殁，仲弓之徒追论夫子之言，谓之《论语》。"由此可知："论语"的"论"是"论纂"的意思，"论语"的"语"是语言的意思。"论语"就是把"接闻于夫子之语""论纂"起来的意思。《论语》是记载孔子及其若干学生言语行事的一部书。"论语"的名字是当时就有的，不是后来别人给的。

《论语》又是若干断片的篇章集合体。这些篇章的排列不一定有什么道理；就是前后两章间，也不一定有什么关连。而且这些断片的篇章绝不是一个人的手笔。《论语》一书，篇幅不大，却出现了不少重复的章节。如"巧言令色，鲜矣仁"一章，先见于《学而》，又重出于《阳货》。又有基本上是重复只是详略不同的。如"君子不重"章，《学而》比《子罕》多出 11 个字。还有意思相同，文字却有异的，如《里仁》说："不患莫己知，求为可知也。"《宪问》又说："不患人之不己知，患其不能也。"《卫灵公》又说："君子病无能焉，不病人之不己知也。"如果加上《学而》的"人不知而不愠，不亦君子乎"，便是重复四次。这种现象只有下面这个推论合理：孔子的言论，当时弟子各有记载，后来才汇集成书。所以，《论语》绝不能看作某一个人的著作。《论语》的作者有孔子的学生。《子罕》："牢曰：'子云：吾不试，故艺。'""牢"是人名，相传他姓琴，字子开，又字子张。这里不称姓氏只称名，这种记述方式和《论语》的一般体例不相吻合。因此，便可以作这样的推论，这一章是琴牢本人的记载，编辑《论语》的人，"直取其所记而载之耳"（日本学者安井息轩《论语集说》中语）。又,《宪问》说:"宪问耻。子曰:'邦有道，谷；邦无道，谷，耻也。'""宪"是原宪，字子思。显然，这也是原宪自己的笔墨。

《论语》的篇章不但出自孔子的不同学生之手，而且还出自他的不同的再传弟子之手。这里面不少是曾参的学生的记载。如《泰伯》说:"曾子有疾，召门弟子曰:'启予足！启予手！《诗》云:"战战兢兢，如临深渊，如履薄冰。"而今而后，吾知免夫！小子！'"这一章不能不说是曾参的门弟子的记载。又如《子张》:"子夏之门人问交于子张。子张曰:'子夏云何？'对曰:'子夏曰:"可者与之，其不可者拒之。"'子张曰:'异乎吾所闻：君子尊贤而容众。嘉善而矜不能。我之大贤与，于人何所不容？我之不贤与，人将拒我，如之何其拒人也？'"这一段又像子张或子夏的学生的记载。又如《先进》中说:"子曰:'孝哉闵子骞！人不间于其父母昆弟之言。'""闵子侍侧，訚訚如也；子路，行行如也；冉有、子贡，侃侃如也。子乐。"孔子称学生从来直呼其名，独独这里对闵损称字，不能不启人疑窦，我们认为这一章是闵损的学生追记的，因而有这一不经意的失实。至于《闵子侍侧》一章，不但闵子骞称"子"，而且列在子路、冉有、子贡三人之前，这是难以理解的。以年龄而论，子路最长；以仕宦而论，闵子更赶不上这三人。他凭什么能在这一段记载上居于首位而且得到“子”的尊称呢?合理的推论是，这也是闵子骞的学生把平日闻于老师之言追记下来而成的。

《论语》一书有孔子弟子的笔墨，也有孔子再传弟子的笔墨，那么，著作年代便有先有后了。这点，在词义的运用上也适当地反映了出来。譬如“夫子”一词，在较早的年代一般指第三者，相当于“他老人家”，直到战国，才普遍用为指称对话者，相当于“你老人家”。《论语》的一般用法都是相当于“他老人家”的，孔子学生当面称孔子为“子”，背后才称“夫子”，别人对孔子也是背后才称“夫子”。只是在《阳货》中有两处例外，言偃对孔子说，“昔者偃也闻诸夫子”；子路对孔子也说，“昔者由也闻诸夫子”，都是当面称“夫子”，开战国时运用“夫子”一词的词义之端。《论语》著笔有先有后，其间相距或者不止于三五十年，由此可以窥见一斑。

《论语》一书的最后编定者，应是曾参的学生。第一，《论语》不但对曾参无一处不称“子”，而且记载他的言行较孔子其他弟子为多。《论语》中单独记载曾参言行的，共有十三章。第二，在孔子弟子中，不但曾参最年轻，而且有一章记载着曾参将死之前对孟敬子的一段话。孟敬子是鲁大夫孟武伯的儿子仲孙捷的谥号。假定曾参死在鲁元公元年(前436)，则孟敬子之死更在其后，那么，这一事的记述者一定是在孟敬子死后才著笔的。孟敬子的年岁我们已难考定，但《檀弓》记载着当鲁悼公死时，孟敬子对答季昭子的一番话，可见当曾子年近七十之时，孟敬子已是鲁国执政大臣之一了。则这一段记载之为曾子弟子所记，毫无可疑。《论语》所叙的人物和事迹，再没有比这更晚的，那么，《论语》的编定者就是这些曾参的学生。因此，我们说《论语》的著笔当开始于春秋末期，而编辑成书则在战国初期。

《论语》传到汉朝，有三种不同的本子：(1)《鲁论语》20篇；(2)《齐论语》22篇，其中20篇的章句很多和《鲁论语》相同，但是多出《问王》和《知道》两篇；(3)《古文论语》21篇，也没有《问王》和《知道》两篇，但是把《尧曰篇》的“子张问”另分为一篇，于是有了两个《子张篇》。篇次也和《齐论》、《鲁论》不一样，文字不同的计四百多字。《鲁论》和《齐论》最初各有师传，到西汉末年，安昌侯张禹先学习了《鲁论》，后来又讲习《齐论》，于是把两个本子融合为一，但是篇目以《鲁论》为根据，号为《张侯论》。张禹是汉成帝的师傅，其时极为尊贵，所以他的这一个本子便为当时一般儒生所尊奉，后汉灵帝时所刻的《熹平石经》就是用的《张侯论》。《古文论语》是在汉景帝时由鲁恭王刘馀在孔子旧宅壁中发现的，当时并没有传授。直到东汉末年，大学者郑玄以《张侯论》为依据，参照《齐论》、《古论》，作了《论语注》。在残存的郑玄《论语注》中我们还可以略略窥见《鲁》、《齐》、《古》三种《论语》本子的异同。今天，我们所用的《论语》本子，基本上就是《张侯论》。

《论语》自汉代以来，便有不少人注解它。《论语》和《孝经》是汉朝初学者必读之书，一定要先读这两部书，才进而学习“五经”。“五经”就是今天的《诗经》、《尚书》(除去伪古文)、《易经》、《仪礼》和《春秋》。看来，《论语》是汉人启蒙书的一种。汉朝人所注释的《论语》，基本上全部亡佚，今日所残存的，以郑玄(127—200，《后汉书》有传)注为较多，因为敦煌和日本发现了一些唐写本残卷，估计十存六七；其他各家，在何晏(190—249)《论语集解》以后，就多半只存于《论语集解》中。现在《十三经注疏》中的《论语注疏》就是用何晏《集解》和宋人邢昺(932—1010，《宋史》有传)的《疏》。至于何晏、邢昺前后还有不少专注《论语》的书，可以参看清人朱彝尊(1629—1709，《清史稿》有传)的《经义考》、纪昀(1724—1805)等人的《四库全书总目提要》以及唐代陆德明(550左右—630左右)的《经典释文序录》和吴检斋(承仕)先生的《疏证》。

《论语译注》的作者杨伯峻先生是一位语言学家和文献学家。他对语言学(尤其是语法学)和文献学两门学问都有精深研究。《论语译注》是在国内外产生过重大影响的著作，已成为世界上许多大学的文科教材或重要参考书。该书旁搜远绍，博采古今学人的研究成果，间下己意，于注释中尽量将历史知识、地理沿革、名物制度、古代民俗以及古代哲学思想考证交代清楚；作为语言学家，他尤其注意字音词义、语法修辞规律的介绍，并时常对这方面的疑难问题进行论证。惟其如此，故能突破前修，独树一帜。如“好之者不如乐之者”(《雍也》)的“乐”字，旧时从《经典释文》的所谓“叶音”读“五教切”或“义效切”，释为“爱好”，这无疑是错误的。对此，杨先生在解放前即发表过《破音略考》一文于《国文月刊》,予以辩正。在《论语译注》中，他仍认为应读 lè，为意动用法。此句便译为“喜爱它的人又不如以它为乐的人”。《论语译注》的译文明白晓畅，并能保持原文的语录体风格。书末附有《论语词典》,尤便读者。

著名的古文字学家张政烺先生赞誉《论语译注》和《孟子译注》为同类著作的典范，40年来，一版再版，历久不衰。正由于这样，我们才将它选入《大中华文库》。

关于《论语》的书，真是汗牛充栋，举不胜举。读者如果认为看了《论语译注》还有进一步研究的必要，可以再看下列几种书：

(1)《论语注疏》——即何晏《集解》、邢昺《疏》,在《十三经注疏》中，除武英殿本外，其他各本多沿袭阮元南昌刻本，因它有《校勘记》，可以参考。

(2)《论语集注》——宋代朱熹(1130—1200)从《礼记》中抽出《大学》和《中庸》,合《论语》、《孟子》为《四书》,自己用很大功力作《集注》。从明朝至清末，科举考试，题目都从《四书》中出；所做文章的义理，也不能违背朱熹的见解，这叫做“代圣人立言”，影响很大。另外朱熹对于《论语》，不但讲“义理”，也注意训诂，故这书无妨参看。

(3)刘宝楠(1791—1855)《论语正义》——清代儒生多不满意唐、宋人的注疏，所以陈奂(1786—1863)作《毛诗传疏》，焦循(1763—1820)作《孟子正义》。刘宝楠便依焦循作《孟子正义》之法，作《论语正义》。后因病而停笔，由他的儿子刘恭冕(1821—1880)继续写定。所以这书实为刘宝楠父子共著。征引广博，折中大体恰当。只因学问日益进展，昔日的好书，今天便可以指出不少缺点，但参考价值仍然不小。

(4)程树德《论语集释》,征引书籍达680种，虽仍有疏略可商之处，因其广征博引，故可参考。

(5)杨树达(1885—1956)《论语疏证》。这书把三国以前所有征引《论语》或者和《论语》的有关资料都依《论语》原文疏列，时出己意，加案语，值得参考。④

三

《论语》流传至国外,有一个由近及远，先东亚，后欧美的过程。

自汉武帝采纳董仲舒的建议,“罢黜百家，独尊儒术”之后，孔子和《论语》逐渐获得了至高无上的地位。随着中国文化向周边国家扩散，《论语》也先后传至越南、朝鲜和日本。

公元前111年(汉武帝元鼎六年)，南越国灭亡，越南北方从此成为中国的一部分，达一千余年，获得独尊地位的儒术，包括《论语》等经典，也随之传入越南。

公元374年，朝鲜半岛上的百济开始设立“博士”一职。此职专掌儒家经典的传授，《论语》传入朝鲜，当在此时。640年(唐贞观十四年)，半岛上的高句丽、新罗、百济三国遣世子和贵族子弟至唐，入国子监研习《论语》等儒家经典。

公元513、516、554年，百济三次遣“五经博士”赴日本传授儒家学说,《论语》当于此时传入日本。768年(唐大历三年)，天皇依唐朝国子监的规定，诏称孔子为“文宣王”。此前，日本依唐律称孔子为“先圣文宣父”。

《论语》之译为西方语言是在16世纪末。艾儒略(J. Aleni)在《大西利先生行述》一文中介绍意大利人利玛窦(Matteo Ricci，1552—1610)“曾将中国《四书》译为西文，寄回本国，国人读而悦之，知中国古书，能识真源……皆利子之力也”。所谓“西文”，这里指拉丁文。1591年(明万历十九年)利玛窦着手翻译《四书》，1594年完成，但不幸未能出版而散佚了。

清初，曾在中国传教的意大利耶稣会士殷铎泽(Prosper Intercetta，1625—1696)和葡萄牙耶稣会士郭纳爵(Ignatius da Casta，1599—1666)用拉丁文合译了《论语》。该译本于1687年由比利时耶稣会士柏应理(Philippus Couplet，1624—1692)出版于巴黎，是为《论语》首次在欧洲刊行。书名为《中国哲学家孔子》(Confucius, Sinarum Philosophus)，中文标题为《西文四书解》，另收有《大学》和《中庸》。出版之后，反响强烈。1688、1691年，《中国哲学家孔子》分别在法英两国出版了法文、英文的节译本。广大民众于是有了接触孔子思想的机会，这引起了整个西欧对中国的赞扬。到18世纪，谈到整个世界，人们总是说“从中国到秘鲁”。

1711年，布拉格大学刊印了比利时传教士卫方济(Franciscus Noël，1651—1729)用拉丁文译的《四书》。卫氏1687年来华，15年后回欧洲。

第九届驻北京东正教传道团修士大司祭雅金夫·比丘林(Н. Я. Ъичурин，1777—1853)和俄罗斯科学院院士王西里(В. Л. Васипъеь，1818—1900)分别于1821年之后和1840—

1850 年间将《论语》译为俄文出版。列夫·托尔斯泰读《论语》时，写信给契诃夫说："我在读儒家著作，这是第二天了。难以想象，它们达到了不同寻常的精神高度。""我正沉湎于中国的智慧之中，极想告诉您和大家这些书籍给我带来的精神上的教益。"他承认，在他成年以后，在东方哲学家中，孔子、孟子对他影响"很大"。

包括《论语》在内的《四书》传到美国是在 18 世纪末或 19 世纪初，有英、法、拉丁等译本。美国超验主义代表人物爱默生(R. W. Emerson，1803—1882) 和梭罗 (H. D. Thoreau，1817—1862)对这些经典都爱不释手，诗人维切尔·林赛(V. Lindsay，1879—1931)则以引吭高歌来表达他对孔子的热爱：愿我们是孔子时代的学士，眼望着古老的中国倾倒如山……

此外，18 世纪初至 19 世纪中叶，《论语》还出版了瑞典语、德语、罗马尼亚语的译本。

今天，《论语》已被译成几十种文字，它的总印数仅次于《圣经》，而高于其他任何一部畅销书。随着以《论语》为主的儒家经典的传播，儒学已成为世界人文科学的热点。1994 年孔子诞辰 2545 周年之际，国际儒学联合会在北京成立了。新加坡内阁资政李光耀任名誉理事长，韩国成均馆馆长崔德根任理事长。洙泗之水"盈科而后进"的涓涓细流，终于汹涌澎湃地"放乎四海"。

上世纪至本世纪将《论语》译为英文的还有英国传教士马歇曼(J. Marshman，1768—1837)、柯大卫(David Collie)以及汉学家翟理思(翟林奈 L. Giles，1875—1958)等人，质量较高的则有理雅各、韦利(亚瑟·威利)及刘殿爵三人的译本。

理雅各(James Legge，1815—1897)，苏格兰人，1839年由伦敦教会派往马六甲布道，任该会所办英华书院(香港中文大学前身)院长，1843年随书院迁往香港。1848年起，在其他教士及华人黄胜等帮助下，开始翻译中国典籍。1861年到1886年出版《中国经典》28卷，内容是四书(包括《论语》)五经及老庄著作，共14种。有鉴于此，牛津大学聘请他为首席汉学教授。

韦利(Arthur David Waley，1889—1996)曾长期任大英博物馆东方部馆员，负责研究整理敦煌文物，同时在伦敦大学东方研究学院授课。他早在剑桥大学皇家学院读书时，受名教授迪金森与摩尔影响，便仰慕中国古代文明，决心研究中国文化，并刻苦自修中文。他关于中国文化的译著，除《论语》外，多达七八种。

刘殿爵(D. C. Lau，1915—)，广东番禺人，生于香港，毕业于香港大学。1949年在苏格兰格拉斯哥大学修完哲学硕士学位课程，随后执教于伦敦大学。1970年升为中文系讲座教授，1978年返港，历任中文大学讲座教授、文学院院长、中国语文研究中心主任。译作有《论语》等七种。

以上三位学者都对《论语》作过深入研究，不仅是翻译而已；译文质量也均属上乘。理氏所译为19世纪书面语体英文，喜用复句，措词古雅，对于年轻读者，未免有些难懂；刘译出版于1979年，用口语语体，喜用单句，通俗易懂，但风格上与原文不免有所出入。韦利所译在时间和风格上都介于二者之间：文字比较简练，接近原文风格，甚至在表达方式上也力争逼肖原文。基于此,《大中华文库》选用了韦利的译本,威利译本中的引言、注释以及名词解释极有学术价值,也在附录中予以保留。和理、刘所译一样,韦译本也有若干值得商榷之处,有些我们已经注意到了,出版时当尽可能地予以改正。[5]

杨逢彬

1999.4

注释:

① 雅斯贝斯:《历史的起源与目标》,华夏出版社 1989 年版,第 3 页。

② 雅斯贝斯:《历史的起源与目标》,华夏出版社 1989 年版,第 14 页。

③ 参见杨伯峻的《试论孔子》,中华书局 1980 年版《论语译注》,第 17 页。

④ 这一部分多是《论语译注·导言》的缩写。

⑤ 这一部分参考了十余部著作和打印稿。其中重点参考了马祖毅、任荣珍著《汉籍外译史》(湖北教育出版社 1997 年版)和刘重德教授所撰《〈论语〉韦利英译本审读意见》(打印件)。

Introduction

Part Ⅰ

As is said in the tradition, the Chinese civilization has a long history of 5,000 years. But now, in China and the Chinese communities overseas, any Chinese tradition, be the major tradition held by the social elite or the minor tradition understood by common citizens or countryside peasants, is just the same. Every Chinese, every act and every move of his or hers may be originated in one book—*The Confucian Analects*, a canon formed 2,400 years ago. That is one of the so-called Axial Periods.

"Axial Period" is a concept put forth by Karl Jaspers, a German philosopher. As he pointed out, after the pre-history and the civilization of remote antiquity, in about 500 BC, some very remarkable events occurred in the scale of the whole world.

In China, Confucius and Laozi were very active, all the Chinese philosophical schools including Mozi, Zhuangzi, Liezi and the other various schools all came into being. So also is the case with India, there appeared Upanishad and Buddha; people probed into the whole philosophical probability from scepticism, materialism, sophism to nihilism. In Iran, Zoroaster taught a challenging viewpoint that human life in this world is a struggle between good and evil. In Palestine, from Elijah, via Isaiah, to the second Isaiah, many prophets came out. As for Greek philosophers, Homer, Parmenides, Herakleitos, Plato, and many tragedians, and Thoucydides and Archimedes, all came out. In these centuries, what were embodied in these names developed almost simultaneously in China,

India and the West which were unaware of one another.[1]

Jaspers calls this period the "axis" of the world history.

The mankind always lives in dependence on what people thought and created in the axial period, and people tend to review this period at every new leap forward and they are rekindled by it. After that, so always is the case, the revival of and the return to the potentiality of the axial period, or its renaissance, always provides us with some new spiritual impetus.[2]

As Talcatt Parsons says, in this brilliant period, the four sources of the world civilization, namely, Greece, Babylonia, India and China, all underwent a "philosophical breakthrough." That is to say, mankind acquired a more reasonable recognition of the origin of the universe in which man lives, and the position which man occupies, and the reason why man is called man.

In China, without Confucius and his *Analects*, we can say nothing of "philosophical breakthrough." As is heard usually, Chinese philosophy is rather ethical. Truly the core of Chinese philosophy is the doctrines of ethics and morality. If we take it that the various forms of Western culture lay stress on the seeking for truth, we may say, the various forms of Chinese culture lay stress on the seeking for goodness. In the ancient times, the first lesson a disciple was taught by any teacher was to cultivate the *virtue*, be the latter a learned scholar or a master of martial arts. Teachers might let his disciples or students recite some maxims or mottoes, which, in most cases, are quoted from the *Analects*.

The resources of traditional Chinese morality have been cast away as rubbish in the past decades. So nowadays even in the big cities, it is hard to find the books of relevant contents. If you are particular in morality, you must be regarded as "a big fool." As a result, some people say, the world today is a world stinking of money every day. But in some "underdeveloped" rural places, the moral ideas contained in the ancient classics still remain. A countryside couple, though they may be little educated, embody the Confucian moralities, in either their speech or their behavior. And their children are brought up in such an atmosphere unconscious of the fact that this is a teaching of traditional morality. In some memoirs of the Cultural Revolution, we may read such scenes describing how someone was sent down to the countryside as a criticized target drawing a wounded body, but the peasants treated him or her as their relatives. It is the reflection of the reality. It is something happened "when people seek for rites in the countryside after having lost them." Such a phenomenon shows that the traditional moralities dwell deeply in man's heart and it is everlastingly green and new. Meanwhile it tells us that "we must not cast away everything in our household, so as to imitate the beggar in the street." (Quoted from a poem by Zhu Xi) So we must read the *Confucian Analects*; it is a textbook of life for all the Chinese people.

What is the *Confucian Analects* about?

As for the fundamental thought of *Confucian Analects*, people have invariably insisted that there are two points of view. One is the *ren* (benevolence). The other is *li* (rite).

Of the scholars studying *The Confucian Analects* from ancient to present, many hold that the book is in the main about benevolence, only some hold that it is a book about rite. Among the latter there are ancient scholars Wang Yuan, Dai Zhen, Chen Feng, Wang Xianqian, and modern scholars Liu Yizheng, Li Dazhao, Chen Duxiu, Hou Wailu, Cai Shangsi, Zhao Jibin and so on.

Mr. Yang Bojun thinks that the core of *Confucian Analects* is benevolence. Below is his statistic result. In *Zuo Qiuming's Chronicle*, the character *rite* is used 462 times, while the character *benevolence* 33 times only. In *Confucian Analects*, the character *rite* is used 75 times only (according to *A Dictionary of Confucian Analects*, 74 times), while the character *benevolence* as many as 109 times (*A Tentative Exposition of Confucius*, see Yang Bojun's *Confucian Analects with Translation and Annotation*, p.16).

We think that the core of *Confucian Analects* is, for a certainty, benevolence.

The benevolence in *Confucian Analects* does not refer to only one thing. Extensively speaking, it means to apply a policy of benevolence in all lands under heaven. Intensively speaking, it means to love people. It refers to loyalty and consideration, and the fundamental way to be a real human being, namely, filial piety to one's parents and love and respect to one's elder brothers. To be a benevolent man in true sense is very difficult, but everyone can do something to achieve it, that is to say, to do good, it is the practice of keeping the benevolent virtue. Let's discuss the problem at four points.

Below is the first point. Benevolence is the very nature by which the human distinguishes himself from the animal, if one is living, he should put the benevolent virtue in practice; and meanwhile, benevolence is the lofty goal one should try to achieve all his life. On one side, people with high ideals are those who exist with benevolence all the time; on the other, they take it for a duty to apply a policy of benevolence in all lands under heaven.

Confucius says, "Benevolence is the humanity." ("The Doctrine of the Mean") Again he says, "Riches and honors are what men desire. If it cannot be obtained in the proper way, they should not be held. Poverty and meanness are what men dislike. If it cannot be obtained in the proper way, they should not be avoided. If a superior man abandons virtue, how can he fulfill the requirements of that name? The superior man does not, even for the space of a single meal, act contrary to virtue. In moments of haste, he cleaves to it. In seasons of danger, he cleaves to it." ("Li Ren") Confucius once praised that Yan Hui was his best student by an exclamation "admirable indeed!" ("Yong Ye")"Benevolence" is a goal worth one's pursuing all his life. "The scholar may not be without breadth of mind and vigorous endurance. His burden is heavy and his course is long. Perfect virtue is the burden, which he considers it is his to sustain;—is it not heavy? Only with death does his course stop;—is it not long?" ("Tai Bo")In order to achieve the benevolent virtue, one should not hesitate to sacrifice his all. "The determined scholar and the man of virtue will not seek to live at the expense of injuring their virtue. They will even sacrifice their lives to preserve their virtue complete." ("Wei Ling Gong") Benevolence is the highest goal and the most ideal state that man may reach. Righteousness, loyalty, forbearance, filial piety, and loving consideration are concrete items under the extensive concept of benevolence.

The second point of view says, benevolence is the important procedure to realize the highest goal to the effect that "the whole world is one community."

The Book of Rites records the conception of Confucius that the whole world is one community, the chapter entitled "Li Yun" says as follows.

When the great Tao prevailed, the whole world was one community. Then people might select the worthy and promote the capable, and have regard for credit and amity, so people would love not only their own kinsmen and children, but also do their duties to the others. As a result, the aged would live their full span, the able-bodied would be of some use, the young would grow up, and the spouse-bereaved, the orphan, the single, the invalid and the diseased would be supported, the male had a sufficient share, and the female had proper marriage. Goods seemed to dislike to lie on the ground, so there was no need to keep them in one's own house; the strength seemed to dislike not to come from the body, so there was no need to use it for one's own purpose. Therefore nobody would plot anymore; there were no robbers and bandits, thus it was unnecessary to close the gate. If so, we may say, the whole world has truly become one community.

I think that such a conception is the same as "the case of a man who extensively confers benefits on the people, and is able to assist all." "Yong Ye" also says as follows: Zigong said, "Suppose the case of a man extensively conferring benefits on the people, and is able to assist all, what would you say of him? Might he be called perfectly virtuous?" The Master said, "Why speak only of virtue in connection with him? Must he not have the qualities of a sage? Even Yao and Shun were still solicitous about this." If one may be able to "extensively confer the benefits on the people," he is more than a "benevolent" person, he may be called a "sage" now. Maybe Yao and Shun were not able to accomplish so much. This tells us that the sage contains the benevolence, and the benevolence is in accordance with the sage. Confucius gave us the answer. He thought that Zilu, Ran You, Gongxi Hua, Chen Wen and Minister Ziwen, did not achieve the benevolent state, and what Yan Yuan reached is only "not contrary to the benevolence." ("Yong Ye") But Confucius praised Guan Zhong as a benevolent man.

Zigong said, "Guan Zhong, I apprehend, was wanting in virtue. When the prince Huan caused his brother Jiu to be killed, Guan Zhong was not able to die with him. Moreover, he became prime minister to Huan." The Master said, "Guan Zhong acted as prime minister to the prince Huan, made him leader of all the princes, and united and rectified the whole kingdom. Down to the present day, the people enjoy the gifts which he conferred. But for Guan Zhong we should now be wearing our hair unbound, and the lappets of our coats buttoning on the left side!"("Xian Wen")

Zilu said, "The prince Huan caused his brother Jiu to be killed, when Shao Hu died with his master, but Guan Zhong did not die. May not I say that he was wanting in virtue?" The Master said, "The prince Huan assembled all the princes together, and that not with weapons of war and chariots:—it was through the influence of Guan Zhong. Whose benevolence was like his? Whose benevolence was like his?" ("Xian Wen")

In Confucius' opinion, Guan Zhong is benevolent in that he helped the prince Huan to bring about a stable situation in the whole country for a rather long period so that people might recuperate and multiply, though he was not parsimonious and did not know the rules of propriety.[3]

The following is the third point. Benevolence may be accumulated bit by bit in everyday life. Benevolence means to love people. The way to carry out the benevolent virtue is to put oneself in the place of another, and from the near to the distant.

Confucius never regarded anybody as a "benevolent" person carelessly. Is "benevolence" a state too high for people to reach? No. Although it is difficult to become a benevolent person or a sage, it is quite easy to practice benevolence by doing every trifle well in everyday life. "The practice of perfect virtue is from a man himself." ("Yan Yuan") "Is virtue a thing remote? I wish to be virtuous, and lo! Virtue is at hand." ("Shu Er") "The man of perfect virtue is cautious and slow in his speech."

("Yan Yuan") "The man of virtue makes the difficulty to be overcome his first business." ("Yong Ye") "The firm, the enduring, the simple, and the modest, are near to virtue." ("Zilu") "Fine words and an insinuating appearance are seldom associated with true virtue." ("Xue Er") "Zizhang asked Confucius about perfect virtue. Confucius said, 'To be able to practice five things everywhere under heaven constitutes perfect virtue.' He begged to ask what they were, and was told, 'Gravity, generosity, sincerity, earnestness, and kindness. If you are grave, you will not be treated with disrespect. If you are generous, you will win all. If you are sincere, people will repose trust in you. If you are earnest, you will accomplish much. If you are kind, this will enable you to employ the services of others.'"("Yang Huo") Of course, benevolence is by no means trifling moral norms, it is "of an all-pervading unity." ("Li Ren") Concretely speaking, "benevolence" is to "love all men." ("Yan Yuan") "The stable being burned down, when he was at court, on his return he said, 'Has many man been hurt?' He did not ask about the horses." ("Xiang Dang") The source of "benevolence" is filial piety and fraternal submission. "The superior man bends his attention to what is radical. That being established, all practical courses naturally grow up. Filial piety and fraternal submission! —Are they not the root of all benevolent actions?" ("Xue Er") Why do we say that filial piety and fraternal submission are the source of benevolence? This is because the way to practice benevolence is the expanded way to love one's kinsmen; it is just the same by doing it from near to remote and from ego to people. "When those who are in high positions perform well all their duties to their relations, the people are aroused to virtues." ("Tai Bo") Negatively speaking, it means, do not do unto others what would not have them do unto you. This is loyalty and consideration. "The doctrine of our master is to be true to the principles of our nature and the benevolent exercise of them to others, —this and nothing more." ("Li Ren") "What you do not want done to yourself, do not do to others." ("Yan Yuan," "Wei Ling Gong") Positively speaking, it means, live and let live. "Now the man of perfect virtue, wishing to be established himself, seeks also to establish others; wishing to be enlarged himself, he seeks also to enlarge others. To be able to judge of others by what is nigh in ourselves;—this may be called the art of virtue." ("Yong Ye") As is said by Mencius, "He is lovingly disposed to people generally, and kind to creatures."("Jin Xin," Part I) "Treat with the reverence due to age the elders in your own family, so that the elders in the families of others shall be similarly treated. Treat with the kindness due to youth the young in your own family, so that the young in the families of others shall be similarly treated." ("King Hui of Liang," Part I) As is also said by Zhang Zai, a scholar in the Song dynasty, "The people are my blood brothers, I shall give them what I have." This is the fraternity that expands the love as kinsfolk feelings to the utmost, and promotes the human spirit to the altitude of the "integrity of heaven and man." This spirit can not only cure the human society of materialism today, but also save earth, our homeland, which is facing the doom for man has been extorting too much from it.

The fourth point is like this. Judging from the relationship of benevolence and rite, the former is the root, the latter the branch; the former is the ins, the latter the outs; the former is the content, the latter the form. Benevolence is the ultimate aim, rite is a kind of binding force and norms and system which guarantee the achievement of the purpose.

According to Mr. Yang Bojun's *A Dictionary of Confucian Analects*, the word *rite* has been used for 74 times, meaning ritual intention, ceremony and propriety, system, and discipline. We think that ceremony and propriety, system, and discipline rites and law all serve the aim—"all under heaven will converge at benevolence."

Zixia asked, saying, "What is the meaning of the passage—The pretty dimples of her arftul smile! The well defined black and white of her eye! The plain ground for the colors?" The Master said, "The business of laying on the colors follows the preparation of the plain ground." Zixia said, "Are ceremonies then a subsequent thing?" The Master said, "It is Shang who can bring out my meaning! Now I can begin to talk about the Odes with him." ("Ba Yi")

Here, the word "subsequent" tells us that rite should come after benevolence. Although Confucius, quoting Meng Xi's words, said, "If you do not learn the rules of Propriety, your character cannot be established," ("Ji Shi") more emphatically he said, "If a man be without the virtues proper to humanity, what has he to do with the rites of propriety? If a man be without the virtues proper to humanity, what has he to do with music?" ("Ba Yi") If one fails to learn rules of etiquette and ceremony, he cannot have a foothold in the society. If one learns the rules of etiquette and ceremony well but nothing of benevolence, he can be nothing but a hypocrite. A superior man should learn the rules of etiquette and ceremony in that he wants to practice the benevolence under heaven. "To subdue one's self and return to propriety is perfect virtue. If a man can for one day subdue himself and return to propriety, all under heaven will ascribe perfect virtue to him." ("Yan Yuan") Namely, only by controlling one's self and returning to ritual system can benevolence be realized in the whole world. Confucius advocated the return of propriety, but he had no idea to restore the rite of the Zhou dynasty, he intended to make some adjustments ("Wei Zheng"). For example, there were cases to bury alive with the dead from the Western Zhou dynasty to the Spring and Autumn Period, the practice was in accordance with the then ritual system. The prince Mu of Qin, though able and virtuous, was buried with three good men at his funeral. Confucius lived in an age not far from the antiquity, he must know such a practice. Nevertheless, he hated bitterly when he saw pottery figurines were buried with the dead. "Zhongni said, 'Was he not without posterity who first made wooden images to bury with the dead?' So he added, because that man made the semblances of men, and used them for that purpose." ("King Hui of Liang," Part I, *The Works of Mencius*) Benevolence means to love people. Confucius angrily condemned all the inhuman actions, even if they were in accordance with the "ritual system." Again he said, "The linen cap is that prescribed by the rules of ceremony, but now a silk one is worn. It is economical, and I follow the common practice." ("Zi Han") The linen cap can be substituted by a silk one, which costs less, what Confucius values is the essence of rite. "It is according to the rules of propriety, they say. It is according to the rules of propriety, they say. Are gems and silk all that is meant by propriety? It is music, they say. It is music, they say. Are bells and drums all that is meant by music?" ("Yang Huo") What is the essence of rite that Confucius approves? As stated above, it is benevolence and righteousness. When Confucius taught his students, he always took benevolence for the ultimate aim. As for literature and etiquette, they are secondary. "A youth, when at home, should be filial, and, abroad, respectful to the elders. He should be earnest and truthful. He should overflow in love to all, and cultivate friendship of the good. When he has time and opportunity after the performance of these things, he should employ them in polite studies." ("Xue Er") "The superior man extensively studying all learning, and keeping himself under the restraint of the rules of propriety, may thus likewise not overstep what is right."

("Yong Ye") And Yan Yuan also said, "The Master, by orderly method, skillfully leads men on. He enlarged my mind with learning, and taught me the restraints of propriety. When I wish to give over the study of his doctrines, I cannot do so··· "("Zi Han") "Filial piety and fraternal love" are the fundamentals of benevolence. Benevolence means to love people, this asks us to love people extensively. It is quite natural for those who seek for benevolence to be close to the benevolent. Only after cultivating yourself in this way can you be qualified to study concrete disciplines, to follow the rules of propriety. In the *Confucian Analects*, the term *rite* has some other usage than *to restrain*, for example, it also means *to regulate, to unify, to accomplish* and so on. "In practicing the rules of propriety, appropriateness is to be prized. In the ways prescribed by the ancient kings, this is the excellent quality, and in things small and great we follow them. Yet it is not to be observed in all cases. If one, knowing how such appropriateness should be prized, manifests it, without regulating it by the rules of propriety, this likewise is not to be done." ("Xue Er") "If the people be led by laws, and uniformity sought to be given them by punishments, they will try to avoid the punishment, but have no sense of shame. If they be led by virtue, and uniformity sought to be given them by the rules of propriety, they will have the sense of shame, and moreover will become good." ("Wei Zheng") "Suppose a man with the knowledge of Zang Wuzhong, the freedom from covetousness of Gongchuo, the bravery of Zhuangzi of Bian, and the varied talents of Ran Qiu; add to these the accomplishments of the rules of propriety and music—such a one might be reckoned a complete man." ("Xian Wen") From the above examples, we may see that rite always functions to restrain, to regulate, to rectify, and to accomplish, its ultimate aim is always benevolence. "Meng Yi asked what filial piety was. The Master said, 'It is not being disobedient.' …The Master replied, 'That parents, when alive, should be served according to propriety; that, when dead, they should be buried according to propriety; and that they should be sacrificed to according to propriety.'" ("Wei Zheng") "Let there be a careful attention to perform the funeral rites to parents, and let them be followed when long gone with the ceremonies of sacrifice; then the virtue of the people will resume its proper excellence." ("Xue Er") Here we see clearly that funeral and sacrifice must be according to propriety is only for the purpose to begin and end an affair earnestly, to cultivate the virtue of man abundantly, namely, "When those who are in high stations perform well all their duties to their relations, the people are aroused to virtue." ("Tai Bo")

In short, the core of the *Confucian Analects* is benevolence. While rite is secondary and it serves benevolence only.

Part Ⅱ

In "Descriptive Accounts of Books," *The History of the Han Dynasty* by Ban Gu, there is a record as follows: "*The Analects* is a book of the answers Confucius gave to his disciples and contemporaries as well as the dialogue between the disciples and their Master. The disciples had their own records. When Confucius passed away, his disciples got together and edited these words, so the book is called the *Confucian Analects*." In "Bian Ming Lun," *Wen Xuan*, Li Shan quoted from *Fuzi* as follows, "When Confucius passed away, Zhonggong and some other disciples recollected their Master's words, and edited a book entitled *Confucian Analects*." As we know, analects come from Greek *analegein*, to collect up, and *legein*, to gather. It is truly interesting enough! So also is the case with *lun yu*, the Chinese pronunciation of *analects. Lun*, means to collect up, to gather; *yu*, speech, words; *lun yu*, to collect up, to edit the words relative to Confucius. *The Confucian Analects* is a book about dialogues and actions of Confucius and some of his students. And the book was called *Lun Yu* then. It is the original title.

The Confucian Analects is also a collection of fragments. These fragments were collected together at random, there is no unified reason of the order of a given book of it; and even in one book there is no unified reason between its two successive chapters. And what is more, these fragments were recorded by more than one person. *The Confucian Analects* is not a big book, but there are many recurrent passages in it. For example, the chapter of "fine words and an insinuating appearance" is first seen in "Xue Er, " and then in "Yang Huo." And there are some passages repeating one another on the whole, the only difference among them is that some are detailed, and some sketchy. For example, the chapter of "if the scholar is not grave" is seen in "Xue Er" and "Zi Han," but in the former there are eleven characters more than in the latter. There are some passages of the same meaning but different in words. For example, "Li Ren" says, "I am not concerned that I am not known; I seek to be worthy to be known." "Xian Wen" says, "I will not be concerned at men's not knowing me; I will be concerned at my own want of ability." "Wei Ling Gong" says, "The superior man is distressed by his want of ability. He is not distressed by men's not knowing him." And "Xue Er" says, "Is he not a man of complete virtue, who feels no discomposure though men may take no note of him?" The same idea was repeatedly recorded for four times. This phenomenon can only be reasonably deduced as follows. Confucius' words were recorded separately by his disciples in that very age, later a book was made on basis of the various records. Therefore we cannot regard the *Analects* as a book written by a certain author. Among the authors, there are Confucius' students. "Zi Han" says, "Lao said,—The Master said, 'Having no official employment, I acquired many arts.'" According to legend, Lao's family name is Qin, who is also called Zikai, or Zizhang. Here the family name is not mentioned, but only his personal name. The recording style here is different from the general style of the *Analects*. Therefore we may deduce that this chapter was recorded by Qin Lao himself, and those who edited the *Analects* "directly put the recorded materials into the book." (*Rongo Shusetsu*, by Yasui Sokken, 1799 - 1876, a Japanese scholar) Again, "Xian Wen" says, "Xian asked what was shameful. The Master said, 'When good government prevails in a state, to be thinking only of his salary; and, when bad government prevails, to be thinking, in the same way, only of his salary; — this is shamful.'" Here Xian refers to Yuan Xian, who is also called Zisi. It is obvious that this is also a record by Yuan Xian himself.

The sections and chapters of the *Analects* were recorded not only by his students, but also by his students' students. Quite a few were recorded by Zeng Shen's students. For example, "Tai Bo" says, "The philosopher Zeng being sick, he called to him the disciples of his school, and said, 'Uncover my feet, uncover my hands. It is said in the *Book of Poetry*, "We should be apprehensive and cautious, as if standing on the brink of a deep gulf, as if treading on thin ice." And so have I been. Now and hereafter, I know my escape from all injury to my person. O! ye, my little children.'" Nobody can deny this chapter is recorded by one of Zeng Shen's disciples. For another example, "Zizhang" says, "The disciples of Zixia asked Zizhang about the principles of intercourse. Zizhang asked, 'What does Zixia say on the subject?' They replied, 'Zixia says,

— "Associate with those who can advantage you. Put away from you those who cannot do so." Zizhang observed, 'This is different from what I have learned. The superior man honors the talented and virtuous and bears with all. He praises the good, and pities the incompetent. Am I possessed of great talent and virtue? — Who is there among men whom I will not bear with? Am I devoid of talents and virtue? — Men will put me away from them. What have we to do with the putting away of others?'" This long passage looks like a record by a certain disciple of Zizhang or Zixia. Again, "Xian Jin"says, "The Master said, 'Filial indeed is Min Ziqian! Other people say nothing of him different from the report of his parents and brothers.'" " Minzi was standing by his side, looking bland and precise; Zilu looking bold and soldierly; Ran You and Zigong with a free and straightforward manner. The Master was pleased." As we know, when Confucius called his students, his habit is to call them by their personal names directly. But here, we see a peculiar instance, he called Min Sun by his style — Ziqian. This arouses our suspicion. I think this chapter was recorded by one of Min Sun's students afterwards from memory, so there remains such a careless trace. As for the chapter of "Minzi was standing by his side," we find Min Sun is called *zi* (the ancient title of respect for learned and virtuous man), and he is mentioned before the other three— Zilu, Ran You and Zigong. This is hard to understand. By age, Zilu is the oldest. By official rank, Min Sun is inferior to the other three. Why should he be mentioned before them? Why should he be styled *zi*?A reasonable deduction may be that Min Ziqian's students recorded what they often heard from their teacher.

Since among the authors of the *Analects* there are disciples of Confucius, and also disciples of disciples, the whole book must be written at different dates. This may also be seen in the vocabulary. For example, the word "master" referred to the third person in the earlier days, meaning "that granddad." Not until the period of Warring States did it begin to refer to the direct dialogist, meaning "you Granddad." In the *Analects*, in most cases, it refers to "that granddad," too.The disciples of Confucius called him "Sir" to his face. When behind his back, they called him "Master." The other people also called Confucius "Master" when behind his back. But in "Yang Huo," there are two exceptions. One reads as follows: Ziyou replied, "Formerly, Master, I heard you say …" The other reads as follows. Zilu said, "Master, formerly I have heard you say…" Both are examples of calling a person" Master" to his face, and this starts a new usage of the word "master" in this way, which prevails formally in the period of Warring States. People wrote the *Analects* at different dates, the time between the earliest and the latest is more than scores of years. You can visualize this by seeing these two examples.

The last editors of the *Analects* must be some students of Zeng Shen. Firstly, whenever Zeng Shen is mentioned, the title *zi* is used. And the passages recording his words and actions are more than others'. The record of Zeng Shen's words and actions amounts to thirteen chapters.Secondly, among the disciples of Confucius, Zeng Shen is the youngest, and what is more, there is a chapter recording his speech to Meng Jing before his death. Meng Jing is the posthumous title of Zhongsun Jie, a son of Meng Wu. Suppose Zeng Shen died in 436 BC, Meng Jing's death must be later than the former. Therefore, the recorder of this event must write so only after Meng Jing's death. It is hard to ascertain how many years Meng Jing lived for. But in "Tan Gong," *The Book of Rites*, there is a record. It says, when duke Dao of Lu died, Meng Jing said much to Ji Zhao, from which we know, when Zeng Shen was near to seventy years old, Meng Jing had already become one of the ministers in power in Lu. Nobody has ever had any doubt of this record. No persons and events recorded in *Analects* are later than this, so it is sure that the last editors of the *Analects* are some of Zeng Shen's students. Therefore we say, the date of the *Analects* started from the late Spring and Autumn Period, and ended with the early Warring States.

Down to the Han dynasty, there were three editions of the *Analects*. The first is the *Analects of Lu*, containing twenty books. The second is the *Analects of Qi*, containing twenty-two books, many sentences and phrases are the same as the first, but there are two books more than the first, namely, "Wen Wang" and "Zhi Dao." The third is the *Analects of Ancient Script*, containing twenty-one books, without "Wen Wang" and "Zhi Dao". But in this edition "Zizhang" is divided into two, so there are two books entitled "Zizhang." The order of books is also different from the editions of Qi and Lu, and over 400 characters are different. At first the editions of Qi and Lu were transmitted down under the guidance of respective teachers of their own. Down to the late years of the Western Han dynasty, there occurred a scholar named Zhang Yu, who was the marquis of Anchang. He first studied the Lu edition, and then he studied and lectured the Qi edition. After that he combined the two editions into one but he adopted the order of the Lu edition. People called the new edition the *Analects of Marquis Zhang*. Zhang Yu was the master of Emperor Cheng of Han. He was held in great respect. Most scholars followed his edition then. And in the Xi Ping Reign (172-177) of Emperor Ling of Han, this edition was inscribed on the stone. This is the famous *Xi Ping Stone Scripture. The Analects of Ancient Script* was discovered in the wall of Confucian old house by Liu Yu, King Gong of Lu, in the reign (157-141BC) of Emperor Jing of Han, and nobody taught it then. During the last years of the Eastern Han dynasty, Zheng Xuan, the then greatest scholar, wrote his *Commentary to the Analects* on basis of the *Analects of Marquis Zhang,* with reference to the *Analects of Qi* and the *Analects of Ancient Script*. Now in the remainder of *Commentary to* the *Analects*, we may find similarities and differences of the three editions, namely, the *Analects of Lu,* the *Analects of Qi*, and the *Analects of Ancient Script*. The edition we use today is fundamentally the *Analects of Marquis Zhang*.

Since the Han dynasty, many people have been making their commentaries to the *Confucian Analects*. The beginners must first read *the Analects* and the *Classic of Filial Piety* in the Han dynasty before they started to read the "Five Classics," namely, *The Book of Poetry, The Book of History*, *The Book of Changes*, *The Book of Rites, The Spring and Autumn Annals*. Evidently the *Analects* served as one of the Children's primers in the Han dynasty. The commentaries written by people of the Han dynasty have been basically lost, what remains until today is on the whole the commentaries by Zheng Xuan (127-200, biographized in *Hou Han Shu*). This is because some incomplete handwritten copies have been found in Dunhuang and Japan, of which more than a half belong to Zheng Xuan's commentaries. As for the ideas of the other schools to commentate *The Analects*, it is hard to find them now, except for what has already been absorbed by He Yan (190-249) in his *Collected Commentaries on the Analects. Commentary and Subcommentary to the Analects*, a work exists in *Commentary and Subcommentary to the Thirteen Classics*, is made up of He Yan's collected commentaries and of subcommentary by a scholar of the Song dynasty named Xing Bing (932-1010, biographized in *Song Shi*). As for quite a few books which specially commentate *The Analects* written by contemporaries of He Yan and Xing Bing, we may consult the following books: *Jing Yi Kao* by Zhu

Yizun (1629-1709, biographized in *Qing Shi Gao), An Outline of Complete Library in Four Divisions* by Ji Yun (1724-1805) and his colleagues, *Jing Dian Shi Wen Xu Lu* by a Tang scholar named Lu Deming (c.550-c.630), and *Shu Zheng* by Mr. Wu Jianzhai (also called Chengshi).

Mr. Yang Bojun, the author of the *Confucian Analects with Translation and Annotation*, is a linguist and a bibliographer. He made a comprehensive and profound study of two disciplines, namely, bibliography and linguistics, and especially of grammar of the latter. *Confucian Analects with Translation and Annotation* is a work having exerted a tremendous influence both at home and abroad, and it is used as a textbook or as an important reference book for the students of liberal arts in many universities in the world. This book is well documented by quoting copiously and inserting the author's own ideas sometimes, so in the annotation are contained as much as possible the knowledge and relative research of history, geographical change, name and description of things, ancient folkways and ancient philosophy. Since the author was a linguist, he paid much attention to introducing the laws of phonetics, etymology, grammar and rhetoric, and in his introduction he frequently proved some difficult problems. Only by doing so, he surpassed his forerunners and flied his own colors. For example, in "Yong Ye," there is a sentence"好之者不如乐之者." As for the character 乐， those old scholars who followed the"叶音"method of *Jing Dian Shi Wen*, read it as"五教切"or as"义效切"and explained it as"to love," it is of course wrong. In view of this, Mr. Yang published an essay entitled *Po Yin Lüe Kao* in *Guo Wen Yue Kan*, to authenticate the problem. In *Confucian Analects with Translation and Annotation*, he persists in reading it as *le*. Here the character itself is not a verb, but a noun used as a verb. Therefore the whole sentence means"they who love it are not equal to those who find *pleasure* in it." The modern Chinese version of *Confucian Analects with Translation and Annotation* is smooth and clear, and it keeps the style of quotation of the original. It is very convenient for the reader because of the appendix— *A Dictionary of Confucian Analects*.

Mr. Zhang Zhenglang, a famous palaeograhper, praises *Confucian Analects with Translation and Annotation* and *Mencius with Translation and Annotation* to be two examples among the books of the same kind. This book is a long lasting book, for in the past forty years it was printed and reprinted time and again. Just owing to this, we put it in the *Library of Chinese Classics*.

The books relative to the *Analects* are too numerous to mention individually. If you desire to read more after you finish reading *Confucian Analects with Translation and Annotation*, you may read the following books.

1 *Commentary and Subcommentary to the Analects* It is made up of *Collected Commentaries on the Analects* by He Yan and of *Subcommentary to the Analects* by Xing Bing. The book is contained in *Commentary and Subcommentary to the Thirteen Classics*. Apart from the Wu Ying Dian edition, many printers use the Nanchang block-print edition by Ruan Yuan. It is appendixed with *Textual Criticism Record*, which the reader may use.

2 *Collected Commentaries on the Analects* It is a book by Zhu Xi (1130-1200), a Song scholar. Out of the *Book of Rites*, he took a part, namely, the "Great Learning," and added it to the "Doctrine of the Mean," *Analects*, and *Mencius*, and called them the *Four Books*, and then he put a lot of work in making his *Collected Commentaries*. From the Ming to the Qing, all the topics for the imperial examination are taken from the sentences or phrases of the *Four Books*, the argumentation of the examinees cannot go against Zhu Xi's ideas, and this is called to speak in

place of the sages. So this book has exercised a great influence. Besides, Zhu Xi not only made his argumentation upon the *Analects*, but also paid some attention to exegesis, so this book is valued for reference.

3 *Rectified Interpretation of the Analects* It is a book by Liu Baonan (1791-1855). In the Qing dynasty, many scholars were not satisfied with the commentaries and subcommentaries made by Tang and Song scholars, so Chen Huan (1786-1863) wrote *Mao Shi Zhuan Shu*, and Jiao Xun (1763-1820) wrote *Rectified Interpretation of Mencius*. After the manner of Jiao Xun's *Rectified Interpretation of Mencius*, Liu Baonan started to write his *Rectified Interpretation of the Annals.* When he was sick, he stopped writing, his son Liu Gongmian (1821-1880) finished writing the whole book. So it is a book written by father and son of the Liu. Truly it is a well documented book, and its argumentation is basically reliable. Anyhow, since the research is progressing day by day, a good book yesterday may be found defective today, nevertheless it remains to be rather referential.

4 *Collected Interpretations of the Analects* It is a book by Cheng Shude, who quoted 680 books. Although there is some room for further discussion, it may serve as a book for reference even today, for it is very well documented.

5 *Reorganized Subcommentaries to the Analects* It is a book by Yang Shuda (1885-1956). The author sought through all the documents written before the period of the Three Kingdoms, so he was able to reorganize all the materials produced then which quote or are relative to the *Analects.* All useful materials are arranged in the same order of the original *Analects*, and the author sometimes wrote down his own realization in the form of "author's comment," therefore it is referential indeed.[4]

Part III

The circulation of the *Confucian Analects* in the whole world follows such a process—from the near to the distant, and first in East Asia and then in Europe and America.

Since Emperor Wu of the Han dynasty proscribed all non-Confucian schools of thought and espoused Confucianism as the orthodox state ideology according to Dong Zhongshu's suggestion, Confucius the man and the *Analects* the book had gradually been promoted to the supreme status. Along with the Chinese culture spreading to the neighboring countries, the *Confucian Analects* was brought to Vietnam, Korea and Japan at different times.

In 111 BC, the sixth year of Yuan Ding Reign of Emperor Wu of the Han dynasty, a country named Nan Yue perished, since then the northern part of Vietnam had become a part of China for more than one thousand years. Confucianism, including the *Confucian Analects* and some other classics, which had already acquired the supreme status, spread to Vietnam accordingly.

In 374 AD, in the Korean peninsula, a country named Bai Ji established the post of "Bo-shi," namely, court academician. Because this is a post in charge of teaching the Confucian classics, we may believe that the *Confucian Analects* must be spread to Korea then. In 640 AD, the three kingdoms on the peninsula, namely, Gao Gou Li, Xin Luo, and Bai Ji, sent the eldest sons of the kings and princes as well as the noble youths to China during the Tang dynasty, they studied the *Analects* and other Confucian classics in the Imperial College.

Separately in 513, 516 and 554 AD, Bai Ji Kingdom sent"Bo-shi of five classics" to Japan to teach the doctrines of Confucian school. We may believe that the *Confucian Analects* spread to Japan then. In 768 AD, the third year of the Da Li Reign of the Tang, according to the regulation of the Imperial College of Tang, the emperor of Japan instructed, in the form of an imperial edict, that Confucius should be called"Wen-xuan-wang"— the king propagating the civilization. Before this, following the law of Tang, Japan had already called Confucius"Xian-sheng-wen-xuan-fu"—the father prior to all saints to propagate the civilization.

By the end of the 16th century the translation of the *Confucian Analects* into Western languages had begun. Julio Aleni (1582-1649), in his article entitled *Da Xi Li Xian Sheng Xing Shu*, told us that Matteo Ricci (1552-1610), an early Italian missioner,"who had translated the *Four Books* from Chinese into a Western language and sent them to his homeland, when his countrymen read them, they felt enjoyable, they came to know that the Chinese classics might lead people to the true origin … All these should be ascribed to Matteo Ricci." The so-called Western language refers to Latin. Matteo Ricci started with the translation of the *Four Books* in 1591, the nineteenth year of Wan Li Reign of the Ming, and he finished his translation in 1594. Unfortunately his translation was scattered and lost before publication.

In the first years of the Qing dynasty, Prosper Intercetta(1625-1696), an Italian Jesuit and Ignatius da Casta (1599-1666), a Portugese Jesuit, jointly translated the *Confucian Analects* into Latin. Philippus Couplet (1624-1692), a Belgian Jesuit, published their translation in Paris in 1687. This is the first publication of the *Confucian Analects* in Europe. The title is *Confucius, Sinarum Philosophus*, together with a Chinese title—*Xi Wen Si Shu Jie*, in which are included *The Great Learning* and *The Doctrine of the Mean*. The abridged French and English versions of *Confucius, Sinarum Philosophus* were separately published in France and England in 1688 and 1691. So the common people might come into contact with the Confucian thought, and this aroused a praise of Confucius in the whole Western Europe. In the 18th century, whenever the whole world was mentioned, people would use the phrase "from China to Peru."

In 1711, the University of Prague published the Latin version of the *Four Books* translated by Franciscus Noël (1651-1729), a Belgian missioner. He came to China in 1687 and fifteen years later he returned to Europe.

N. Ya. Bichurin (1777-1853, i. e. Ioakinf), the great priest, friar, of the Ninth Mission of the Russian Orthodox Eastern Church to Beijing, translated the *Confucian Analects* into Russian and published it in some time after 1821. V. P. Vasilyev (1818-1900), a member of the Russian Academy, also did so from 1840 to 1850. When Lev Tolstoy read the *Analects*, he wrote to A. P. Chekhov, saying,"I am reading one of the works of Confucian school. Now it is the second day. It is hard to imagine that they have reached an extraordinary height." "I have indulged myself in the wisdom of China, extremely I want to tell you and everybody that these books have given me a spiritual benefit." As he acknowledged, when he became adult, among the Eastern philosophers, Confucius and Mencius had *greatly* influenced him.

Towards the end of the 18th century or at the beginning of the 19th century, the *Four Books*, including the *Confucian Analects*, spread to America, and there were translations of English, French, Latin and other languages. R. W. Emerson (1803-1882) and H. D. Thoreau (1817-1862) were two representatives of American transcendentalism, the moment they saw these books they both took a fancy to them and would not let them go. V. Lindsay (1879-1931), a poet, sang heartily to express his ardent love of Confucius: May we be students of the Confucian times, let's prostrate and prostrate for ever, only with our head lifted to look up to the ancient China!

Besides, from the early 18th century to mid 19th century, the Swedish, German and Romanian versions of the *Confucian Analects* were also published.

Today, the general impression of the *Confucian Analects* is higher than any other best seller, it is only next to the Bible. Alongside the spreading of the classics of the Confucian school headed by the *Analects*, Confucianism has already become a hot spot of the humanities in the world. In 1994, on the occasion to celebrate the 2545th anniversary of the birth of Confucius, the International Confucian Association was established in Beijing. Li Guangyao, the veteran statesman of Singapore was elected honorary chairman, and Choe Tok-kun, the head of Song Kyun Kwan, was elected chairman. Quietly trickle through the two brooks, the Zhushui River and the Sishui River. You see, their water "fills up every hole." And then they become streams, "and then they advance, flowing on to the four seas."

In the recent two centuries, there are some other people who translated the *Confucian Analects* into English. For example, there are J. Marshman (1768-1837), David Collie, two English missioners, and L. Giles (1875-1958), a Sinologist. Among so many translators, James Legge, Arthur David Waley and D. C. Lau are generally acknowledged to have put forth their versions of English in high quality.

James Legge (1815-1897) is a Scottish missionary. The London Church sent him to Malacca as a missionary in 1839. Later he became the president of the Ying Hua Academy (from which grew out the Hong Kong Chinese University). In 1843 the academy was moved to Hong Kong, he went there too. Since 1848 he had started to translate Chinese classics with the help of some other missionaries and a Chinese named Huang Sheng. From 1861 to 1886 he published the *Chinese Classics* in 28 volumes, in which 14 Chinese classics are contained, including the *Four Books* (the *Analects* is one of the four), the *Five Classics* and the works by Laozi and Zhuangzi. In view of this, the University of Oxford got him to act as the first professor of Chinese in 1876.

Arthur David Waley (1889-1996) served as a research fellow in the Oriental Section of the British Museum for a long time, in charge of sifting the Dunhuang manuscripts, meanwhile he taught in the Faculty of Oriental Studies, London University. When a young student at King's College, Cambridge, he was greatly influenced by famous professors such as G. L. Dickinson (lecturer at Cambridge, 1896-1920) and G. E. Moore (lecturer, 1911-1925, professor, 1925-1939, Cambridge). He longed eagerly for the ancient Chinese civilization and so he decided to research the Chinese culture, so he diligently studied Chinese on his own. Except for the *Confucian Analects*, the books he translated of Chinese culture amount to seven or eight kinds.

D. C. Lau (b.1915) was born in Hong Kong, while Panyu, a county in Guangdong Province, is his ancestors' homeland. He graduated from Hong Kong University. In 1949, having finished the courses of master degree, he went to teach at London University. In 1970 he was promoted to be professor of lectures in Chinese Department there. In 1978 he returned to Hong Kong, successively he served as the professor of lectures in Hong Kong Chinese University, the chairman of College of Literature, and the director of the Center of the Chinese Language. He has already translated seven books including the *Confucian Analects*.

The three scholars mentioned above have all made a profound research into the *Confucian Analects*. What they have done is by no means translation only, and their translations belong to first-class. When James Legge translated something, he would like to use the written English of the 19th century, compound and complex sentences were his like, and archaic words were his like, too. Therefore the readers today may find it somewhat difficult to read his translation. D. C. Lau's translation was published in 1979. He uses spoken English, and he prefers using the simple sentences, so his version is easy to understand. But there is some discrepancy between his version and the original in style. A. D. Waley's version has strong points of both the two modernity and style, it is comparatively a terse version, close to the original in style, and what is more, even in expression it bears a close resemblance to the original, too. In view of this, we adopt it while editing the *Library of Chinese Classics*. The "Introduction," "Notes" and "Terms" in Waley's translation is of great scholarstic value, so they are kept in the appendixes. As there are some shortcomings in the other two translations, there is some room for further discussion in the translation by A. D. Waley. We shall try our best to correct the inappropriate translation that we have found.[5]

Yang Fengbin

Translated by Zhang Siqi

Notes:

1 q. v. Karl Theodor Jaspers, *Vom Ursprung und Zeit der Geschichte*, 1949.

2 Ibid.

3 *Lun Yu Yi Zhu*, China Book Company, 1980, p.17.

4 This is an adaption of *Introduction to Lun Yu Yi Zhu*.

5 In this part more than ten books and typewritten copies are conferred. Among them there are the following worth special mentioning; Ma Zuyi and Ren Rongzhen, *Han Ji Wai Yi Shi*, Hubei Education Press, 1997; Professor Liu Zhongde, *Opinions after Reading and Evaluating A. D. Waley's Translation of the Analects* ,typewritten copy.

目　录

CONTENTS

孔子（前 551 —前 479 年）

Confucius (551 — 479 B.C.)

学而篇第一

【原文】

1.1 子曰:“学而时习之，不亦说乎?有朋自远方来，不亦乐乎?人不知，而不愠，不亦君子乎?”

1.2 有子曰:“其为人也孝悌，而好犯上者，鲜矣；不好犯上，而好作乱者，未之有也。君子务本，本立而道生。孝悌也者，其为仁之本与!”

1.3 子曰:“巧言令色，鲜矣仁!”

1.4 曾子曰:“吾日三省吾身——为人谋而不忠乎?与朋友交而不信乎?传不习乎?”

1.5 子曰:“道千乘之国，敬事而信，节用而爱人，使民

【今译】

1.1 孔子说:“学了，然后按一定的时间去实习它，不也高兴吗?有志同道合的人从远处来，不也快乐吗?人家不了解我，我却不怨恨，不也是君子吗?”

1.2 有子说:“他的为人，孝顺爹娘，敬爱兄长，却喜欢触犯上级，这种人是很少的；不喜欢触犯上级，却喜欢造反，这种人从来没有过。君子专心致力于基础工作，基础树立了，‘道’就会产生。孝顺爹娘，敬爱兄长，这就是‘仁’的基础吧!”

1.3 孔子说:“花言巧语，伪善的面貌，这种人，‘仁德’是不会多的。”

1.4 曾子说:“我每天多次自己反省：替别人办事是否尽心竭力了呢?同朋友往来是否诚实呢?老师传授我的学业是否复习了呢?”

1.5 孔子说:“治理具有一千辆兵车的国家，就要严肃认真地对待工作，信实无欺，节约费用，爱护官吏，役使老百姓要在农闲

BOOK I

1.1 The Master said, "To learn and at due times to repeat what one has learnt, is that not after all[1] a pleasure? That friends should come to one from afar,[2] is this not after all delightful? To remain unsoured even though one's merits are unrecognized by others, is that not after all what is expected of a gentleman?"

1.2 Master You[3] said, "Those who in private life behave well towards their parents and elder brothers, in public life seldom show a disposition to resist the authority of their superiors. And as for such men starting a revolution, no instance of it has ever occurred. It is upon the trunk[4] that a gentleman works. When that is firmly set up, the Way grows. And surely proper behaviour towards parents and elder brothers is the trunk of Goodness?"

1.3 The Master said,"'Clever talk and a pretentious manner' are seldom found in the Good."

1.4 Master Zeng[5] said, "Every day I examine myself on these three points: in acting on behalf of others, have I always been loyal to their interests? In intercourse with my friends, have I always been true to my word? Have I failed to repeat[6] the precepts that have been handed down to me?"

1.5 The Master said, "A country of a thousand war-chariots cannot be administered unless the ruler attends strictly to business, punctually observes his promises, is economical in expenditure, shows affection to-

【原文】

以时。”

1.6 子曰:“弟子，入则孝，出则悌，谨而信，泛爱众，而亲仁。行有余力，则以学文。”

1.7 子夏曰:“贤贤易色；事父母，能竭其力；事君，能致其身；与朋友交，言而有信，虽曰未学，吾必谓之学矣。”

1.8 子曰:“君子不重，则不威；学则不固。主忠信。无友不如

【今译】

时间。”

1.6 孔子说:“后生小子，在父母跟前，就孝顺父母；离开自己房子，便敬爱兄长；寡言少语，说则诚实可信，博爱大众，亲近有仁德的人。这样躬行实践之后，有剩余力量，就再去学习文献。”

1.7 子夏说:“对妻子，重品德，不重容貌；侍奉爹娘，能尽心竭力；服事君上，能豁出生命；同朋友交往，说话诚实守信。这种人，虽说没学习过，我一定说他已经学习过了。”

1.8 孔子说:“君子，如果不庄重，就没有威严；即使读书，所学的也不会巩固。要以忠和信两种道德为主。不要跟不如自己的人

wards his subjects in general, and uses the labour of the peasantry only at the proper times of year[7]."

1.6 The Master said, "A young man's duty is to behave well to his parents at home and to his elders abroad, to be cautious in giving promises and punctual in keeping them, to have kindly feelings towards everyone, but seek the intimacy of the Good. If, when all that is done, he has any energy to spare, then let him study the polite arts[8]."

1.7 Zixia said, "A man who

> Treats his betters as betters,
> Wears an air of respect,
> Who into serving father and mother
> Knows how to put his whole strength,
> Who in the service of his prince will lay
>   down his life,
> Who in intercourse with friends is true
>   to his word——

others may say of him that he still lacks education[9], but I for my part should certainly call him an educated man."

1.8 The Master said, "If a gentleman is frivolous[10], he will lose the respect of his inferiors and lack firm ground upon which to build up his education. First and foremost he must learn to be faithful to his superiors, to keep promises, to refuse the friendship of all who are not like him[11]. And if he finds he has made a mistake, then he must not be afraid

【原文】

己者。过，则勿惮改。”

1.9 曾子曰：“慎终，追远，民德归厚矣。”

1.10 子禽问于子贡曰：“夫子至于是邦也，必闻其政，求之与？抑与之与？”子贡曰：“夫子温、良、恭、俭、让以得之。夫子之求之也，其诸异乎人之求之与？”

1.11 子曰：“父在，观其志；父没，观其行；三年无改于父之道，可谓孝矣。”

1.12 有子曰：“礼之用，和为贵。先王之道，斯为美；小大由之。有所不行，知和而和，不以礼节之，亦不可行也。”

1.13 有子曰：“信近于义，言可复也。恭近于礼，远耻辱也。因

【今译】

交朋友。有了过错，就不要怕改正。”

1.9 曾子说：“谨慎地对待父母的死亡，追念远代祖先，自然会导致老百姓归于忠厚老实了。”

1.10 子禽向子贡问道：“他老人家一到哪个国家，必然听得到那个国家的政事，求来的呢？还是别人自动告诉他的呢？”子贡道：“他老人家是靠温和、善良、严肃、节俭、谦逊来取得的。他老人家获得的方法，和别人获得的方法，不相同吧？”

1.11 孔子说：“当他父亲活着，[因为他无权独立行动，]要观察他的志向；他父亲死了，要考察他的行为；若是他对他父亲的合理部分，长期地不加改变，可以说做到孝了。”

1.12 有子说：“礼的作用，以遇事都做得恰当为可贵。过去圣明君王的治理国家，可宝贵的地方就在这里；他们小事大事都做得恰当。但是，如有行不通的地方，便为恰当而求恰当，不用一定的规矩制度来加以节制，也是不可行的。”

1.13 有子说：“所守的约言符合义，说的话就能兑现。态度容貌的庄矜合于礼，就不致遭受侮辱。依靠关系深的人，也就可

of admitting the fact and amending his ways."

1.9 Master Zeng said, "When proper respect towards the dead is shown at the End and continued after they are far away the moral force(*de*德)[12] of a people has reached its highest point."

1.10 Ziqin said to Zigong[13], "When our Master arrives in a fresh country he always manages to find out about its policy.[14] Does he do this by asking questions, or do people tell him of their own accord?" Zigong said, "Our Master gets things by being cordial, frank, courteous, temperate, deferential. That is our Master's way of enquiring — a very different matter, certainly, from the way in which enquiries are generally made."

1.11 The Master said, "While a man's father is alive, you can only see his intentions; it is when his father dies that you discover whether or not he is capable of carrying them out. If for the whole three years of mourning he manages to carry on the household exactly as in his father's day, then he is a good son indeed."[15]

1.12 Master You said, "In the usages of ritual it is harmony that is prized; the Way of the Former Kings from this got its beauty. Both small matters and great matters depend upon it. If things go amiss, he who knows the harmony will be able to attune them. But if harmony itself is not modulated by ritual, things will still go amiss."

1.13 Master You said,

"In your promises cleave to what is right,
And you will be able to fulfil your word.

【原文】

不失其亲，亦可宗也。”

1.14　子曰:“君子食无求饱，居无求安，敏于事而慎于言，就有道而正焉，可谓好学也已。”

1.15　子贡曰:“贫而无谄，富而无骄，何如?”子曰:“可也；未若贫而乐，富而好礼者也。”

子贡曰:“《诗》云:‘如切如磋，如琢如磨’，其斯之谓与?”子曰:“赐也，始可与言《诗》已矣，告诸往而知来者。”

1.16　子曰:“不患人之不己知，患不知人也。”

【今译】

靠了。”

1.14　孔子说:“君子，吃食不要求饱足，居住不要求舒适，对工作勤劳敏捷，说话却谨慎，到有道的人那里去匡正自己，这样，可以说是好学了。”

1.15　子贡说:“贫穷却不巴结奉承，有钱却不骄傲自大，怎么样?”孔子说:“可以了；但是还不如虽贫穷却乐于道，纵有钱却谦虚好礼哩。”

子贡说:“《诗经》上说:‘要像对待骨、角、象牙、玉石一样，先开料，再糙锉、细刻，然后磨光。’那就是这样的意思吧?”孔子道：“赐呀，现在可以同你讨论《诗经》了，告诉你一件，你能有所发挥，举一反三了。”

1.16　孔子说:“别人不了解我，我不急；我急的是自己不了解别人。”

In your obeisances cleave to ritual,
And you will keep dishonour at bay.
Marry one who has not betrayed her own kin,
And you may safely present her to your ancestors."

1.14 The Master said, "A gentleman who never goes on eating till he is sated, who does not demand comfort in his home, who is diligent in business and cautious in speech, who associates with those that possess the Way and thereby corrects his own faults — such a one may indeed be said to have a taste for learning."

1.15 Zigong said, "'Poor without cadging, rich without swagger.' What of that?" [16] The Master said, "Not bad. But better still, 'Poor, yet delighting in the Way; rich, yet a student of ritual.'" Zigong said, "The saying of the *Songs*[17],

As thing cut, as thing filed,
As thing chiselled, as thing polished

refers, I suppose, to what you have just said?" The Master said, "Ci, now I can really begin to talk to you about the *Songs*, for when I allude to sayings of the past, you see what bearing they have on what was to come after."

1.16 The Master said, "(The good man) Does not grieve that other people do not recognize his merits. His only anxiety is lest he should fail to recognize theirs."

为政篇第二

【原文】

2.1　子曰："为政以德，譬如北辰居其所而众星共之。"

2.2　子曰："《诗》三百，一言以蔽之，曰：'思无邪'。"

2.3　子曰："道之以政，齐之以刑，民免而无耻；道之以德，齐之以礼，有耻且格。"

2.4　子曰："吾十有五而志于学，三十而立，四十而不惑，五十而知天命，六十而耳顺，七十而从心所欲，不逾矩。"

2.5　孟懿子问孝。子曰："无违。"

樊迟御，子告之曰："孟孙问孝于我，我对曰，无违。"樊迟

【今译】

2.1　孔子说："用道德来治理国政，自己便会像北极星一般，在一定的位置上，别的星辰都环绕着它。"

2.2　孔子说："《诗经》三百篇，用一句话来概括它，就是'思想纯正'。"

2.3　孔子说："用政法来诱导他们，使用刑罚来整顿他们，人民只是暂时地免于罪过，却没有廉耻之心。如果用道德来诱导他们，使用礼教来整顿他们，人民不但有廉耻之心，而且人心归服。"

2.4　孔子说："我十五岁，有志于学问；三十岁，[懂礼仪，]说话做事都有把握；四十岁，[掌握了各种知识，]不致迷惑；五十岁，得知天命；六十岁，一听别人言语，便可以分别真假，判明是非；到了七十岁，便随心所欲，任何念头不越出规矩。"

2.5　孟懿子向孔子问孝道。孔子说："不要违背礼节。"

不久，樊迟替孔子赶车子，孔子便告诉他说："孟孙向我问孝道，

BOOK II

2.1 The Master said, "He who rules by moral force (*de*) is like the pole-star, which remains in its place while all the lesser stars do homage to it."

2.2 The Master said, "If out of the three hundred *Songs* I had to take one phrase to cover all my teaching, I would say 'Let there be no evil in your thoughts.'"

2.3 The Master said, "Govern the people by regulations, keep order among them by chastisements, and they will flee from you, and lose all self-respect. Govern them by moral force, keep order among them by ritual and they will keep their self-respect and come to you of their own accord."

2.4 The Master said, "At fifteen I set my heart upon learning. At thirty, I had planted my feet firm upon the ground. At forty, I no longer suffered from perplexities. At fifty, I knew what were the biddings of Heaven. At sixty, I heard them with docile ear. At seventy, I could follow the dictates of my own heart; for what I desired no longer overstepped the boundaries of right."

2.5 Meng Yi[1] asked about the treatment of parents. The Master said, "Never disobey! " When Fan Chi[2] was driving his carriage for him, the Master said, "Meng asked me about the treatment of parents and I said, 'Never disobey!'" Fan Chi said, "In what sense did you mean it?" The Master said, "While they are alive, serve them according to ritual. When

【原文】

曰:“何谓也?”子曰:“生，事之以礼；死，葬之以礼，祭之以礼。”

2.6　孟武伯问孝。子曰:“父母唯其疾之忧。”

2.7　子游问孝。子曰:“今之孝者，是谓能养。至于犬马，皆能有养；不敬，何以别乎?”

2.8　子夏问孝。子曰:“色难。有事，弟子服其劳；有酒食，先生馔，曾是以为孝乎?”

2.9　子曰:“吾与回言终日，不违，如愚。退而省其私，亦足以发，回也不愚。”

2.10　子曰:“视其所以，观其所由，察其所安。人焉廋哉?人焉廋哉?”

【今译】

我答复说，不要违背礼节。”樊迟道:“这是什么意思?”孔子道:“父母活着，依规定的礼节侍奉他们；死了，依规定的礼节埋葬他们，祭祀他们。”

2.6　孟武伯向孔子请教孝道。孔子道:“做爹娘的只是为孝子的疾病发愁。”

2.7　子游问孝道。孔子说:“现在的所谓孝，就是说能够养活爹娘便行了。对于狗马都能够得到饲养；若不存心严肃地孝顺父母，那养活爹娘和饲养狗马怎样去分别呢?”

2.8　子夏问孝道。孔子道:“儿子在父母前经常有愉悦的容色，是件难事。有事情，年轻人效劳；有酒有肴，年长的人吃喝，难道这竟可认为是孝么?”

2.9　孔子说:“我整天和颜回讲学，他从不提反对意见和疑问，像个蠢人。等他退回去自己研究，却也能发挥，可见颜回并不愚蠢。”

2.10　孔子说:“考查一个人所结交的朋友；观察他为达到一定目的所采用的方式方法；了解他的心情，安于什么，不安于什么。那么，这个人怎么隐藏得住呢?这个人怎么隐藏得住呢?”

they die, bury them according to ritual and sacrifice to them according to ritual."[3]

2.6 Meng Wu[4] asked about the treatment of parents. The Master said, "Behave in such a way that your father and mother have no anxiety about you, except concerning your health."

2.7 Ziyou[5] asked about the treatment of parents. The Master said, " 'Filial sons' nowadays are people who see to it that their parents get enough to eat. But even dogs and horses are cared for to that extent. If there is no feeling of respect, wherein lies the difference?"

2.8 Zixia[6] asked about the treatment of parents. The Master said, "It is the demeanour that is difficult. Filial piety does not consist merely in young people undertaking the hard work, when anything has to be done, or serving their elders first with wine and food. It is something much more than that."

2.9 The Master said, " I can talk to Yan Hui[7] a whole day without his ever differing from me. One would think he was stupid. But if I enquire into his private conduct when he is not with me I find that it fully demonstrates what I have taught him. No, Hui is by no means stupid."

2.10 The Master said, "Look closely into his aims, observe the means by which he pursues them, discover what brings him content — and can the man's real worth[8] remain hidden from you, can it remain hidden from you?"

【原文】

2.11　子曰:“温故而知新，可以为师矣。”

2.12　子曰:“君子不器。”

2.13　子贡问君子。子曰:“先行其言而后从之。”

2.14　子曰:“君子周而不比，小人比而不周。”

2.15　子曰:“学而不思则罔，思而不学则殆。”

2.16　子曰:“攻乎异端，斯害也已。”

2.17　子曰:“由！诲女知之乎！知之为知之，不知为不知，是知也。”

2.18　子张学干禄。子曰:“多闻阙疑，慎言其余，则寡尤；多见阙殆，慎行其余，则寡悔。言寡尤，行寡悔，禄在其中矣。”

【今译】

2.11　孔子说:“在温习旧知识时，能有新体会、新发现，就可以做老师了。”

2.12　孔子说:“君子不像器皿一般[只有一定的用途]。”

2.13　子贡问怎样才能做一个君子。孔子道:“对于你要说的话，先实行了，再说出来[这就够说是一个君子了]。”

2.14　孔子说:“君子是团结，而不是勾结；小人是勾结，而不是团结。”

2.15　孔子说:“只是读书，却不思考，就会受骗；只是空想，却不读书，就会缺乏信心。”

2.16　孔子说:“批判那些不正确的议论，祸害就可以消灭了。”

2.17　孔子说:“由！教给你对待知或不知的正确态度吧！知道就是知道，不知道就是不知道，这就是聪明智慧。”

2.18　子张向孔子学求官职得俸禄的方法。孔子说:“多听，有怀疑的地方，加以保留；其余足以自信的部分，谨慎地说出，就能减少错误。多看，有怀疑的地方，加以保留；其余足以自信的部分，谨慎地实行，就能减少懊悔。言语的错误少，行动的懊悔少，官职俸禄就在这里面了。”

2.11 The Master said, “He who by reanimating[9] the Old can gain knowledge of the New is fit to be a teacher.”

2.12 The Master said, “A gentleman is not an implement[10].”

2.13 Zigong asked about the true gentleman. The Master said, “He does not preach what he practises till he has practised what he preaches.”

2.14 The Master said, “A gentleman can see a question from all sides without bias. The small man[11] is biased and can see a question only from one side.”

2.15 The Master said, “He who learns but does not think[12] is lost. He who thinks but does not learn is in great danger.”

2.16 The Master said, “He who sets to work upon a different strand destroys the whole fabric.”[13]

2.17 The Master said, “You,[14] shall I teach you what knowledge is? When you know a thing, to recognize that you know it, and when you do not know a thing, to recognize that you do not know it. That is knowledge.”[15]

2.18 Zizhang was studying the *Song* Ganlu[16] .The Master said, “Hear much, but maintain silence[17] as regards doubtful points and be cautious in speaking of the rest; then you will seldom get into trouble. See much, but ignore what it is dangerous to have seen, and be cautious in acting upon the rest; then you will seldom want to undo your acts. He who seldom gets into trouble about what he has said and seldom does any-

【原文】

2.19　哀公问曰:“何为则民服?”孔子对曰:“举直错诸枉,则民服;举枉错诸直,则民不服。”

2.20　季康子问:“使民敬、忠以劝,如之何?”子曰:“临之以庄,则敬;孝慈,则忠;举善而教不能,则劝。”

2.21　或谓孔子曰:“子奚不为政?”子曰:“《书》云:‘孝乎惟孝,友于兄弟,施于有政。’是亦为政,奚其为为政?”

2.22　子曰:“人而无信,不知其可也。大车无輗,小车无軏,其何以行之哉?”

2.23　子张问:“十世可知也?”子曰:“殷因于夏礼,所损益,可知

【今译】

2.19　鲁哀公问道:“要做些什么事才能使百姓服从呢?”孔子答道:“把正直的人提拔出来,放在邪曲的人之上,百姓就服从了;若是把邪曲的人提拔出来,放在正直的人之上,百姓就会不服从。”

2.20　季康子问道:“要使人民严肃认真、尽心竭力和互相勉励,应该怎么办呢?”孔子说:“你对待人民的事情严肃认真,他们对待你的政令也会严肃认真了;你孝顺父母,慈爱幼小,他们也就会对你尽心竭力了;你提拔好人,教育能力弱的人,他们也就会劝勉了。”

2.21　有人对孔子道:“你为什么不参与政治?”孔子道:“《尚书》上说,‘孝呀,只有孝顺父母,友爱兄弟,把这种风气影响到政治上去。’这也就是参与政治了呀,为什么定要做官才算参与政治呢?”

2.22　孔子说:“作为一个人,却不讲信誉,不知那怎么可以。譬如大车子没有安横木的輗,小车子没有安横木的軏,如何能走呢?”

2.23　子张问:“今后十代[的礼仪制度]可以预先知道吗?”孔子说:“殷朝沿袭夏朝的礼仪制度,所废除的,所增加的,是可以知道

thing that he afterwards wishes he had not done, will be sure incidentally[18] to get his reward."

2.19 Duke Ai[19] asked, "What can I do in order to get the support of the common people?" Master Kong[20] replied, "If you 'raise up the straight and set them on top of the crooked,' the commoners will support you. But if you raise the crooked and set them on top of the straight, the commoners will not support you."

2.20 Ji Kang[21] asked whether there were any form of encouragement by which he could induce the common people to be respectful and loyal. The Master said, "Approach them with dignity, and they will respect you. Show piety towards your parents and kindness towards your children, and they will be loyal to you. Promote those who are worthy, train those who are incompetent; that is the best form of encouragement."

2.21 Someone, when talking to Master Kong, said, "How is it that you are not in the public service?" The Master said, "The *Books*[22] says, 'Be filial, only be filial and friendly towards your brothers, and you will be contributing to government.' There are other sorts of service quite different from what you mean by 'service.'"

2.22 The Master said, "I do not see what use a man can be put to, whose word cannot be trusted. How can a waggon be made to go if it has no yoke-bar or a carriage, if it has no collar-bar?"

2.23 Zizhang[23] asked whether the state of things ten generations hence could be foretold. The Master said, "We know in what ways the Yin

【原文】

也；周因于殷礼，所损益，可知也。其或继周者，虽百世，可知也。”

2.24　子曰："非其鬼而祭之，谄也。见义不为，无勇也。"

【今译】

的；周朝沿袭殷朝的礼仪制度，所废除的，所增加的，也是可以知道的。那么，假定有继承周朝而当政的人，就是以后一百代，也是可以预先知道的。”

2.24　孔子说："不是我所应该祭祀的鬼神，却去祭祀他，这是献媚。眼见应该挺身而出的事情，却袖手旁观，这是怯懦。"

modified ritual when they followed upon the Xia[24] .We know in what ways the Zhou[25] modified ritual when they followed upon the Yin[26]. And hence we can foretell what the successors of Zhou will be like, even supposing they do not appear till a hundred generations from now."

2.24 The Master said, "Just as to sacrifice to ancestors other than one's own is presumption, so to see what is right and not do it is cowardice."

八佾篇第三

【原文】

3.1　孔子谓季氏，“八佾舞于庭，是可忍也，孰不可忍也?”

3.2　三家者以《雍》彻。子曰:“‘相维辟公，天子穆穆’，奚取于三家之堂?”

3.3　子曰:“人而不仁，如礼何?人而不仁，如乐何?”

3.4　林放问礼之本。子曰:“大哉问!礼，与其奢也，宁俭；丧，与其易也，宁戚。”

3.5　子曰:“夷狄之有君，不如诸夏之亡也。”

【今译】

3.1　孔子谈到季氏，说:“他用六十四人在庭院中奏乐舞蹈，这都可以狠心做出来，什么事不可以狠心做出来呢?”

3.2　仲孙、叔孙、季孙三家，当他们祭祀祖先的时候，[也用天子的礼,]唱着《雍》这篇诗来撤除祭品。孔子说:“[《雍》诗上有这样的话：]‘助祭的是诸侯，天子严肃静穆地在那儿主祭。’这两句话，用在三家祭祖的大厅上在意义上取它哪一点呢?”

3.3　孔子说:“做了人，却不仁，怎样来对待礼仪制度呢?做了人，却不仁，怎样来对待音乐呢?”

3.4　林放问礼的本质。孔子说:“你的问题意义重大呀!就一般礼仪说，与其铺张浪费，宁可朴素俭约；就丧礼说，与其仪文周到，宁可过度悲哀。”

3.5　孔子说:“文化落后国家虽然有个君主，还不如中国没有君主哩。”

BOOK Ⅲ

3.1 Master Kong said of the head of the Ji family[1] when he had eight teams[2] of dancers performing in his courtyard, "If this man can be endured, who cannot be endured!"

3.2 The Three Families used the *Yong Song*[3] during the removal of the sacrificial vessels. The Master said,

"*By rulers and lords attended,*
The Son of Heaven, mysterious —

What possible application can such words have in the hall of the Three Families?"

3.3 The Master said, "A man who is not Good, what can he have to do with ritual? A man who is not Good, what can he have to do with music?"

3.4 Lin Fang asked for some main principles in connexion with ritual. The Master said, "A very big question. In ritual at large it is a safe rule always to be too sparing rather than too lavish; and in the particular case of mourning-rites, they should be dictated by grief rather than by fear."

3.5 The Master said, "The barbarians of the East and North have retained their princes. They are not in such a state of decay as we in China[4]."

【原文】

3.6 季氏旅于泰山。子谓冉有曰:“女弗能救与?”对曰:“不能。”子曰:“呜呼!曾谓泰山不如林放乎?”

3.7 子曰:“君子无所争。必也射乎!揖让而升,下而饮。其争也君子。”

3.8 子夏问曰:“‘巧笑倩兮,美目盼兮,素以为绚兮。’何谓也?”子曰:“绘事后素。”

曰:“礼后乎?”子曰:“起予者商也!始可与言《诗》已矣。”

3.9 子曰:“夏礼,吾能言之,杞不足征也;殷礼,吾能言之,宋不足征也。文献不足故也。足,则吾能征之矣。”

【今译】

3.6 季氏要去祭祀泰山。孔子对冉有说道:“你不能阻止吗?”冉有答道:“不能。”孔子道:“哎呀!竟可以说泰山之神还不及林放[懂礼,居然接受这不合规矩的祭祀]吗?”

3.7 孔子说:“君子没有什么可争的事情。如果有所争,一定是比箭吧![但是当射箭的时候,]相互作揖然后登堂;[射箭完毕,]走下堂来,然后[作揖]喝酒。那一种竞赛是很有礼貌的。”

3.8 子夏问道:“‘有酒涡的脸笑得美呀,黑白分明的眼流转得媚呀,洁白的底子上画着花卉呀。’这几句诗是什么意思?”孔子道:“先有白色底子,然后画花。”

子夏道:“那么,是不是礼乐的产生在[仁义]以后呢?”孔子道:“卜商呀,你真是能启发我的人。现在可以同你讨论《诗经》了。”

3.9 孔子说:“夏代的礼,我能说出来,它的后代杞国不足以作证;殷代的礼,我能说出来,它的后代宋国不足以作证。这是他们的历史文件和贤者不够的缘故。若有足够的文件和贤者,我就可以引来作证了。”

3.6 The head of the Ji family was going to make the offerings on Mount Tai[5]. The Master said to Ran Qiu[6], "Cannot you save him from this? "Ran Qiu replied, "I cannot." The Master said, "Alas, we can hardly suppose Mount Tai to be ignorant of matters that even Lin Fang enquires into!"[7]

3.7 The Master said, "Gentlemen never compete. You will say that in archery they do so. But even then they bow and make way for one another when they are going up to the archery-ground, when they are coming down and at the subsequent drinking-bout. Thus even when competing, they still remain gentlemen."

3.8 Zixia asked, saying, "What is the meaning of

Oh the sweet smile dimpling,
The lovely eyes so black and white!
Plain silk that you would take for coloured stuff."

The Master said, "The painting comes after the plain groundwork." Zixia said, "Then ritual comes afterwards?" The Master said, "Shang[8] it is who bears me up. At last I have someone with whom I can discuss the *Songs*!"

3.9 The Master said, "How can we talk about the ritual of the Xia? The State of Qi[9] supplies no adequate evidence. How can we talk about the ritual of Yin? The State of Song supplies no adequate evidence. For there is a lack both of documents and of learned men. But for this lack we should be able to obtain evidence from these two States."

【原文】

3.10　子曰："禘自既灌而往者，吾不欲观之矣。"

3.11　或问禘之说。子曰："不知也；知其说者之于天下也，其如示诸斯乎！"指其掌。

3.12　祭如在，祭神如神在。子曰："吾不与祭，如不祭。"

3.13　王孙贾问曰："与其媚于奥，宁媚于灶，何谓也？"子曰："不然；获罪于天，无所祷也。"

3.14　子曰："周监于二代，郁郁乎文哉！吾从周。"

3.15　子入太庙，每事问。或曰："孰谓鄹人之子知礼乎？入太庙，每事问。"子闻之，曰："是礼也。"

【今译】

3.10　孔子说："禘祭的礼，从第一次献酒以后，我就不想看了。"

3.11　有人向孔子请教关于禘祭的理论。孔子说："我不知道；知道的人对于治理天下，会好像把东西摆在这里一样容易吧！"一面说，一面指着手掌。

3.12　孔子祭祀祖先的时候，便好像祖先真在那里；祭神的时候，便好像神真在那里。孔子又说："我若是不能亲自参加祭祀，是不请别人代理的。"

3.13　王孙贾问道："'与其巴结房屋里西南角的神，宁可巴结灶君司命'，这两句话是什么意思？"孔子道："不对；若是得罪了上天，祈祷也没用。"

3.14　孔子说："周朝的礼仪制度是以夏商两代为根据，然后制定的，多么丰富多彩呀！我主张周朝的。"

3.15　孔子到周公庙，每件事情都发问。有人便说："谁说叔梁纥的这个儿子懂得礼呢？他到了太庙，每件事都要向别人请教。"孔子听到了这话，便道："这正是礼呀。"

3.10 The Master said, "At the Ancestral Sacrifice, as for all that comes after the libation, I had far rather not witness it!"

3.11 Someone asked for an explanation of the Ancestral Sacrifice. The Master said, "I do not know. Anyone who knew the explanation could deal with all things under Heaven as easily as I lay this here"; and he laid his finger upon the palm of his hand.

3.12 Of the saying, "The word 'sacrifice' is like the word 'present'; one should sacrifice to a spirit as though that spirit was present," the Master said, "If I am not present at the sacrifice, it is as though there were no sacrifice[10]."

3.13 Wangsun Jia[11] asked about the meaning of the saying,

Better pay court to the stove
Than pay court to the Shrine.[12]

The Master said, "It is not true. He who has put himself in the wrong with Heaven has no means of expiation left."

3.14 The Master said, "Zhou could survey the two preceding dynasties. How great a wealth of culture! And we follow upon Zhou."[13]

3.15 When the Master entered the Grand Temple[14] he asked questions about everything there. Someone said, "Do not tell me that this son of a villager from Zou[15] is expert in matters of ritual. When he went to the Grand Temple, he had to ask about everything." The Master hearing of

【原文】

3.16　子曰："射不主皮，为力不同科，古之道也。"

3.17　子贡欲去告朔之饩羊。子曰："赐也！尔爱其羊，我爱其礼。"

3.18　子曰："事君尽礼，人以为谄也。"

3.19　定公问："君使臣，臣事君，如之何？"孔子对曰："君使臣以礼，臣事君以忠。"

3.20　子曰："《关雎》，乐而不淫，哀而不伤。"

3.21　哀公问社于宰我。宰我对曰："夏后氏以松，殷人以柏，周

【今译】

3.16　孔子说："比箭，不一定要穿破箭靶子，因为各人的气力大小不一样，这是古时的规矩。"

3.17　子贡要把鲁国每月初一告祭祖庙的那只活羊去而不用。孔子道："赐呀！你可惜那只羊，我可惜那种礼。"

3.18　孔子说："服事君主，一切依照做臣子的礼节去做，别人却以为他在谄媚哩。"

3.19　鲁定公问："君主使用臣子，臣子服事君子，各应该怎么样？"孔子答道："君主应该依礼来使用臣子，臣子应该忠心地服事君主。"

3.20　孔子说："《关雎》这诗，快乐而不放荡，悲哀而不痛苦。"

3.21　鲁哀公问宰我，作社主用什么木。宰我答道："夏代用松木，

this said, "Just so! Such is the ritual."[16]

3.16 The Master said, "The saying

In archery it is not the hide that counts,
For some men have more strength than others,

is the way of the Ancients."[17]

3.17 Zigong wanted to do away with the presentation of a sacrificial sheep at the announcement of each new moon. The Master said, "Ci! You grudge sheep, but I grudge ritual."

3.18 The Master said, "Were anyone to-day to serve his prince according to the full prescriptions of ritual, he would be thought a sycophant."

3.19 Duke Ding(died 495 B.C.)asked for a precept concerning a ruler's use of his ministers and a minister's service to his ruler. Master Kong replied saying, "A ruler in employing his ministers should be guided solely by the prescriptions of ritual. Ministers in serving their ruler, solely by devotion to his cause."

3.20 The Master said, "The Ospreys![18] Pleasure not carried to the point of debauch; grief not carried to the point of self-injury."

3.21 Duke Ai asked Zai Yu[19] about the Holy Ground. Zai Yu replied, "The Xia sovereigns marked theirs with a pine, the men of Yin used a cypress, the men of Zhou used a chestnut-tree, saying,'This will cause

【原文】

人以栗，曰，使民战栗。”子闻之，曰：“成事不说，遂事不谏，既往不咎。”

3.22　子曰：“管仲之器小哉！”

或曰：“管仲俭乎？”曰：“管氏有三归，官事不摄，焉得俭？”

“然则管仲知礼乎？”曰：“邦君树塞门，管氏亦树塞门。邦君为两君之好，有反坫，管氏亦有反坫。管氏而知礼，孰不知礼？”

3.23　子语鲁大师乐，曰：“乐其可知也：始作，翕如也；从之，纯如也，皦如也，绎如也，以成。”

3.24　仪封人请见，曰：“君子之至于斯也，吾未尝不得见也。”从者见之。出曰：“二三子何患于丧乎？天下之无道也久矣，天将以夫子为木铎。”

【今译】

殷代用柏木，周代用栗木，意思是使人民战战栗栗。”孔子听到了这话，[责备宰我]说：“已经做了的事不便再解释了，已经完成的事不便再挽救了，已经过去的事不便再追究了。”

3.22　孔子说：“管仲的器量狭小得很呀！”

有人便问：“他是不是很节俭呢？”孔子道：“他收取了人民的大量的市租，他手下的人员，[一人一职，]从不兼差，如何能说是节俭呢？”

那人又问：“那末，他懂得礼节么？”孔子又道：“国君宫殿门前，立了一个塞门，管氏也立了个塞门；国君设宴招待外国的君主，在堂上有放置酒杯的设备，管氏也有这样的设备。假若说他懂得礼节，那谁不懂得礼节呢？”

3.23　孔子把演奏音乐的道理告给鲁国的太师，说道：“音乐，那是可以晓得的：开始演奏，翕翕地热烈；继续下去，纯纯地和谐，皦皦地清晰，绎绎地不绝，这样，然后完成。”

3.24　仪这个地方的边防官请求孔子接见他，说道：“所有到了这个地方的有道德学问的人，我从没有不和他见面的。”孔子的随行学生请求孔子接见了他。他辞出以后，对孔子的学生们说：“你们这些人为什么着急没有官位呢？天下黑暗日子也长久了，[圣人也该有得意的时候了，]上天会要把他老人家做人民的导师哩。”

the common people to be in fear and trembling.'"[20] The Master hearing of it said, "What is over and done with, one does not discuss; what has already taken its course, one does not criticize; what already belongs to the past, one does not censure."

3.22 The Master said, "Guan Zhong[21] was in reality a man of very narrow capacities." Someone said, "Surely he displayed an example of frugality? " The Master said, "Guan had three lots of wives[22] , his State officers performed no double duties. How can he be cited as an example of frugality?" " That may be," the other said, " but surely he had a great knowledge of ritual? " The Master said, "Only the ruler of a State may build a screen to mask his gate; but Guan had such a screen. Only the ruler of a State, when meeting another such ruler, may use cup-mounds[23]; but Guan used one. If even Guan is to be cited as an expert in ritual, who is not an expert in ritual?"

3.23 When talking to the Grand Master[24] of Lu about music, the Master said, "Their music in so far as one can find out about it began with a strict unison. Soon the musicians were given more liberty[25] ; but the tone remained harmonious, brilliant, consistent, right on till the close."

3.24 The guardian of the frontier-mound at Yi[26] asked to be presented to the Master, saying, "No gentleman arriving at this frontier has ever yet failed to accord me an interview. "The Master's followers presented him. On going out the man said, "Sirs, you must not be disheartened by his failure. It is now a very long while[27] since the Way prevailed in the world. I feel sure that Heaven intends to use your Master as a wooden bell[28]."

【原文】

3.25　子谓《韶》:“尽美矣，又尽善也。”谓《武》:“尽美矣，未尽善也。”

3.26　子曰:“居上不宽，为礼不敬，临丧不哀，吾何以观之哉?”

【今译】

3.25　孔子论到《韶》，说:“美极了，而且好极了。”论到《武》，说:“美极了，却还不够好。”

3.26　孔子说:“居于统治地位不宽宏大量，行礼的时候不严肃认真，参加丧礼的时候不悲哀，这种样子我怎么看得下去呢?”

3.25 The Master spoke of the Succession Dance[29] as being perfect beauty and at the same time perfect goodness; but of the War Dance as being perfect beauty, but not perfect goodness.

3.26 The Master said, "High office filled by men of narrow views, ritual performed without reverence, the forms of mourning observed without grief — these are things I cannot bear to see!"

里仁篇第四

【原文】

4.1　子曰："里仁为美。择不处仁，焉得知?"

4.2　子曰："不仁者不可以久处约，不可以长处乐。仁者安仁，知者利仁。"

4.3　子曰："唯仁者能好人，能恶人。"

4.4　子曰："苟志于仁矣，无恶也。"

4.5　子曰："富与贵，是人之所欲也；不以其道得之，不处也。贫与贱，是人之所恶也；不以其道得之，不去也。君子去仁，恶乎成名?君子无终食之间违仁，造次必于是，颠沛必于是。"

【今译】

4.1　孔子说："住的地方，要有仁德这才好。选择住处，没有仁德，怎么能是聪明呢?"

4.2　孔子说："不仁的人不可以长久地居于穷困中，也不可以长久地居于安乐中。有仁德的人安于仁[实行仁德便心安，不实行仁德心便不安]；聪明人利用仁[他认识到仁德对他长远而巨大的利益，他便实行仁德]。"

4.3　孔子说："只有仁人才能够喜爱某人，厌恶某人。"

4.4　孔子说："假如立定志向实行仁德，总没有坏处。"

4.5　孔子说："发大财，做大官，这是人人所盼望的；不用正当的方法去得到它，君子不接受。穷困和下贱，这是人人所厌恶的；不用正当的方法去抛掉它，君子不摆脱。君子抛弃了仁德，怎样去成就他的声名呢?君子没有吃完一餐饭的时间离开仁德，就是在仓猝匆忙的时候一定和仁德同在，就是在颠沛流离的时候一定和仁德同在。"

BOOK IV

4.1 The Master said, "It is Goodness that gives to a neighbourhood its beauty. One who is free to choose, yet does not prefer to dwell among the Good — how can he be accorded the name of wise?"[1]

4.2 The Master said, "Without Goodness a man

> Cannot for long endure adversity,
> Cannot for long enjoy prosperity.

The Good Man rests content with Goodness; he that is merely wise pursues Goodness in the belief that it pays to do so."

4.3, 4.4 Of the adage "Only a Good Man knows how to like people, knows how to dislike them," the Master said, "He whose heart is in the smallest degree set upon Goodness will dislike no one."

4.5 Wealth and rank are what every man desires; but if they can only be retained to the detriment of the Way he professes, he must relinquish them. Poverty and obscurity are what every man detests; but if they can only be avoided to the detriment of the Way he professes, he must accept them. The gentleman who ever parts company with Goodness does not fulfil that name. Never for a moment does a gentleman quit the way of Goodness. He is never so harried but that he cleaves to this; never so tottering but that he cleaves to this.

【原文】

4.6 子曰:“我未见好仁者，恶不仁者。好仁者，无以尚之；恶不仁者，其为仁矣，不使不仁者加乎其身。有能一日用其力于仁矣乎?我未见力不足者。盖有之矣，我未之见也。”

4.7 子曰:“人之过也，各于其党。观过，斯知仁矣。”

4.8 子曰:“朝闻道，夕死可矣。”

4.9 子曰:“士志于道，而耻恶衣恶食者，未足与议也。”

4.10 子曰:“君子之于天下也，无适也，无莫也，义之与比。”

4.11 子曰:“君子怀德，小人怀土；君子怀刑，小人怀惠。”

【今译】

4.6 孔子说:“我不曾见到过爱好仁德的人和厌恶不仁德的人。爱好仁德的人，那是再好也没有的了；厌恶不仁德的人，他行仁德，只是不使不仁德的东西加在自己身上。有谁能在某一天使用他的力量于仁德呢?我没见过力量不够的。大概这种人还是有的，我不曾见到罢了。”

4.7 孔子说:“[人是各种各样的，人的错误也是各种各样的。]什么样的错误就是由什么样的人犯的。仔细考察某人所犯的错误，就可以知道他是什么样式的人了。”

4.8 孔子说:“早晨得知真理，要我当晚死去，都可以。”

4.9 孔子说:“读书人有志于真理，但又以自己吃粗粮穿破衣为耻辱，这种人，不值得同他商议了。”

4.10 孔子说:“君子对于天下的事情，没规定要怎样干，也没规定不要怎样干，只要怎样干合理恰当，便怎样干。”

4.11 孔子说:“君子怀念道德，小人怀念乡土；君子关心法度，小人关心恩惠。”

4.6 The Master said, "I for my part have never yet seen one who really cared for Goodness, nor one who really abhorred wickedness. One who really cared for Goodness would never let any other consideration come first. One who abhorred wickedness would be so constantly doing Good that wickedness would never have a chance to get at him. Has anyone ever managed to do Good with his whole might even as long as the space of a single day? I think not. Yet I for my part have never seen anyone give up such an attempt because he had not the *strength* to go on. It may well have happened, but I for my part have never seen it[2]."

4.7 The Master said, "Every man's faults belong to a set.[3] If one looks out for faults it is only as a means of recognizing Goodness."

4.8 The Master said, "In the morning, hear the Way; in the evening, die content!"

4.9 The Master said, "A Knight whose heart is set upon the Way, but who is ashamed of wearing shabby clothes and eating coarse food, is not worth calling into counsel."

4.10 The Master said, "A gentleman in his dealings with the world has neither enmities nor affections; but wherever he sees Right he ranges himself beside it."

4.11 The Master said, "Where gentlemen set their hearts upon moral force(*de*),[4] the commoners set theirs upon the soil.[5] Where gentlemen think only of punishments, the commoners think only of exemptions."

【原文】

4.12 子曰:“放于利而行，多怨。”

4.13 子曰:“能以礼让为国乎?何有?不能以礼让为国，如礼何?”

4.14 子曰:“不患无位，患所以立。不患莫己知，求为可知也。”

4.15 子曰:“参乎!吾道一以贯之。”曾子曰:“唯。”

子出，门人问曰:“何谓也?”曾子曰:“夫子之道，忠恕而已矣。”

4.16 子曰:“君子喻于义，小人喻于利。”

4.17 子曰:“见贤思齐焉，见不贤而内自省也。”

4.18 子曰:“事父母几谏，见志不从，又敬不违，劳而不怨。”

【今译】

4.12 孔子说:“依据个人利益而行动，会招致很多的怨恨。”

4.13 孔子说:“能够用礼让来治理国家吗?这有什么困难呢?如果不能用礼让来治理国家，又怎样来对待礼仪呢?”

4.14 孔子说:“不发愁没有职位，只发愁没有任职的本领；不怕没有人知道自己，去追求足以使别人知道自己的本领好了。”

4.15 孔子说:“参呀!我的学说贯穿着一个基本观念。”曾子说:“是。”

孔子走出去以后，别的学生便问曾子道:“这是什么意思?”曾子道:“他老人家的学说，只是忠和恕罢了。”

4.16 孔子说:“君子懂得的是义，小人懂得的是利。”

4.17 孔子说:“看见贤人，便应该想向他看齐；看见不贤的人，便应该自己反省[有没有同他类似的毛病]。”

4.18 孔子说:“侍奉父母，[如果他们有不对的地方，]得轻微婉转地劝止，看到自己的心意没有被听从，仍然恭敬地不触犯他们，虽然忧愁，但不怨恨。”

4.12 The Master said, "Those whose measures are dictated by mere expediency will arouse continual discontent."

4.13 The Master said, "If it is really possible to govern countries by ritual and yielding, there is no more to be said. But if it is not really possible, of what use is ritual?"

4.14 The Master said, "He does not mind not being in office; all he minds about is whether he has qualities that entitle him to office. He does not mind failing to get recognition; he is too busy doing the things that entitle him to recognition."

4.15 The Master said, "Shen! My Way has one(thread)that runs right through it." Master Zeng said, "Yes." When the Master had gone out, the disciples asked saying, "What did he mean?" Master Zeng said, " Our Master's Way is simply this: loyalty, consideration."

4.16 The Master said, "A gentleman takes as much trouble to discover what is right as lesser men take to discover what will pay."

4.17 The Master said, "In the presence of a good man, think all the time how you may learn to equal him. In the presence of a bad man, turn your gaze within[6]!"

4.18 The Master said, "In serving his father and mother a man may gently remonstrate with them. But if he sees that he has failed to change their opinion, he should resume an attitude of deference and not thwart them; may feel discouraged, but not resentful."

【原文】

4.19　子曰:“父母在，不远游，游必有方。”

4.20　子曰:“三年无改于父之道，可谓孝矣。”

4.21　子曰:“父母之年，不可不知也。一则以喜，一则以惧。”

4.22　子曰:“古者言之不出，耻躬之不逮也。”

4.23　子曰:“以约失之者鲜矣。”

4.24　子曰:“君子欲讷于言而敏于行。”

4.25　子曰:“德不孤，必有邻。”

4.26　子游曰:“事君数，斯辱矣；朋友数，斯疏矣。”

【今译】

4.19　孔子说:“父母在世，不出远门，如果要出远门，必须有一定的去处。”

4.20　见学而篇第一。

4.21　孔子说:“父母的年纪不能不时时记在心里：一方面因[其高寿]而喜欢，另一方面又因[其寿高]而有所恐惧。”

4.22　孔子说:“古时候言语不轻易出口，就是怕自己的行动赶不上。”

4.23　孔子说:“因为对自己节制、约束而犯过失的，这种事情总不会多。”

4.24　孔子说:“君子言语要谨慎迟钝，工作要勤劳敏捷。”

4.25　孔子说:“有道德的人不会孤单，一定会有[志同道合的人来和他做]伙伴。”

4.26　子游说:“对待君主过于烦琐，就会招致侮辱；对待朋友过于烦琐，就会反被疏远。”

4.19 The Master said, “While father and mother are alive, a good son does not wander far afield; or if he does so, goes only where he has said he was going[7].”

4.20 The Master said, “If for the whole three years of mourning a son manages to carry on the household exactly as in his father’s day, then he is a good son indeed.”

4.21 The Master said, “It is always better for a man to know the age of his parents. In the one case[8] such knowledge will be a comfort to him; in the other,[9] it will fill him with a salutary dread.”

4.22 The Master said, “In old days a man kept a hold on his words, fearing the disgrace that would ensue should he himself fail to keep pace with them.”

4.23 The Master said, “Those who err on the side of strictness are few indeed!”

4.24 The Master said, “A gentleman covets the reputation of being slow in word but prompt in deed.”

4.25 The Master said, “Moral force(*de*)never dwells in solitude; it will always bring neighbours.”[10]

4.26 Ziyou said, “In the service of one’s prince repeated scolding[11] can only lead to loss of favour; in friendship, it can only lead to estrangement.”

公冶长篇第五

【原文】

5.1 子谓公冶长,“可妻也。虽在缧绁之中,非其罪也。”以其子妻之。

5.2 子谓南容:“邦有道,不废;邦无道,免于刑戮。”以其兄之子妻之。

5.3 子谓子贱:“君子哉若人!鲁无君子者,斯焉取斯?”

5.4 子贡问曰:“赐也何如?”子曰:“女,器也。”曰:“何器也?”曰:“瑚琏也。”

5.5 或曰:“雍也仁而不佞。”子曰:“焉用佞?御人以口给,屡憎于人。不知其仁,焉用佞?”

5.6 子使漆雕开仕。对曰:“吾斯之未能信。”子说。

【今译】

5.1 孔子说公冶长,“可以把女儿嫁给他。他虽然曾被关在监狱之中,但不是他的罪过。”便把自己的女儿嫁给他。

5.2 孔子说南容,“国家政治清明,[总有官做,]不被废弃;国家政治黑暗,也不致被刑罚。”于是把自己的侄女嫁给他。

5.3 孔子评论宓子贱,说:“这人是君子呀!假若鲁国没有君子,这种人从哪里取来这种好品德呢?”

5.4 子贡问道:“我是一个怎样的人?”孔子道:“你好比是一个器皿。”子贡道:“什么器皿?”孔子道:“宗庙里盛黍稷的瑚琏。”

5.5 有人说:“冉雍这个人有仁德,却没有口才。”孔子道:“何必要口才呢?强嘴利舌地同人家辩驳,常常被人讨厌。冉雍未必仁,但为什么要有口才呢?”

5.6 孔子叫漆雕开去做官。他答道:“我对这个还没有信心。”孔子听了很欢喜。

BOOK V

5.1 The Master said of Gongye Chang, "Though he has suffered imprisonment, he is not an unfit person to choose as a husband; for it was not through any fault of his own. " He married him to his daughter.

The Master said of Nan Rong[1], "In a country ruled according to the Way, he would not be overlooked; in a country not ruled according to the Way, he would manage to avoid capital punishment or mutilation." He married him to his elder brother's[2] daughter.

5.2 Of Zijian[3] he said, "A gentleman indeed is such a one as he! If the land of Lu were indeed without gentlemen, how could he have learnt this?"

5.3 Zigong asked saying, "What do you think of me?" The Master said, "You are a vessel."[4] Zigong said, "What sort of vessel?" The Master said, "A sacrificial vase of jade!"[5]

5.4 Someone said, "Ran Yong is Good, but he is a poor talker." The Master said, "What need has he to be a good talker? Those who down others with clap-trap are seldom popular. Whether he is Good, I do not know. But I see no need for him to be a good talker."

5.5 The Master gave Qidiao Kai leave to take office, but he replied, "I have not yet sufficiently perfected myself in the virtue of good faith."The Master was delighted.

【原文】

5.7 子曰:“道不行，乘桴浮于海。从我者，其由与?”子路闻之喜。子曰:“由也好勇过我，无所取材。”

5.8 孟武伯问子路仁乎?子曰:“不知也。”又问。子曰:“由也，千乘之国，可使治其赋也，不知其仁也。”

“求也何如?”子曰:“求也，千室之邑，百乘之家，可使为之宰也，不知其仁也。”

“赤也何如?”子曰:“赤也，束带立于朝，可使与宾客言也，不知其仁也。”

5.9 子谓子贡曰:“女与回也孰愈?”对曰:“赐也何敢望回?回也闻一以知十，赐也闻一以知二。”子曰:“弗如也；吾与女弗如也。”

5.10 宰予昼寝。子曰:“朽木不可雕也，粪土之墙不可杇也。于予与何诛?”子曰:“始吾于人也，听其言而信其行；今吾于人也，听其

【今译】

5.7 孔子道:“主张行不通了，我想坐个木排到海外去，跟随我的恐怕只有仲由吧!”子路听到这话，高兴得很。孔子说:“仲由这个人太好勇敢了，好勇的精神大大超过了我，这就没有什么可取的呀!”

5.8 孟武伯向孔子问子路有没有仁德。孔子道:“不晓得。”他又问。孔子道:“仲由啦，如果有一千辆兵车的国家，可以叫他负责兵役和军政的工作。至于他有没有仁德，我不晓得。”

孟武伯继续问:“冉求又怎么样呢?”孔子道:“求啦，千户人口的私邑，可以叫他当县长；百辆兵车的大夫封地，可以叫他当总管。至于他有没有仁德，我不晓得。”

“公西赤又怎么样呢?”孔子道:“赤啦，穿着礼服，立于朝廷之中，可以叫他接待外宾，办理交涉。至于他有没有仁德，我不晓得。”

5.9 孔子对子贡道:“你和颜回，哪一个强些?”子贡答道:“我么，怎敢和回相比?他啦，听到一件事，可以推演知道十件事；我咧，听到一件事，只能推知两件事。”孔子道:“赶不上他；我同意你的话，是赶不上他。”

5.10 宰予在白天睡觉。孔子说:“腐烂了的木头雕刻不得，粪土似的墙壁粉刷不得；对于宰予么，不值得责备呀。”又说:“最初，我对人家，听到他的话，便相信他的行为；今天，我对人家，听到他的

5.6 The Master said, "The Way makes no progress. I shall get upon a raft and float out to sea.[6] I am sure You would come with me." Zilu on hearing of this was in high spirits. The Master said, "That is You indeed! He sets far too much store by feats of physical daring. It seems as though I should never get hold of the right sort of people."

5.7 Meng Wu[7] asked whether Zilu was Good. The Master said, "I do not know." On his repeating the question the Master said, "In a country of a thousand war-chariots You could be trusted to carry out the recruiting. But whether he is Good, I do not know." "What about Qiu[8]? "The Master said, "In a city of a thousand families or a baronial family with a hundred chariots he might do well as Warden. But whether he is Good, I do not know." "What about Chi[9]?" The Master said, "Girt with his sash, standing in his place at Court he might well be charged to converse with strangers and guests. But whether he is Good, I do not know."[10]

5.8 The Master in discussing Zigong said to him, "Which do you yourself think is the better, you or Hui?" He answered saying, "I dare not so much as look at Hui. For Hui has but to hear one part in ten, in order to understand the whole ten. Whereas if I hear one part, I understand no more than two parts. "The Master said, "Not equal to him — you and I are not equal to him!"

5.9 Zai Yu[11] used to sleep during the day. The Master said, "Rotten wood cannot be carved, nor a wall of dried dung be trowelled. What use is there in my scolding him any more?"

The Master said, "There was a time when I merely listened attentively to what people said, and took for granted that they would carry out

【原文】

言而观其行。于予与改是。”

5.11 子曰:“吾未见刚者。”或对曰:“申枨。”子曰:“枨也欲，焉得刚?”

5.12 子贡曰:“我不欲人之加诸我也，吾亦欲无加诸人。”子曰:“赐也，非尔所及也。”

5.13 子贡曰:“夫子之文章，可得而闻也；夫子之言性与天道，不可得而闻也。”

5.14 子路有闻，未之能行，唯恐有闻。

5.15 子贡问曰:“孔文子何以谓之‘文’也?”子曰:“敏而好学，不耻下问，是以谓之‘文’也。”

5.16 子谓子产，“有君子之道四焉：其行己也恭，其事上也敬，

【今译】

话，却要考察他的行为。从宰予的事件以后，我改变了态度。”

5.11 孔子道:“我没见过刚毅不屈的人。”有人答道:“申枨是这样的人。”孔子道:“申枨啦，他欲望太多，哪里能够刚毅不屈?”

5.12 子贡道:“我不想别人欺侮我，我也不想欺侮别人。”孔子说:“赐，这不是你能做到的。”

5.13 子贡说:“老师关于文献方面的学问，我们听得到；老师关于天性和天道的言论，我们听不到。”

5.14 子路有所闻，还没有能够去做，只怕又有所闻。

5.15 子贡问道:“孔文子凭什么谥他为‘文’?”孔子道:“他聪敏灵活，爱好学问，又谦虚下问，不以为耻，所以用‘文’字做他的谥号。”

5.16 孔子评论子产，说:“他有四种行为合于君子之道：他自己的容颜态度庄严恭敬，他对待君上负责认真，他教养人民有恩惠，

their words. Now I am obliged not only to give ear to what they say, but also to keep an eye on what they do. It was my dealings with Zai Yu that brought about the change."

5.10 The Master said, "I have never yet seen a man who was truly steadfast[12]."Someone answered saying,"Shen Cheng."The Master said, "Cheng! He is at the mercy of his desires. How can *he* be called steadfast?"

5.11 Zigong said, "What I do not want others to do to me, I have no desire to do to others." The Master said, "Oh Ci! You have not quite got to that point yet."

5.12 Zigong said, "Our Master's views concerning culture[13] and the outward insignia[14] of goodness, we are permitted to hear; but about Man's nature[15] and the ways of Heaven he will not tell us anything at all."

5.13 When Zilu heard any precept and was still trying unsuccessfully to put it into practice, his one fear was that he might hear some fresh precept.

5.14 Zigong asked saying, "Why was Kong Wen called Wen('The Cultured')?"[16]The Master said, "Because he was diligent and so fond of learning that he was not ashamed to pick up knowledge even from his inferiors."

5.15 Of Zichan[17] the Master said that in him were to be found four of the virtues that belong to the Way of the true gentleman. In his private conduct he was courteous, in serving his master he was punctilious, in pro-

【原文】

其养民也惠，其使民也义。”

5.17 子曰：“晏平仲善与人交，久而敬之。”

5.18 子曰：“臧文仲居蔡，山节藻棁，何如其知也？”

5.19 子张问曰：“令尹子文三仕为令尹，无喜色；三已之，无愠色。旧令尹之政，必以告新令尹。何如？”子曰：“忠矣。”曰：“仁矣乎？”曰：“未知；——焉得仁？”

“崔子弑齐君，陈文子有马十乘，弃而违之。至于他邦，则曰，‘犹吾大夫崔子也。’违之。之一邦，则又曰：‘犹吾大夫崔子也。’违之。何如？”子曰：“清矣。”曰：“仁矣乎？”曰：“未知；——焉得仁？”

【今译】

他役使人民合于道理。”

5.17 孔子说：“晏平仲善于和别人交朋友，相交越久，别人越发敬重他。”

5.18 孔子说：“臧文仲替一种叫蔡的大乌龟盖了一间屋，有雕刻着像山一样的斗拱和画着藻草的梁上短柱，这个人的聪明怎么这样呢？”

5.19 子张问道：“楚国的令尹子文三次做令尹的官，没有高兴的颜色；三次被罢免，没有怨恨的颜色。[每次交代，]一定把自己的一切政令全部告诉接位的人。这个人怎么样？”孔子道：“可算尽忠于国家了。”子张道：“算不算仁呢？”孔子道：“不晓得；——这怎么能算是仁呢？”

子张又问：“崔杼无理地杀掉齐庄公，陈文子有四十匹马，舍弃不要，离开齐国。到了另一个国家，说道：‘这里的执政者同我们的崔子差不多。’又离开。又到了一国，又说道：‘这里的执政者同我们的崔子差不多。’于是又离开。这个人怎么样？”孔子道：“清白得很。”子张道：“算不算仁呢？”孔子道：“不晓得；——这怎么能算是仁呢？”

viding for the needs of the people he gave them even more than their due; in exacting service from the people, he was just.

5.16 The Master said, "Yan Pingzhong is[18] a good example of what one's intercourse with one's fellowmen should be. However long he has known anyone he always maintains the same scrupulous courtesy."

5.17 The Master said, "Zang Wenzhong[19] kept a Cai tortoise[20] in a hall with the hill-pattern on its pillar tops and the duckweed pattern on its king-posts.[21] Of what sort, pray, was his knowledge[22]?"

5.18 Zizhang asked saying, "The Grand Minister Ziwen [23] was appointed to this office on three separate occasions, but did not on any of these three occasions display the least sign of elation. Three times he was deposed; but never showed the least sign of disappointment. Each time, he duly informed his successor concerning the administration of State affairs during his tenure of office. What should you say of him?" The Master said, "He was certainly faithful to his prince's interests." Zizhang said, "Would you not call him Good? "The Master said, "I am not sure. I see nothing in that to merit the title Good."

(Zizhang said) "When Cui assassinated the sovereign of Qi[24] ,Chen Wen[25] who held a fief of ten war chariots gave it up and went away. On arriving in another State, he said,'I can see they are no better here than our minister Cui'; and he went away. On arriving in the next country, he said,'I can see they are no better here than our minister Cui'; and went away. What should you say of him? " The Master said, "He was certainly scrupulous." Zizhang said, "Would you not call him Good? "The Master said, "I am not sure. I see nothing in that to merit the title Good."

【原文】

5.20　季文子三思而后行。子闻之，曰："再，斯可矣。"

5.21　子曰："宁武子，邦有道，则知；邦无道，则愚。其知可及也，其愚不可及也。"

5.22　子在陈，曰："归与！归与！吾党之小子狂简，斐然成章，不知所以裁之。"

5.23　子曰："伯夷、叔齐不念旧恶，怨是用希。"

5.24　子曰："孰谓微生高直？或乞醯焉，乞诸其邻而与之。"

5.25　子曰："巧言、令色、足恭，左丘明耻之，丘亦耻之。匿怨而友其人，左丘明耻之，丘亦耻之。"

【今译】

5.20　季文子每件事考虑多次才行动。孔子听到了，说："想两次也就可以了。"

5.21　孔子说："宁武子在国家太平时节，便聪明；在国家昏暗时节，便装傻。他那聪明，别人赶得上；那装傻，别人就赶不上了。"

5.22　孔子在陈国，说："回去吧！回去吧！我们那里的学生们志向高大得很，文采又都斐然可观，我不知道怎样去指导他们。"

5.23　孔子说："伯夷、叔齐这两兄弟不记念过去的仇恨，别人对他们的怨恨也就很少。"

5.24　孔子说："谁说微生高这个人直爽？有人向他讨点醋，[他不说自己没有，]却到邻人那里转讨一点给人。"

5.25　孔子说："花言巧语，伪善的容貌，十足的恭顺，这种态度，左丘明认为可耻，我也认为可耻。内心藏着怨恨，表面上却同他要好，这种行为，左丘明认为可耻，我也认为可耻。"

5.19 Ji Wen used to think thrice before acting. The Master hearing of it said, "Twice is quite enough."

5.20 The Master said, "Ning Wu[26] so long as the Way prevailed in his country showed wisdom; but when the Way no longer prevailed, he showed his folly. To such wisdom as his we may all attain; but not to such folly!"

5.21 When the Master was in Chen[27] he said, "Let us go back, let us go back! The little ones at home are headstrong and careless. They are perfecting themselves in all the showy insignia of culture without any idea how to use them."

5.22 The Master said, "Boyi and Shuqi[28] never bore old ills in mind and had but the faintest feelings of rancour."

5.23 The Master said, "How can we call even Weisheng Gao upright? When someone asked him for vinegar he went and begged it from the people next door, and then gave it as though it were his own gift."[29]

5.24 The Master said, "Clever talk, a pretentious manner and a reverence that is only of the feet — Zuo Qiuming[30] was incapable of stooping to them, and I too could never stoop to them. Having to conceal one's indignation and keep on friendly terms with the people against whom one feels it — Zuo Qiuming was incapable of stooping to such conduct, and I too am incapable of stooping to such conduct."

【原文】

5.26 颜渊季路侍。子曰:“盍各言尔志?”

子路曰:“愿车马衣轻裘与朋友共敝之而无憾。”

颜渊曰:“愿无伐善,无施劳。”

子路曰:“愿闻子之志。”

子曰:“老者安之,朋友信之,少者怀之。”

5.27 子曰:“已矣乎!吾未见能见其过而内自讼者也。”

5.28 子曰:“十室之邑,必有忠信如丘者焉,不如丘之好学也。”

【今译】

5.26 孔子坐着,颜渊、季路两人站在孔子身边。孔子道:“何不各人说说自己的志向?”

子路道:“愿意把我的车马衣服同朋友共同使用,坏了也没有什么不满。”

颜渊道:“愿意不夸耀自己的好处,不表白自己的功劳。”

子路向孔子道:“希望听到您的志向。”

孔子道:“[我的志向是,]老者使他安逸,朋友使他信任我,年青人使他怀念我。”

5.27 孔子说:“算了吧!我没有看见过能够看到自己的错误便自我责备的哩。”

5.28 孔子说:“就是十户人家的地方,一定有像我这样又忠心又信实的人,只是赶不上我的喜欢学问罢了。”

5.25 Once when Yan Hui and Zilu were waiting upon him the Master said, "Suppose each of you were to tell his wish. "Zilu said, "I should like to have carriages and horses, clothes and fur rugs, share them with my friends and feel no annoyance if they were returned to me the worse for wear." Yan Hui said, "I should like never to boast of my good qualities nor make a fuss about the trouble I take on behalf of others." Zilu said, "A thing I should like is to hear the Master's wish. "The Master said, "In dealing with the aged, to be of comfort to them; in dealing with friends, to be of good faith with them; in dealing with the young, to cherish them."

5.26 The Master said, "In vain have I looked for a single man capable of seeing his own faults and bringing the charge home against himself."

5.27 The Master said, "In a hamlet of ten houses you may be sure of finding someone quite as loyal and true to his word as I. But I doubt if you would find anyone with such a love of learning[31]."

雍也篇第六

【原文】

6.1　子曰:“雍也可使南面。”

6.2　仲弓问子桑伯子。子曰:“可也简。”

仲弓曰:“居敬而行简，以临其民，不亦可乎?居简而行简，无乃大简乎?”子曰:“雍之言然。”

6.3　哀公问:“弟子孰为好学?”孔子对曰:“有颜回者好学，不迁怒，不贰过。不幸短命死矣，今也则亡，未闻好学者也。”

6.4　子华使于齐，冉子为其母请粟。子曰:“与之釜。”

请益。曰:“与之庾。”

冉子与之粟五秉。

子曰:“赤之适齐也，乘肥马，衣轻裘。吾闻之也：君子周急不继富。”

6.5　原思为之宰，与之粟九百，辞。子曰:“毋!以与尔邻里乡党乎!”

【今译】

6.1　孔子说:“冉雍这个人，可以让他做一部门或一地方的长官。”

6.2　仲弓问到子桑伯子这个人。孔子道:“他简单得好。”

仲弓道:“若存心严肃认真，而以简单行之，[抓大体，不烦琐，]来治理百姓，不也可以吗?若存心简单，又以简单行之，不是太简单了吗?”孔子道:“你这番话正确。”

6.3　鲁哀公问:“你的学生中，哪个好学?”孔子答道:“有一个叫颜回的人好学，不拿别人出气，也不再犯同样的过失。不幸短命死了，现在再没有这样的人了，再也没听过好学的人了。”

6.4　公西华被派到齐国去做使者，冉有替他母亲向孔子请求要小米。孔子道:“给他六斗四升。”

冉有请求增加。孔子道:“再给他二斗四升。”

冉有却给了他八十石。

孔子道:“公西赤到齐国去，坐着由肥马驾的车辆，穿着又轻又暖的皮袍。我听说过：君子只是雪里送炭，不去锦上添花。”

6.5　原思任孔子家的总管，孔子给他小米九百，他不肯受。孔子道:“别辞!有多的，给你地方上[的穷人]吧!”

BOOK VI

6.1 The Master said, "Now Yong[1] ,for example. I should not mind setting him with his face to the south[2]." Ran Yong then asked about Zisang Bozi. The Master said, "He too would do. He is lax." Ran Yong said, "I can understand that such a man might do as a ruler, provided he were scrupulous in his own conduct and lax only in his dealings with the people. But you would admit that a man who was lax in his own conduct as well as in government would be too lax[3] ." The Master said, "What Yong says is quite true."

6.2 Duke Ai asked which of the disciples had a love of learning. Master Kong answered him saying, "There was Yan Hui. He had a great love of learning. He never vented his wrath upon the innocent nor let others suffer for his faults. Unfortunately the span of life allotted to him by Heaven was short, and he died. At present there are none or at any rate I have heard of none who are fond of learning."

6.3 When Gongxi Hua was sent on a mission to Qi, Master Ran asked that Hua's mother might be granted an allowance of grain. The Master said, "Give her a cauldron[4] full." Ran said that was not enough. The Master said, "Give her a measure[5] ." Master Ran gave her five bundles[6]. The Master said, "When Chi[7] went to Qi he drove sleek horses and was wrapped in light furs. There is a saying, 'A gentleman helps out the necessitous; he does not make the rich richer still.'"

When Yuan Si was made a governor, he was given an allowance of nine hundred measures of grain, but declined it. The Master said, "Surely

【原文】

6.6 子谓仲弓,曰:“犁牛之子骍且角，虽欲勿用，山川其舍诸?”

6.7 子曰:“回也，其心三月不违仁，其余则日月至焉而已矣。”

6.8 季康子问:“仲由可使从政也与?”子曰:“由也果，于从政乎何有?”

曰:“赐也可使从政也与?”曰:“赐也达，于从政乎何有?”

曰:“求也可使从政也与?”曰:“求也艺，于从政乎何有?”

6.9 季氏使闵子骞为费宰。闵子骞曰:“善为我辞焉!如有复我者，则吾必在汶上矣。”

6.10 伯牛有疾，子问之，自牖执其手，曰:“亡之，命矣夫!斯

【今译】

6.6 孔子谈到冉雍，说:“耕牛的儿子长着赤色的毛，整齐的角，虽然不想用它作牺牲来祭祀，山川之神难道会舍弃它吗?”

6.7 孔子说:“颜回呀，他的心长久地不离开仁德，别的学生么，只是短时期偶然想起一下罢了。”

6.8 季康子问孔子:“仲由这人，可以使用他治理政事么?”孔子道:“仲由果敢决断，让他治理政事有什么困难呢?”

又问:“端木赐可以使用他治理政事么?”孔子道:“端木赐通情达理，让他治理政事有什么困难呢?”

又问:“冉求可以使用他治理政事么?”孔子道:“冉求多才多艺，让他治理政事有什么困难呢?”

6.9 季氏叫闵子骞做他采邑费地的县长。闵子骞对来人说道:“好好地替我辞掉吧!若是再来找我的话，那我一定会逃到汶水之北去了。”

6.10 伯牛生了病，孔子去探问他，从窗户里握着他的手，道:“难

you could find people who would be glad of it among your neighbours or in your village?"

6.4 The Master said of Ran Yong, "If the offspring of a brindled[8] ox is ruddy-coated and has grown its horns, however much people might hesitate to use it[9] ,would the hills and streams really reject it?"

6.5 The Master said, "Hui is capable of occupying his whole mind for three months on end with no thought but that of Goodness. The others can do so, some for a day, some even for a month; but that is all."[10]

6.6 Ji Kang[11] asked whether Zilu was the right sort of person to put into office. The Master said, "You is efficient. It goes without saying that he is capable of holding office." Ji Kang said, "How about Zigong? Would he be the right sort of person to put into office?" The Master said, "He can turn his merits to account[12] .It goes without saying that he is capable of holding office." Ji Kang said, "How about Ran Qiu? Would he be the right sort of person to put into office? " The Master said, "He is versatile. It goes without saying that he is capable of holding office."

6.7 The Ji Family[13] wanted to make Min Ziqian governor of Mi[14] .Min Ziqian said, "Invent a polite excuse for me. If that is not accepted and they try to get at me again, I shall certainly install myself on the far side of the Wen[15]."

6.8 When Ran Geng was ill, the Master went to enquire after him, and grasping his hand through the window said, "It is all over with him! Heaven has so ordained it — but that such a man should have such an

【原文】

人也而有斯疾也！斯人也而有斯疾也！”

6.11　子曰：“贤哉，回也！一箪食，一瓢饮，在陋巷，人不堪其忧，回也不改其乐。贤哉，回也！”

6.12　冉求曰：“非不说子之道，力不足也。”子曰：“力不足者，中道而废。今女画。”

6.13　子谓子夏曰：“女为君子儒！无为小人儒！”

6.14　子游为武城宰。子曰：“女得人焉耳乎？”曰：“有澹台灭明者，行不由径，非公事，未尝至于偃之室也。”

6.15　子曰：“孟之反不伐，奔而殿，将入门，策其马，曰：‘非敢后也，马不进也。’”

6.16　子曰：“不有祝鮀之佞，而有宋朝之美，难乎免于今之世矣！”

【今译】

得活了，这是命呀！这样的人竟有这样的病！这样的人竟有这样的病！”

6.11　孔子说：“颜回多么有修养呀！一竹筐饭，一瓜瓢水，住在小巷子里，别人都受不了那穷苦的忧愁，颜回却不改变他自有的快乐。颜回多么有修养呀！”

6.12　冉求道：“不是我不喜欢您的学说，是我力量不够。”孔子道：“如果真是力量不够，走到半道会再走不动了。现在你却没有开步走。”

6.13　孔子对子夏道：“你要去做个君子式的儒者，不要去做那小人式的儒者！”

6.14　子游做武城县县长。孔子道：“你在这儿得到什么人才没有？”他道：“有一个叫澹台灭明的人，走路不插小道，不是公事，从不到我屋里来。”

6.15　孔子说：“孟之反不夸耀自己，［在抵御齐国的战役中，右翼的军队溃退了，］他走在最后，掩护全军，将进城门，便鞭打着马匹，一面说道：‘不是我敢于殿后，是马匹不肯快走的缘故。’”

6.16　孔子说：“假使没有祝鮀的口才，而仅有宋朝的美丽，在今天的社会里怕不易避免祸害了。”

illness! That such a man should have such an illness!"

6.9 The Master said, "Incomparable indeed was Hui! A handful[16] of rice to eat, a gourdful of water to drink, living in a mean street — others would have found it unendurably depressing, but to Hui's cheerfulness it made no difference at all. Incomparable indeed was Hui!"

6.10 Ran Qiu said, "It is not that your Way does not commend itself to me, but that it demands powers I do not possess. " The Master said, "He whose strength gives out collapses during the course of the journey (the Way); but you deliberately draw the line[17]."

6.11 The Master said to Zixia,"You must practise the *ru*[18] of gentlemen, not that of the common people."

6.12 When Ziyou was Warden of the castle of Wu, the Master said, "Have you managed to get hold of the right sort of people there?" Ziyou said, "There is someone called Tantai Mieming who 'walks on no by-paths.'[19] He has not once come to my house except on public business."

6.13 The Master said, "Meng Zhifan is no boaster. When his people were routed[20] he was the last to flee; but when they neared the city-gate, he whipped up his horses, saying, 'It was not courage that kept me behind. My horses were slow.'"

6.14 The Master said, "Without the eloquence of the priest[21] Tuo and the beauty of Prince Chao of Song it is hard nowadays to get through."

【原文】

6.17　子曰："谁能出不由户？何莫由斯道也？"

6.18　子曰："质胜文则野，文胜质则史。文质彬彬，然后君子。"

6.19　子曰："人之生也直，罔之生也幸而免。"

6.20　子曰："知之者不如好之者，好之者不如乐之者。"

6.21　子曰："中人以上，可以语上也；中人以下，不可以语上也。"

6.22　樊迟问知。子曰："务民之义，敬鬼神而远之，可谓知矣。"问仁。曰："仁者先难而后获，可谓仁矣。"

6.23　子曰："知者乐水，仁者乐山。知者动，仁者静。知者乐，

【今译】

6.17　孔子说："谁能够走出屋外不从房门经过？为什么没有人从我这条路行走呢？"

6.18　孔子说："朴实多于文采，就未免粗野；文采多于朴实，又未免虚浮。文采和朴实，配合适当，这才是个君子。"

6.19　孔子说："人的生存由于正直，不正直的人也可以生存，那是他侥幸地免于祸害。"

6.20　孔子说："[对于任何学问和事业，]懂得它的人不如喜爱它的人，喜爱它的人又不如以它为乐的人。"

6.21　孔子说："中等水平以上的人，可以告诉他高深学问；中等水平以下的人，不可以告诉他高深学问。"

6.22　樊迟问怎么样才算聪明。孔子道："把心力专一地放在使人民走向'义'上，严肃地对待鬼神，但并不打算接近他，可以说是聪明了。"

又问怎么样才叫做有仁德。孔子道："仁德的人付出一定的力量，然后收获果实，可以说是仁德了。"

6.23　孔子说："聪明人乐于水，仁人乐于山。聪明人活动，仁人

6.15 The Master said, "Who expects to be able to go out of a house except by the door? How is it then that no one follows this Way of ours?"[22]

6.16 The Master said, "When natural substance prevails over ornamentation,[23] you get the boorishness of the rustic. When ornamentation prevails over natural substance, you get the pedantry of the scribe. Only when ornament and substance are duly blended do you get the true gentleman."

6.17 The Master said, "Man's very life is honesty, in that without it he will be lucky indeed if he escapes with his life."

6.18 The Master said, "To prefer it[24] is better than only to know it. To delight in it is better than merely to prefer it."

6.19 The Master said, "To men who have risen at all above the middling sort, one may talk of things higher yet. But to men who are at all below the middling sort it is useless to talk of things that are above them[25]."

6.20 Fan Chi asked about wisdom. The Master said, "He who devotes himself to securing for his subjects what it is right they should have, who by respect for the Spirits keeps them at a distance[26] ,may be termed wise." He asked about Goodness. The Master said, "Goodness cannot be obtained till what is difficult has been duly done. He who has done this may be called Good."

6.21 The Master said, "The wise man delights in water, the Good man delights in mountains. For the wise move; but the Good stay still. The

【原文】

仁者寿。”

6.24　子曰：“齐一变，至于鲁；鲁一变，至于道。”

6.25　子曰：“觚不觚，觚哉！觚哉！”

6.26　宰我问曰：“仁者，虽告之曰：‘井有仁焉。’其从之也？”子曰：“何为其然也？君子可逝也，不可陷也；可欺也，不可罔也。”

6.27　子曰：“君子博学于文，约之以礼，亦可以弗畔矣夫！”

6.28　子见南子，子路不说。夫子矢之曰：“予所否者，天厌之！天厌之！”

6.29　子曰：“中庸之为德也，其至矣乎！民鲜久矣。”

6.30　子贡曰：“如有博施于民而能济众，何如？可谓仁乎？”子曰：

【今译】

沉静。聪明人快乐，仁人长寿。”

6.24　孔子说：“齐国[的政治和教育]一有改革，便达到鲁国的样子；鲁国[的政治和教育]一有改革，便进而合于大道了。”

6.25　孔子说：“觚不像个觚，这是觚吗！这是觚吗！”

6.26　宰我问道：“有仁德的人，就是告诉他，‘井里掉下一位仁人啦。’他是不是会跟着下去呢？”孔子道：“为什么你要这样做呢？君子可以叫他远远走开不再回来，却不可以陷害他；可以欺骗他，却不可以愚弄他。”

6.27　孔子说：“君子广泛地学习文献，再用礼节来加以约束，也就可以不至于离经叛道了。”

6.28　孔子去和南子相见，子路不高兴。孔子发誓道：“我假若不对的话，天厌弃我吧！天厌弃我吧！”

6.29　孔子说：“中庸这种道德，该是最高的了，大家已经是长久地缺乏它了。”

6.30　子贡道：“假若有这么一个人，广泛地给人民以好处，又能帮助大家生活得很好，怎么样？可以说是仁道了吗？”孔子道：“哪里仅是

wise are happy; but the Good, secure."[27]

6.22 A single change could bring Qi to the level of Lu; and a single change would bring Lu to the Way.

6.23 The Master said, "A horn-gourd that is neither horn nor gourd! A pretty horn-gourd indeed, a pretty horn-gourd indeed[28]."

6.24 Zai Yu asked saying, "I take it a Good Man, even if he were told that another Good Man were at the bottom of a well, would go to join him?" The Master said, "Why should you think so? A gentleman can be broken, but cannot be dented;[29] may be deceived, but cannot be led astray[30]."

6.25 The Master said, "A gentleman who is widely versed in letters and at the same time knows how to submit his learning to the restraints of ritual is not likely, I think, to go far wrong."

6.26 When the Master went to see Nanzi[31] ,Zilu was not pleased. Whereupon the Master made a solemn declaration[32] concerning his visit, saying, "Whatsoever I have done amiss, may Heaven avert it, may Heaven avert it!"

6.27 The Master said, "How transcendent is the moral power of the Middle Use[33]! That it is but rarely found among the common people is a fact long admitted."[34]

6.28 Zigong said, "If a ruler not only conferred wide benefits upon the common people, but also compassed the salvation of the whole State,

【原文】

"何事于仁!必也圣乎!尧舜其犹病诸!夫仁者，己欲立而立人，己欲达而达人。能近取譬，可谓仁之方也已。"

【今译】

仁道!那一定是圣德了!尧舜或者都难以做到哩!仁是什么呢?自己要站得住，同时也使别人站得住；自己要事事行得通，同时也使别人事事行得通。能够就眼下的事实选择例子一步步去做，可以说是实践仁道的方法了。"

what would you say of him? Surely, you would call him Good?" The Master said, "It would no longer be a matter of 'Good.' He would without doubt be a Divine Sage[35]. Even Yao and Shun could hardly criticize him. As for Goodness — you yourself desire rank and standing; then help others to get rank and standing. You want to turn your own merits to account; then help others to turn theirs to account — in fact, the ability to take one's own feelings as a guide — that is the sort of thing that lies in the direction of Goodness[36]."

述而篇第七

【原文】

7.1 子曰:“述而不作,信而好古,窃比于我老彭。”

7.2 子曰:“默而识之,学而不厌,诲人不倦,何有于我哉?”

7.3 子曰:“德之不修,学之不讲,闻义不能徙,不善不能改,是吾忧也。”

7.4 子之燕居,申申如也,夭夭如也。

7.5 子曰:“甚矣吾衰也!久矣吾不复梦见周公!”

7.6 子曰:“志于道,据于德,依于仁,游于艺。”

7.7 子曰:“自行束脩以上,吾未尝无诲焉。”

【今译】

7.1 孔子说:“阐述而不创作,以相信的态度喜爱古代文化,我私自和我那老彭相比。”

7.2 孔子说:“[把所见所闻的]默默地记在心里,努力学习而不厌弃,教导别人而不疲倦,这些事情我做到了哪些呢?”

7.3 孔子说:“品德不培养;学问不讲习;听到义在那里,却不能亲身赴之;有缺点不能改正,这些都是我的忧虑哩!”

7.4 孔子在家闲居,很整齐的,很和乐而舒展的。

7.5 孔子说:“我衰老得多么厉害呀!我好长时间没再梦见周公了!”

7.6 孔子说:“目标在‘道’,根据在‘德’,依靠在‘仁’,而游憩于礼、乐、射、御、书、数六艺之中。”

7.7 孔子说:“只要是主动地给我一点见面薄礼,我从没有不教诲的。”

BOOK VII

7.1, 7.2, 7.3 The Master said, "I have 'transmitted what was taught to me without making up anything of my own.' I have been faithful to and loved the Ancients. In these respects, I make bold to think, not even our old Peng[1] can have excelled me. " The Master said, "I have listened in silence and noted what was said, I have never grown tired of learning nor wearied of teaching others what I have learnt. These at least are merits which I can confidently claim[2] ." The Master said, "The thought that 'I have left my moral power (*de*) untended, my learning unperfected, that I have heard of righteous men, but been unable to go to them; have heard of evil men, but been unable to reform them'[3] — it is these thoughts that disquiet me."

7.4 In his leisure hours the Master's manner was very free-and-easy, and his expression alert and cheerful.

7.5 The Master said, "How utterly have things gone to the bad with me! It is long now indeed since I dreamed that I saw the Duke of Zhou[4]."

7.6 The Master said, "Set your heart upon the Way, support yourself by its power, lean upon Goodness, seek distraction in the arts[5]."

7.7 The Master said, "From the very poorest upwards — beginning even with the man who could bring no better present than a bundle of dried flesh[6] — none has ever come to me without receiving instruction."

【原文】

7.8 子曰："不愤不启，不悱不发。举一隅不以三隅反，则不复也。"

7.9 子食于有丧者之侧，未尝饱也。

7.10 子于是日哭，则不歌。

7.11 子谓颜渊曰："用之则行，舍之则藏，惟我与尔有是夫！"

子路曰："子行三军，则谁与？"

子曰："暴虎冯河，死而无悔者，吾不与也。必也临事而惧，好谋而成者也。"

7.12 子曰："富而可求也，虽执鞭之士，吾亦为之。如不可求，从吾所好。"

【今译】

7.8 孔子说："教导学生，不到他想求明白而不得的时候，不去开导他；不到他想说出来却说不出的时候，不去启发他。教给他东方，他却不能由此推知西、南、北三方，便不再教他了。"

7.9 孔子在死了亲属的人旁边吃饭，不曾吃饱过。

7.10 孔子在这一天哭泣过，就不再唱歌。

7.11 孔子对颜渊道："用我呢，就干起来；不用呢，就藏起来。只有我和你才能这样吧！"

子路道："您若率领军队，找谁共事？"

孔子道："赤手空拳和老虎搏斗，不用船只去渡河，这样死了都不后悔的人，我是不和他共事的。[我所找他共事的，]一定是面临任务便恐惧谨慎，善于谋略而能完成的人哩！"

7.12 孔子说："财富如果可以求得的话，就是做市场的守门卒我也干。如果求它不到，还是我干我的吧。"

7.8 The Master said, "Only one who bursts with eagerness do I instruct; only one who bubbles with excitement do I enlighten. If I hold up one corner and a man cannot come back to me with the other three, I do not continue the lesson."

7.9 If at a meal the Master found himself seated next to someone who was in mourning, he did not eat his fill. When he had wailed at a funeral, during the rest of the day he did not sing.

7.10 The Master said to Yan Hui, "The maxim

When wanted, then go;
When set aside, then hide.

is one that you and I could certainly fulfil. " Zilu said, "Supposing you had command of the Three Hosts[7] ,whom would you take to help you?" The Master said, "The man who was ready to 'beard a tiger or rush a river'[8] without caring whether he lived or died — that sort of man I should not take. I should certainly take someone who approached difficulties with due caution and who preferred to succeed by strategy."

7.11 The Master said, "If any means of escaping poverty presented itself that did not involve doing wrong, I would adopt it, even though my employment were only that of the gentleman who holds the whip[9] .But so long as it is a question of illegitimate means, I shall continue to pursue the quests that I love[10]."

7.12 The rites to which the Master gave the greatest attention were those

【原文】

7.13 子之所慎：齐，战，疾。

7.14 子在齐闻《韶》，三月不知肉味，曰："不图为乐之至于斯也。"

7.15 冉有曰："夫子为卫君乎？"子贡曰："诺；吾将问之。"

入，曰："伯夷、叔齐何人也？"曰："古之贤人也。"曰："怨乎？"曰："求仁而得仁，又何怨？"

出，曰："夫子不为也。"

7.16 子曰："饭疏食饮水，曲肱而枕之，乐亦在其中矣。不义而富且贵，于我如浮云。"

7.17 子曰："加我数年，五十以学《易》，可以无大过矣。"

7.18 子所雅言，《诗》、《书》、执礼，皆雅言也。

【今译】

7.13 孔子所小心慎重的事有三样：斋戒，战争，疾病。

7.14 孔子在齐国听到《韶》的乐章，很长时间尝不出肉味，于是道："想不到欣赏音乐竟到了这种境界。"

7.15 冉有道："老师赞成卫君吗？"子贡道："好吧；我去问问他。"

子贡进到孔子屋里，道："伯夷、叔齐是什么样的人？"孔子道："是古代的贤人。"子贡道："[他们两人互相推让，都不肯做孤竹国的国君，结果都跑到国外，]是不是后来又怨悔呢？"孔子道："他们求仁德，便得到了仁德，又怨悔什么呢？"

子贡走出，答复冉有道："老师不赞成卫君。"

7.16 孔子说："吃粗粮，喝冷水，弯着胳膊做枕头，也有着乐趣。干不正当的事而得来的富贵，我看来好像浮云。"

7.17 孔子说："让我多活几年，到五十岁的时候去学习《易经》，便可以没有大过错了。"

7.18 孔子有用普通话的时候，读《诗》，读《书》，行礼，都用普通话。

connected with purification before sacrifice, with war and with sickness.[11]

7.13 When he was in Qi the Master heard the Succession[12] ,and for three months did not know the taste of meat[13] .He said, "I did not picture to myself that any music existed which could reach such perfection as this."[14]

7.14 Ran Qiu said, "Is our Master on the side of the Prince of Wei[15]?"Zigong said, "Yes, I must ask him about that." He went in and said, "What sort of people were Boyi and Shuqi[16]?" The Master said, "They were good men who lived in the days of old." Zigong said, "Did they repine? "The Master said, "They sought Goodness and got Goodness. Why should they repine? "On coming out Zigong said, "Our Master is not on his side."

7.15 The Master said, "He who seeks only coarse food to eat, water to drink and a bent arm for pillow, will without looking for it find happiness to boot. Any thought of accepting wealth and rank by means that I know to be wrong is as remote from me as the clouds that float above."

7.16 The Master said, "Give me a few more years, so that I may have spent a whole fifty in study, and I believe that after all I should be fairly free from error."

7.17 The occasions upon which the Master used correct pronunciation[17] were when reciting the *Songs* or the *Books* and when practising ritual acts. At all such times he used the correct pronunciation.

【原文】

7.19 叶公问孔子于子路，子路不对。子曰："女奚不曰，其为人也，发愤忘食，乐以忘忧，不知老之将至云尔。"

7.20 子曰："我非生而知之者，好古，敏以求之者也。"

7.21 子不语怪，力，乱，神。

7.22 子曰："三人行，必有我师焉：择其善者而从之，其不善者而改之。"

7.23 子曰："天生德于予，桓魋其如予何？"

7.24 子曰："二三子以我为隐乎？吾无隐乎尔。吾无行而不与二三子者，是丘也。"

7.25 子以四教：文，行，忠，信。

【今译】

7.19 叶公向子路问孔子为人怎么样，子路不回答。孔子对子路道："你为什么不这样说：他的为人，用功便忘记吃饭，快乐便忘记忧愁，不晓得衰老会要到来，如此罢了。"

7.20 孔子说："我不是生来就有知识的人，而是爱好古代文化，勤奋敏捷去求得来的人。"

7.21 孔子不谈怪异、勇力、叛乱和鬼神。

7.22 孔子说："几个人一块走路，其中便一定有可以为我所取法的人：我选取那些优点而学习，看出那些缺点而改正。"

7.23 孔子说："天在我身上生了这样的品德，那桓魋将把我怎样？"

7.24 孔子说："你们这些学生以为我有所隐瞒吗？我对你们是没有隐瞒的。我没有一点不向你们公开，这就是我孔丘的为人。"

7.25 孔子用四种内容教育学生：历代文献，社会生活的实践，对待别人的忠心，与人交际的信实。

7.18 The "Duke of She"[18] asked Zilu about Master Kong (Confucius). Zilu did not reply. The Master said, "Why did you not say 'This is the character of the man: so intent upon enlightening the eager that he forgets his hunger, and so happy in doing so, that he forgets the bitterness of his lot and does not realize that old age is at hand.'[19] That is what he is."

7.19 The Master said, "I for my part am not one of those who have innate knowledge. I am simply one who loves the past and who is diligent in investigating it."

7.20 The Master never talked of prodigies, feats of strength, disorders[20] or spirits.

7.21 The Master said, "Even when walking in a party of no more than three I can always be certain of learning from those I am with. There will be good qualities that I can select for imitation and bad ones that will teach me what requires correction in myself."

7.22 The Master said, "Heaven begat the power (*de*) that is in me. What have I to fear from such a one as Huan Tui[21]?"

7.23 The Master said, "My friends, I know you think that there is something I am keeping from you. There is nothing at all that I keep from you. I take no steps about which I do not consult you, my friends. Were it otherwise, I should not be Qiu[22]."

7.24 The Master took four subjects for his teaching: culture, conduct of affairs, loyalty to superiors and the keeping of promises.

【原文】

7.26　子曰:“圣人，吾不得而见之矣；得见君子者，斯可矣。”

子曰:“善人，吾不得而见之矣；得见有恒者，斯可矣。亡而为有，虚而为盈，约而为泰，难乎有恒矣。”

7.27　子钓而不纲，弋不射宿。

7.28　子曰:“盖有不知而作之者，我无是也。多闻，择其善者而从之;多见而识之；知之次也。”

7.29　互乡难与言，童子见，门人惑。子曰:“与其进也，不与其退也，唯何甚?人洁己以进，与其洁也，不保其往也。”

7.30　子曰:“仁远乎哉?我欲仁，斯仁至矣。”

【今译】

7.26　孔子说:“圣人，我不能看见了；能看见君子，就可以了。”

又说:“善人，我不能看见了，能看见有一定操守的人，就可以了。本来没有，却装做有；本来空虚，却装做充足；本来穷困，却要豪华，这样的人便难于保持一定操守了。”

7.27　孔子钓鱼，不用大绳横断流水来取鱼；用带生丝的箭射鸟，不射归巢的鸟。

7.28　孔子说:“大概有一种自己不懂却凭空造作的人，我没有这种毛病。多多地听，选择其中好的加以接受；多多地看，全记在心里。这样的知，是仅次于‘生而知之’的。”

7.29　互乡这地方的人难于交谈，一个童子得到孔子的接见，弟子们疑惑。孔子道:“我们赞成他的进步，不赞成他的退步，何必做得太过?别人把自己弄得干干净净而来，便应当赞成他的干净，不要死记住他那过去。”

7.30　孔子道:“仁德难道离我们很远吗?我要它，它就来了。”

7.25 The Master said, "A Divine Sage[23] I cannot hope ever to meet; the most I can hope for is to meet a true gentleman." The Master said, "A faultless man I cannot hope ever to meet; the most I can hope for is to meet a man of fixed principles. Yet where all around I see Nothing pretending to be Something[24] ,Emptiness pretending to be Fullness, Penury pretending to be Affluence, even a man of fixed principles will be none too easy to find."

7.26 The Master fished with a line but not with a net; when fowling he did not aim at a roosting bird.[25]

7.27 The Master said, "There may well be those who can do without knowledge; but I for my part am certainly not one of them. To hear much, pick out what is good and follow it, to see much and take due note of it[26], is the lower[27] of the two kinds of knowledge."

7.28 At Hu village[28] the people were difficult to talk to. But an uncapped[29] boy presented himself for an interview. The disciples were in two minds about showing him in. But the Master said, "In sanctioning his entry here I am sanctioning nothing he may do when he retires. We must not be too particular. If anyone purifies[30] himself in order to come to us, let us accept this purification. We are not responsible for what he does when he goes away."

7.29 The Master said, "Is Goodness indeed so far away? If we really wanted Goodness, we should find that it was at our very side."

【原文】

7.31 陈司败问昭公知礼乎,孔子曰:“知礼。”

孔子退，揖巫马期而进之，曰:“吾闻君子不党，君子亦党乎?君取于吴，为同姓，谓之吴孟子。君而知礼，孰不知礼?”

巫马期以告。子曰:“丘也幸，苟有过，人必知之。”

7.32 子与人歌而善，必使反之，而后和之。

7.33 子曰:“文，莫吾犹人也。躬行君子，则吾未之有得。”

7.34 子曰:“若圣与仁，则吾岂敢?抑为之不厌，诲人不倦，则可谓云尔已矣。”公西华曰:“正唯弟子不能学也。”

7.35 子疾病，子路请祷。子曰:“有诸?”子路对曰:“有之;诔曰:

【今译】

7.31 陈司败向孔子问鲁昭公懂不懂礼，孔子道:“懂礼。”

孔子走了出来，陈司败便向巫马期作了个揖，请他走近自己，然后说道:“我听说君子无所偏袒，难道孔子竟偏袒吗?鲁君从吴国娶了位夫人，吴和鲁是同姓国家，[不便叫她做吴姬，]于是叫她做吴孟子。鲁君若是懂得礼，谁不懂得礼呢?”

巫马期把这话转告给孔子。孔子道:“我真幸运，假若有错误，人家一定给指出来。”

7.32 孔子同别人一道唱歌，如果唱得好，一定请他再唱一遍，然后自己又和他。

7.33 孔子说:“书本上的学问，大约我同别人差不多。在生活实践中做一个君子，那我还没有成功。”

7.34 孔子说道:“讲到圣和仁，我怎么敢当?不过是学习和工作总不厌倦，教导别人总不疲劳，就是如此如此罢了。”公西华道:“这正是我们学不到的。”

7.35 孔子病重，子路请求祈祷。孔子道:“有这回事吗?”子路答

7.30 The Minister of Crime in Chen asked whether Duke Zhao of Lu knew the rites. Master Kong said, "He knew the rites." When Master Kong had withdrawn, the Minister motioned Wuma Qi[31] to come forward and said, "I have heard the saying 'A gentleman is never partial.' But it seems that some gentlemen are very partial indeed. His Highness[32] married into the royal family of Wu who belong to the same clan as himself, calling her Wu Mengzi. If his Highness knew the rites, who does not know the rites?" Wuma Qi repeated this to the Master, who said, "I am a fortunate man. If by any chance I make a mistake, people are certain to hear of it!"[33]

7.31 When in the Master's presence anyone sang a song that he liked, he did not join in at once, but asked for it to be repeated and then joined in.

7.32 The Master said, "As far as taking trouble goes, I do not think I compare badly with other people. But as regards carrying out the duties of a gentleman in actual life, I have never yet had a chance to show what I could do."

7.33 The Master said, "As to being a Divine Sage or even a Good Man, far be it from me to make any such claim. As for unwearying effort to learn and unflagging patience in teaching others, those are merits that I do not hesitate to claim." Gongxi Hua said, "The trouble is that we disciples cannot learn!"

7.34 When the Master was very ill, Zilu asked leave to perform the Rite of Expiation. The Master said, "Is there such a thing?"[34] Zilu answered saying, "There is. In one of the Dirges it says,'We performed rites of

【原文】

‘祷尔于上下神祇。’”子曰:“丘之祷久矣。”

7.36　子曰:“奢则不孙，俭则固。与其不孙也，宁固。”

7.37　子曰:“君子坦荡荡，小人长戚戚。”

7.38　子温而厉，威而不猛，恭而安。

【今译】

道:“有的；《诔》文说过:‘替你向天神地祇祈祷。’”孔子道:“我早就祈祷过了。”

7.36　孔子说:“奢侈豪华就显得骄傲，省俭朴素就显得寒伧。与其骄傲，宁可寒伧。”

7.37　孔子说:“君子心地平坦宽广，小人却经常局促忧愁。”

7.38　孔子温和而严厉，有威仪而不凶猛，庄严而安详。

expiation for you, calling upon the sky-spirits above and the earth-spirits below.'" The Master said, "My expiation began long ago!"[35]

7.35 The Master said, "Just as lavishness leads easily to presumption, so does frugality to meanness. But meanness is a far less serious fault than presumption[36]."

7.36 The Master said, "A true gentleman is calm and at ease; the Small Man is fretful and ill at ease."

7.37 The Master's manner was affable yet firm, commanding but not harsh, polite but easy.

泰伯篇第八

【原文】

8.1 子曰:“泰伯,其可谓至德也已矣。三以天下让,民无得而称焉。”

8.2 子曰:“恭而无礼则劳,慎而无礼则葸,勇而无礼则乱,直而无礼则绞。君子笃于亲,则民兴于仁;故旧不遗,则民不偷。”

8.3 曾子有疾,召门弟子曰:“启予足!启予手!《诗》云:‘战战兢兢,如临深渊,如履薄冰。’而今而后,吾知免夫!小子!”

【今译】

8.1 孔子说:“泰伯,那可以说是品德极崇高了。屡次地把天下让给季历,老百姓简直找不出恰当的词语来称赞他。”

8.2 孔子说:“注重容貌态度的端庄,却不知礼,就未免劳倦;只知谨慎,却不知礼,就流于畏葸懦弱;专凭敢作敢为的胆量,却不知礼,就会盲动闯祸;心直口快,却不知礼,就会尖刻刺人。在上位的人能用深厚感情对待亲族,老百姓就会走向仁德;在上位的人不遗弃他的老同事、老朋友,那老百姓就不致对人冷淡无情。”

8.3 曾参病了,把他的学生召集拢来,说道:“看看我的脚!看看我的手!《诗经》上说:‘小心呀!好像面临深深水坑之旁,好像行走薄薄冰层之上。’从今以后,我才晓得自己是可以免于祸害刑戮的了!学生们!”

BOOK Ⅷ

8.1 The Master said, "Of Taibo[1] it may indeed be said that he attained to the very highest pitch of moral power. No less than three times he renounced the sovereignty of all things under Heaven, without the people getting a chance to praise him for it."

8.2 The Master said, "Courtesy not bounded by the prescriptions of ritual becomes tiresome. Caution not bounded by the prescriptions of ritual becomes timidity, daring becomes turbulence, inflexibility becomes harshness."[2]

The Master said, "When gentlemen deal generously with their own kin, the common people are incited to Goodness. When old dependents are not discarded, the common people will not be fickle."

8.3 When Master Zeng was ill he summoned his disciples and said, "Free my feet, free my hands. The *Song* says:

> *In fear and trembling,*
> *With caution and care,*
> *As though on the brink of a chasm,*
> *As though treading thin ice.*

But I feel now that whatever may betide I have got through safely, my little ones."[3]

8.4 When Master Zeng was ill, Meng Jing[4] came to see him. Master

【原文】

8.4　曾子有疾，孟敬子问之。曾子言曰："鸟之将死，其鸣也哀；人之将死，其言也善。君子所贵乎道者三：动容貌，斯远暴慢矣；正颜色，斯近信矣；出辞气，斯远鄙倍矣。笾豆之事，则有司存。"

8.5　曾子曰："以能问于不能，以多问于寡；有若无，实若虚，犯而不校——昔者吾友尝从事于斯矣。"

8.6　曾子曰："可以托六尺之孤，可以寄百里之命，临大节而不可夺也——君子人与？君子人也。"

8.7　曾子曰："士不可以不弘毅，任重而道远。仁以为己任，不亦重乎？死而后已，不亦远乎？"

【今译】

8.4　曾参病了，孟敬子探问他。曾子说："鸟要死了，鸣声是悲哀的；人要死了，说出的话是善意的。在上位的人待人接物有三方面应该注重：严肃自己的容貌，就可以避免别人的粗暴和懈怠；端正自己的脸色，就容易使人相信；说话的时候，多考虑言辞和声调，就可以避免鄙陋粗野和错误。至于礼仪的细节，自有主管人员。"

8.5　曾子说："有能力却向无能力的人请教，知识丰富却向知识缺少的人请教；有学问像没学问一样，满腹知识像空无所有一样；纵被欺侮，也不计较——从前我的一位朋友便曾这样做了。"

8.6　曾子说："可以把幼小的孤儿和国家的命脉都交付给他，面临安危存亡的紧要关头，却不动摇屈服——这种人，是君子人吗？是君子人哩。"

8.7　曾子说："读书人不可以不刚强而有毅力，因为他负担沉重，路程遥远。以实现仁德于天下为己任，不也沉重吗？到死方休，不也遥远吗？"

Zeng spoke to him saying, "When a bird is about to die, its song touches the heart[5] .When a man is about to die, his words are of note. There are three things that a gentleman, in following the Way, places above all the rest: from every attitude, every gesture that he employs he must remove all trace of violence or arrogance; every look that he composes in his face must betoken good faith; from every word that he utters, from every intonation, he must remove all trace of coarseness or impropriety. As to the ordering of ritual vessels and the like, there are those whose business it is to attend to such matters."

8.5 Master Zeng said, "Clever, yet not ashamed to consult those less clever than himself; widely gifted, yet not ashamed to consult those with few gifts; having, yet seeming not to have; full, yet seeming empty; offended against, yet never contesting — long ago I had a friend[6] whose ways were such as this."

8.6 Master Zeng said, "The man to whom one could with equal confidence entrust an orphan not yet fully grown[7] or the sovereignty of a whole State[8], whom the advent of no emergency however great could upset — would such a one be a true gentleman? He I think would be a true gentleman indeed."

8.7 Master Zeng said, "The true Knight of the Way must perforce be both broad-shouldered and stout of heart; his burden is heavy and he has far to go. For Goodness is the burden he has taken upon himself; and must we not grant that it is a heavy one to bear? Only with death does his journey end; then must we not grant that he has far to go?"

【原文】

8.8　子曰:"兴于诗，立于礼，成于乐。"

8.9　子曰:"民可使由之，不可使知之。"

8.10　子曰:"好勇疾贫，乱也。人而不仁，疾之已甚，乱也。"

8.11　子曰:"如有周公之才之美，使骄且吝，其余不足观也已。"

8.12　子曰:"三年学，不至于谷，不易得也。"

8.13　子曰:"笃信好学，守死善道。危邦不入，乱邦不居。天下有道则见，无道则隐。邦有道，贫且贱焉，耻也。邦无道，富且贵焉，耻也。"

【今译】

8.8　孔子说:"诗篇使我振奋，礼使我能在社会上站得住，音乐使我的所学得以完成。"

8.9　孔子说:"老百姓，可以使他们照着我们的道路走去，不可以使他们知道那是为什么。"

8.10　孔子说:"以勇敢自喜却厌恶贫困，是一种祸害。对于不仁的人，痛恨太甚，也是一种祸害。"

8.11　孔子说:"假如才能的美妙真比得上周公，只要骄傲而吝啬，别的方面也就不值得一看了。"

8.12　孔子说:"读书三年并不存做官的念头，这是难得的。"

8.13　孔子说:"坚定地相信我们的道，努力学习它，誓死保全它。不进入危险的国家，不居住祸乱的国家。天下太平，就出来工作；不太平，就隐居。政治清明，自己贫贱，是耻辱；政治黑暗，自己富贵，也是耻辱。"

8.8 The Master said, "Let a man be first incited by the *Songs*, then given a firm footing by the study of ritual, and finally perfected by music."

8.9 The Master said, "The common people can be made to follow it[9]; they cannot be made to understand it."

8.10 The Master said, "One who is by nature daring and is suffering from poverty will not long be law-abiding. Indeed, any men, save those that are truly Good, if their sufferings are very great, will be likely to rebel."

8.11 The Master said, "If a man has gifts as wonderful as those of the Duke of Zhou, yet is arrogant and mean, all the rest is of no account."

8.12 The Master said,

> "One who will study for three years
> Without thought of reward[10]
> Would be hard indeed to find."

8.13 The Master said, "Be of unwavering good faith, love learning, if attacked be ready to die for the good Way. Do not enter a State that pursues dangerous courses, nor stay in one where the people have rebelled. When the Way prevails under Heaven, then show yourself; when it does not prevail, then hide. When the Way prevails in your own land, count it a disgrace to be needy and obscure; when the Way does not prevail in your land, then count it a disgrace to be rich and honoured."

【原文】

8.14　子曰："不在其位，不谋其政。"

8.15　子曰："师挚之始，《关雎》之乱，洋洋乎盈耳哉！"

8.16　子曰："狂而不直，侗而不愿，悾悾而不信，吾不知之矣。"

8.17　子曰："学如不及，犹恐失之。"

8.18　子曰："巍巍乎，舜禹之有天下也而不与焉！"

8.19　子曰："大哉尧之为君也！巍巍乎！唯天为大，唯尧则之。荡荡乎！民无能名焉。巍巍乎其有成功也！焕乎其有文章！"

8.20　舜有臣五人而天下治。武王曰："予有乱臣十人。"孔子曰："才难，不其然乎？唐虞之际，于斯为盛。有妇人焉，九人而已。三

【今译】

8.14　孔子说："不居于那个职位，便不考虑它的政务。"

8.15　孔子说："当太师挚开始演奏的时候，当结尾演奏《关雎》之曲的时候，满耳朵都是音乐呀！"

8.16　孔子说："狂妄而不直率，幼稚而不老实，无能而不讲信用，这种人我是不知道其所以然的。"

8.17　孔子说："做学问好像[追逐什么似的，]生怕赶不上；[赶上了，]还生怕丢掉了。"

8.18　孔子说："舜和禹真是崇高得很呀！贵为天子，富有四海，[却整年地为百姓勤劳，]一点也不为自己。"

8.19　孔子说："尧真是了不得呀！真高大得很呀！只有天最高最大，只有尧能够学习天。他的恩惠真是广博呀！老百姓简直不知道怎样称赞他。他的功绩实在太崇高了，他的礼仪制度也真够美好了！"

8.20　舜有五位贤臣，天下便太平。武王也说过："我有十位能治理天下的臣子。"孔子因此说道："[常言道：]'人才不易得。'不是这样吗？唐尧和虞舜之间以及周武王说那话的时候，人才最兴盛。然而武王十位人才之中还有一位妇女，实际上只是九位罢了。周文王得

8.14 The Master said, "He who holds no rank in a State does not discuss its policies."

8.15 The Master said, "When Zhi the Chief Musician led the climax of the *Ospreys*[11], what a grand flood of sound filled one's ears!"

8.16 The Master said, "Impetuous, but tricky! Ingenuous, but dishonest! Simple-minded, but capable of breaking promises![12] To such men I can give no recognition."

8.17 The Master said, "Learn as if you were following someone whom you could not catch up, as though it were someone you were frightened of losing."

8.18 The Master said, "Sublime were Shun and Yu! All that is under Heaven was theirs, yet they remained aloof from it."

8.19 The Master said, "Greatest, as lord and ruler, was Yao.[13] Sublime, indeed, was he. 'There is no greatness like the greatness of Heaven,' yet Yao could copy it. So boundless was it[14] that the people could find no name for it;[15] yet sublime were his achievements, dazzling the insignia of his culture!"

8.20 Shun had five ministers and all that is under Heaven was well ruled. King Wu said, "I have ten[16] ministers." Master Kong said, "True indeed is the saying that 'the right material is hard to find'; for the turn of the Tang and Yu dynasties[17] was the time most famous for this[18]. (As for King Wu,) There was a woman among his ten, so that in reality there

【原文】

分天下有其二，以服事殷。周之德，其可谓至德也已矣。”

8.21　子曰：“禹，吾无间然矣。菲饮食而致孝乎鬼神，恶衣服而致美乎黻冕，卑宫室而尽力乎沟洫。禹，吾无间然矣。”

【今译】

了天下的三分之二，仍然向商纣称臣，周朝的道德，可以说是最高的了。”

8.21　孔子说：“禹，我对他没有批评了。他自己吃得很坏，却把祭品办得极丰盛；穿得很坏，却把祭服做得极华美；住得很坏，却把力量完全用于沟渠水利。禹，我对他没有批评了。”

were only nine men. Yet of all that is under Heaven he held two parts in three, using them in submissive service to the dynasty of Yin[19]. The moral power (*de*) of Zhou may, indeed, be called an absolutely perfect moral power!"

8.21 The Master said, "In Yu I can find no semblance of a flaw. Abstemious in his own food and drink, he displayed the utmost devotion in his offerings to spirits and divinities[20]. Content with the plainest clothes for common wear, he saw to it that his sacrificial apron and ceremonial headdress were of the utmost magnificence. His place of habitation was of the humblest, and all his energy went into draining and ditching.[21] In him I can find no semblance of a flaw."

子罕篇第九

【原文】

9.1　子罕言利与命与仁。

9.2　达巷党人曰："大哉孔子！博学而无所成名。"子闻之，谓门弟子曰："吾何执？执御乎？执射乎？吾执御矣。"

9.3　子曰："麻冕，礼也；今也纯，俭，吾从众。拜下，礼也；今拜乎上，泰也。虽违众，吾从下。"

9.4　子绝四——毋意，毋必，毋固，毋我。

9.5　子畏于匡，曰："文王既没，文不在兹乎？天之将丧斯文也，后死者不得与于斯文也；天之未丧斯文也，匡人其如予何？"

【今译】

9.1　孔子很少[主动]谈到功利、命运和仁德。

9.2　达街的一个人说："孔子真伟大！学问广博，可惜没有足以树立名声的专长。"孔子听了这话，就对学生们说："我干什么呢？赶马车呢？做射击手呢？我赶马车好了。"

9.3　孔子说："礼帽用麻料来织，这是合于传统的礼的；今天大家都用丝料，这样省俭些，我同意大家的做法。臣见君，先在堂下磕头，然后升堂又磕头，这是合于传统的礼的。今天大家都免除了堂下的磕头，只升堂后磕头，这是倨傲的表现。虽然违反大家，我仍然主张要先在堂下磕头。"

9.4　孔子一点也没有四种毛病——不悬空揣测，不绝对肯定，不拘泥固执，不唯我独是。

9.5　孔子被匡地的群众所拘禁，便道："周文王死了以后，一切文化遗产不都在我这里吗？天若是要消灭这种文化，那我也不会掌握这些文化了；天若是不要消灭这一文化，那匡人将把我怎么样呢？"

BOOK IX

9.1 The Master seldom spoke of profit or fate or Goodness.

9.2 A villager from Daxiang said, "Master Kong is no doubt a very great man and vastly learned. But he does nothing to bear out this reputation." The Master, hearing of it, said to his disciples, "What shall I take up? Shall I take up chariot-driving? Or shall it be archery? I think I will take up driving!"[1]

9.3 The Master said, "The hemp-thread crown is prescribed by ritual.[2] Nowadays people wear black silk, which is economical; and I follow the general practice. Obeisance below the daïs is prescribed by ritual. Nowadays people make obeisance after mounting the daïs. This is presumptuous, and though to do so is contrary to the general practice, I make a point of bowing while still down below."

9.4 There were four things that the Master wholly eschewed: he took nothing for granted, he was never over-positive, never obstinate, never egotistic.

9.5 When the Master was trapped in Kuang[3], he said, "When King Wen perished, did that mean that culture (*wen*文) ceased to exist? If Heaven had really intended that such culture as his should disappear, a latter-day mortal would never have been able to link himself to it as I have done. And if Heaven does not intend to destroy such culture, what have I to fear from the people of Kuang?"

【原文】

9.6　太宰问于子贡曰:“夫子圣者与?何其多能也?”子贡曰:“固天纵之将圣，又多能也。”

子闻之，曰:“太宰知我乎!吾少也贱，故多能鄙事。君子多乎哉?不多也。”

9.7　牢曰:“子云:‘吾不试，故艺。’”

9.8　子曰:“吾有知乎哉?无知也。有鄙夫问于我，空空如也。我叩其两端而竭焉。”

9.9　子曰:“凤鸟不至，河不出图，吾已矣夫!”

9.10　子见齐衰者、冕衣裳者与瞽者，见之，虽少，必作；过之，必趋。

【今译】

9.6　太宰向子贡问道:“孔老先生是位圣人吗?为什么这样多才多艺呢?”子贡道:“这本是上天让他成为圣人，又使他多才多艺。”

孔子听到，便道:“太宰知道我呀!我小时候穷苦，所以学会了不少鄙贱的技艺。真正的君子会有这样多的技巧吗?是不会的。”

9.7　牢说:“孔子说过，我不曾被国家所用，所以学得一些技艺。”

9.8　孔子说:“我有知识吗?没有哩。有一个庄稼汉问我，我本是一点也不知道的；我从他那个问题的首尾两头去盘问，[才得到很多意思，]然后尽量地告诉他。”

9.9　孔子说:“凤凰不飞来了，黄河也没有图画出来了，我这一生恐怕是完了吧!”

9.10　孔子看见穿丧服的人、穿戴着礼帽礼服的人以及瞎了眼睛的人，相见的时候，他们虽然年轻，孔子一定站起来；走过的时候，一定快走几步。

9.6 The Grand Minister (of Wu?) asked Zigong saying, "Is your Master a Divine Sage? If so, how comes it that he has many practical accomplishments[4]?" Zigong said, "Heaven certainly intended[5] him to become a Sage; it is also true that he has many accomplishments." When the Master heard of it he said, "The Grand Minister is quite right about me. When I was young I was in humble circumstances; that is why I have many practical accomplishments in regard to simple, everyday matters. Does it befit a gentleman to have many accomplishments? No, he is in no need of them at all."

Lao says that the Master said, "It is because I have not been given a chance that I have become so handy."

9.7 The Master said, "Do I regard myself as a possessor of wisdom? Far from it. But if even a simple peasant comes in all sincerity and asks me a question, I am ready to thrash the matter out, with all its pros and cons, to the very end."

9.8 The Master said, "The phoenix does not come; the river gives forth no chart.[6] It is all over with me[7]!"

9.9 Whenever he was visited by anyone dressed in the robes of mourning or wearing ceremonial headdress, with gown and skirt, or a blind man, even if such a one were younger than himself, the Master on seeing him invariably rose to his feet, and if compelled to walk past him always quickened his step[8].

9.10 Yan Hui said with a deep sigh, "The more I strain my gaze up to-

【原文】

9.11　颜渊喟然叹曰:“仰之弥高，钻之弥坚。瞻之在前，忽焉在后。夫子循循然善诱人，博我以文，约我以礼，欲罢不能。既竭吾才，如有所立卓尔。虽欲从之，末由也已。”

9.12　子疾病，子路使门人为臣。病间，曰:“久矣哉，由之行诈也!无臣而为有臣。吾谁欺?欺天乎?且予与其死于臣之手也，无宁死于二三子之手乎?且予纵不得大葬，予死于道路乎?”

9.13　子贡曰:“有美玉于斯，韫椟而藏诸?求善贾而沽诸?”子曰:“沽之哉!沽之哉!我待贾者也。”

9.14　子欲居九夷。或曰:“陋，如之何?”子曰:“君子居之，何陋之有?”

【今译】

9.11　颜渊感叹着说:“老师之道，越抬头看，越觉得高;越用力钻研，越觉得深。看看，似乎在前面，忽然又到后面去了。[虽然这样高深和不容易捉摸，可是]老师善于有步骤地诱导我们，用各种文献来丰富我的知识，又用一定的礼节来约束我的行为，使我想停止学习都不可能。我已经用尽我的才力，似乎能够独立地工作。要想再向前迈进一步，又不知怎样着手了。”

9.12　孔子病得厉害，子路便命孔子的学生组织治丧处。很久以后，孔子的病渐渐好了，就道:“仲由干这种欺假的勾当竟太长久了呀!我本不该有治丧的组织，却一定要使人组织治丧处。我欺哄谁呢?欺哄上天吗?我与其死在治丧的人的手里，宁肯死在你们学生们的手里，不还好些吗?即使不能热热闹闹地办理丧葬，我会死在路上吗?”

9.13　子贡道:“这里有一块美玉，把它放在柜子里藏起来呢?还是找一个识货的商人卖掉呢?”孔子道:“卖掉，卖掉!我是在等待识货者哩。”

9.14　孔子想搬到九夷去住。有人说:“那地方非常简陋，怎么好住?”孔子道:“有君子去住，就不简陋了。”

wards it[9], the higher it soars. The deeper I bore down into it, the harder it becomes. I see it in front; but suddenly it is behind. Step by step the Master skilfully lures one on. He has broadened me with culture, restrained me with ritual. Even if I wanted to stop, I could not. Just when I feel that I have exhausted every resource, something seems to rise up, standing out sharp and clear[10]. Yet though I long to pursue it, I can find no way of getting to it at all."

9.11 When the Master was very ill, Zilu caused some of the disciples to get themselves up as official retainers. Coming to himself for a short while, the Master said, "How like You, to go in for this sort of imposture! In pretending to have retainers when I have none, whom do I deceive? Do I deceive Heaven? Not only would I far rather die in the arms of you disciples than in the arms of retainers, but also as regards my funeral — even if I am not accorded a State Burial, it is not as though I were dying by the roadside."

9.12 Zigong said, "Suppose one had a lovely jewel, should one wrap it up, put it in a box and keep it, or try to get the best price one can for it?" The Master said, "Sell it! Most certainly sell it! I myself am one who is waiting for an offer."[11]

9.13 The Master wanted to settle among the Nine Wild Tribes of the East. Someone said, "I am afraid you would find it hard to put up with their lack of refinement." The Master said, "Were a true gentleman to settle among them there would soon be no trouble about lack of refinement."

【原文】

9.15 子曰:“吾自卫反鲁，然后乐正，《雅》《颂》各得其所。”

9.16 子曰:“出则事公卿，入则事父兄，丧事不敢不勉，不为酒困，何有于我哉?”

9.17 子在川上，曰:“逝者如斯夫!不舍昼夜。”

9.18 子曰:“吾未见好德如好色者也。”

9.19 子曰:“譬如为山，未成一篑，止，吾止也。譬如平地，虽覆一篑，进，吾往也。”

9.20 子曰:“语之而不惰者，其回也与!”

9.21 子谓颜渊，曰:“惜乎!吾见其进也，未见其止也。”

【今译】

9.15 孔子说:“我从卫国回到鲁国，才把音乐[的篇章]整理出来，使《雅》归《雅》，《颂》归《颂》，各有适当的安置。”

9.16 孔子说:“出外便服事公卿，入门便服事父兄，有丧事不敢不尽礼，不被酒所困扰，这些事我做到了哪些呢?”

9.17 孔子在河边，叹道:“消逝的时光像河水一样呀!日夜不停地流去。”

9.18 孔子说:“我没有看见过这样的人，喜爱道德赛过喜爱美貌。”

9.19 孔子说:“好比堆土成山，只要再加一筐土便成山了，如果懒得做下去，这是我自己停止的。又好比在平地上堆土成山，纵是刚刚倒下一筐土，如果决心努力前进，还是要自己坚持呵!”

9.20 孔子说:“听我说话始终不懈怠的，大概只有颜回一个人吧!”

9.21 孔子谈到颜渊，说道:“可惜呀[他死了]!我只看见他不断地进步，从没看见他停留。”

9.14 The Master said, "It was only after my return from Wei to Lu that music was revised, Court pieces and Ancestral Recitations being at last properly discriminated."[12]

9.15 The Master said, "I can claim that at Court I have duly served the Duke and his officers; at home, my father and elder brother. As regards matters of mourning, I am conscious of no neglect, nor have I ever been overcome with wine. Concerning these things at any rate my mind is quite at rest[13]."

9.16 Once when the Master was standing by a stream, he said, "Could one but go on and on like this, never ceasing day or night!"

9.17 The Master said, "I have never yet seen anyone whose desire to build up his moral power was as strong as sexual desire."

9.18 The Master said, "The case is like that of someone raising a mound. If he stops working, the fact that it perhaps needed only one more basketful makes no difference; I stay where I am. Whereas even if he has not got beyond levelling the ground, but is still at work, the fact that he has only tilted one basketful of earth makes no difference. I go to help him."

9.19 The Master said, "It was Hui whom I could count on always to listen attentively to anything I said."

9.20 The Master said of Yan Hui, "Alas, I saw him go forward, but had no chance to see whither this progress would have led him in the end."

【原文】

9.22 子曰:“苗而不秀者有矣夫!秀而不实者有矣夫!”

9.23 子曰:“后生可畏，焉知来者之不如今也?四十、五十而无闻焉，斯亦不足畏也已。”

9.24 子曰:“法语之言，能无从乎?改之为贵。巽与之言，能无说乎?绎之为贵。说而不绎，从而不改，吾末如之何也已矣。”

9.25 子曰:“主忠信，毋友不如己者，过则勿惮改。”

9.26 子曰:“三军可夺帅也，匹夫不可夺志也。”

9.27 子曰:“衣敝缊袍，与衣狐貉者立，而不耻者，其由也与?

【今译】

9.22 孔子说:“庄稼生长了，却不吐穗开花的，有过的吧!吐穗开花了，却不凝浆结实的，有过的吧!”

9.23 孔子说:“年少的人是可怕的，怎能断定他的将来赶不上现在的人呢?一个人到了四五十岁还没有什么名望，也就值不得惧怕了。”

9.24 孔子说:“严肃而合乎原则的话，能够不接受吗?改正错误才可贵。顺从己意的话，能够不高兴吗?分析一下才可贵。盲目高兴，不加分析;表面接受，实际不改，这种人我是没有办法对付他的了。”

9.25 见学而篇第一。

9.26 孔子说:“一国军队，可以使它丧失主帅;一个男子汉，却不能强迫他放弃主张。”

9.27 孔子说道:“穿着破烂的旧丝绵袍子和穿着狐貉裘的人一道站着，不觉得惭愧的，恐怕只有仲由吧!《诗经》上说:‘不嫉妒，不

9.21 The Master said, "There are shoots whose lot it is to spring up but never to flower; others whose lot it is to flower, but never bear fruit[14]."

9.22 The Master said, "Respect the young. How do you know that they will not one day be all that you are now? But if a man has reached forty or fifty and nothing has been heard of him, then I grant there is no need to respect him."

9.23 The Master said, "The words of the *Fa Yu*[15] (Model Sayings) cannot fail to stir us; but what matters is that they should change our ways. The words of the *Xun Yu*[16] cannot fail to commend themselves to us; but what matters is that we should carry them out. For those who approve but do not carry out, who are stirred but do not change, I can do nothing at all."

9.24 The Master said, "First and foremost, be faithful to your superiors, keep all promises, refuse the friendship of all who are not like you; and if you have made a mistake, do not be afraid of admitting the fact and amending your ways."

9.25 The Master said, "You may rob the Three Armies of their commander-in-chief, but you cannot deprive the humblest peasant of his opinion."

9.26 The Master said, "'Wearing a shabby hemp-quilted gown, yet capable of standing unabashed with those who wore fox and badger.' That would apply quite well to You, would it not?

【原文】

'不忮不求，何用不臧？'"子路终身诵之。子曰："是道也，何足以臧？"

9.28　子曰："岁寒，然后知松柏之后凋也。"

9.29　子曰："知者不惑，仁者不忧，勇者不惧。"

9.30　子曰："可与共学，未可与适道；可与适道，未可与立；可与立，未可与权。"

9.31　"唐棣之华，偏其反而。岂不尔思？室是远而。"子曰："未之思也，夫何远之有？"

【今译】

贪求，为什么不会好？'"子路听了，便老念着这两句诗。孔子又道："仅仅这个样子，怎样能够好得起来？"

9.28　孔子说："天冷了，才晓得松柏树是最后落叶的。"

9.29　孔子说："聪明人不致疑惑，仁德的人经常乐观，勇敢的人无所畏惧。"

9.30　孔子说："可以同他一道学习的人，未必可以同他一道取得某种成就；可以同他一道取得某种成就的人，未必可以同他一道事事依体而行；可以同他一道事事依体而行的人，未必可以同他一道通权达变。"

9.31　古代有几句这样的诗："唐棣树的花，翩翩地摇摆。难道我不想念你？因为家住得太遥远。"孔子道："他是不去想念哩，真的想念，有什么遥远呢？"

"Who harmed none, was foe to none,
Did nothing that was not right."[17]

Afterwards Zilu (You) kept on continually chanting those lines to himself. The Master said, "Come now, the wisdom contained in them is not worth treasuring[18] to that extent!"

9.27 The Master said, "Only when the year grows cold do we see that the pine and cypress are the last to fade."

9.28 The Master said, "He that is really Good can never be unhappy. He that is really wise can never be perplexed. He that is really brave is never afraid."

9.29 The Master said, "There are some whom one can join in study but whom one cannot join in progress along the Way; others whom one can join in progress along the Way, but beside whom one cannot take one's stand[19]; and others again beside whom one can take one's stand, but whom one cannot join in counsel."

9.30 *The flowery branch of the wild cherry*
How swiftly it flies back![20]
It is not that I do not love you;
But your house is far away.

The Master said, "He did not really love her. Had he done so, he would not have worried about the distance."[21]

乡党篇第十

【原文】

10.1　孔子于乡党，恂恂如也，似不能言者。

其在宗庙朝廷，便便言，唯谨尔。

10.2　朝，与下大夫言，侃侃如也；与上大夫言，訚訚如也。君在，踧踖如也，与与如也。

10.3　君召使摈，色勃如也，足躩如也。揖所与立，左右手，衣前后，襜如也。趋进，翼如也。宾退，必复命曰："宾不顾矣。"

10.4　入公门，鞠躬如也，如不容。

立不中门，行不履阈。

过位，色勃如也，足躩如也，其言似不足者。

摄齐升堂，鞠躬如也，屏气似不息者。

出，降一等，逞颜色，怡怡如也。

【今译】

10.1　孔子在本乡的地方上非常恭顺，好像不能说话的样子。

他在宗庙里、朝廷上，有话便明白而流畅地说出，只是说得很少。

10.2　上朝的时候，[君主还没有到来，]同下大夫说话，温和而快乐的样子；同上大夫说话，正直而恭敬的样子。君主已经来了，恭敬而心中不安的样子，行步安祥的样子。

10.3　鲁君召他去接待外国的贵宾，面色矜持庄重，脚步也快起来。向两旁的人作揖，或者向左拱手，或者向右拱手，衣裳一俯一仰，却很整齐。快步向前，好像鸟儿舒展了翅膀。贵宾辞别后一定向君主回报说："客人已经不回头了。"

10.4　孔子走进朝廷的门，害怕而谨慎的样子，好像没有容身之地。

站，不站在门的中间；走，不踩门坎。

经过国君的坐位，面色便矜庄，脚步也快，言语也好像中气不足。

提起下摆向堂上走，恭敬谨慎的样子，憋住气好像不呼吸一般。

走出来，降下台阶一级，面色便放松，怡然自得。

BOOK X

10.1 At home in his native village his manner is simple and unassuming, as though he did not trust himself to speak. But in the ancestral temple and at Court he speaks readily, though always choosing his words with care.

10.2 At Court when conversing with the Under Ministers his attitude is friendly and affable; when conversing with the Upper Ministers, it is restrained and formal. When the ruler is present it is wary, but not cramped.

10.3 When the ruler summons him to receive a guest, a look of confusion comes over his face and his legs seem to give beneath his weight. When saluting his colleagues he passes his right hand to the left, letting his robe hang down in front and behind; and as he advances with quickened step, his attitude is one of majestic dignity.

When the guest has gone, he reports the close of the visit, saying, "The guest is no longer looking back."

10.4 On entering the Palace Gate he seems to shrink into himself, as though there were not room. If he halts, it must never be in the middle of the gate, nor in going through does he ever tread on the threshold. As he passes the Stance[1] a look of confusion comes over his face, his legs seem to give way under him and words seem to fail him. While, holding up the hem of his skirt, he ascends the Audience Hall, he seems to double up and keeps in his breath, so that you would think he was not breathing at all. On coming out, after descending the first step his expression relaxes

【原文】

没阶，趋进，翼如也。

复其位，踧踖如也。

10.5 执圭，鞠躬如也，如不胜。上如揖，下如授。勃如战色，足蹜蹜如有循。

享礼，有容色。

私觌，愉愉如也。

10.6 君子不以绀緅饰，红紫不以为亵服。当暑，袗絺绤，必表而出之。缁衣，羔裘；素衣，麑裘；黄衣，狐裘。亵裘长，短右袂。必有寝衣，长一身有半。狐貉之厚以居。去丧，无所不佩。非帷裳，必杀之。羔裘玄冠不以吊。吉月，必朝服而朝。

10.7 齐，必有明衣，布。

齐必变食，居必迁坐。

【今译】

走完了台阶，快快地向前走几步，好像鸟儿舒展翅膀。

回到自己的位置，恭敬而内心不安的样子。

10.5 [孔子出使到外国，举行典礼，]拿着圭，恭敬谨慎地，好像举不起来。向上举好像在作揖，向下拿好像在交给别人。面色矜庄好像在作战。脚步也紧凑狭窄，好像在沿着[一条线]走过。

献礼物的时候，满脸和气。

用私人身份和外国君臣会见，显得轻松愉快。

10.6 君子不用[近乎黑色的]天青色和铁灰色作镶边，[近乎赤色的]浅红色和紫色不用来作平常居家的衣服。暑天，穿着粗的或者细的葛布单衣，但一定裹着衬衫，使它露在外面。黑色的衣配紫羔，白色的衣配麑裘，黄色的衣配狐裘。居家的皮袄身材较长，可是右边的袖子要做得短些。睡觉一定有小被，长度合本人身长的一又二分之一。用狐貉皮的厚毛作坐垫。丧服满了以后，什么东西都可以佩带。不是[上朝和祭祀穿的]用整幅布做的裙子，一定裁去一些布。紫羔和黑色礼帽都不穿戴着去吊丧。大年初一，一定穿着上朝的礼服去朝贺。

10.7 斋戒沐浴的时候，一定有浴衣，用布做的。

斋戒的时候，一定改变平常的饮食；居住也一定搬移地方[不和妻妾同房]。

into one of satisfaction and relief. At the bottom of the steps he quickens his pace, advancing with an air of majestic dignity. On regaining his place he resumes his attitude of wariness and hesitation.

10.5 When carrying the tablet of jade[2], he seems to double up, as though borne down by its weight. He holds it at the highest as though he were making a bow[3], at the lowest, as though he were proffering a gift. His expression, too, changes to one of dread and his feet seem to recoil, as though he were avoiding something. When presenting ritual-presents, his expression is placid. At the private audience his attitude is gay and animated.

10.6 A gentleman[4] does not wear facings of purple or mauve, nor in undress does he use pink or roan[5]. In hot weather he wears an unlined gown of fine thread loosely woven, but puts on an outside garment before going out-of-doors[6]. With a black robe he wears black lambskin; with a robe of undyed silk, fawn. With a yellow robe, fox fur. On his undress robe the fur cuffs are long; but the right is shorter than the left.[7] His bedclothes must be half as long again as a man's height. The thicker kinds of fox and badger are for home wear. Except when in mourning, he wears all his girdle-ornaments[8]. Apart from his Court apron, all his skirts are wider at the bottom than at the waist. Lambskin dyed black and a hat of dark-dyed silk must not be worn when making visits of condolence.[9] At the Announcement of the New Moon he must go to Court in full Court dress.

10.7, 10.8 When preparing himself for sacrifice he must wear the Bright Robe[10], and it must be of linen. He must change his food and also the

【原文】

10.8　食不厌精，脍不厌细。

食饐而餲，鱼馁而肉败，不食。色恶，不食。臭恶，不食。失饪，不食。不时，不食。割不正，不食。不得其酱，不食。

肉虽多，不使胜食气。

唯酒无量，不及乱。

沽酒市脯不食。

不撤姜食，不多食。

10.9　祭于公，不宿肉。祭肉不出三日。出三日，不食之矣。

10.10　食不语，寝不言。

10.11　虽疏食菜羹，必祭，必齐如也。

10.12　席不正，不坐。

10.13　乡人饮酒，杖者出，斯出矣。

10.14　乡人傩，朝服而立于阼阶。

【今译】

10.8　粮食不嫌舂得精，鱼和肉不嫌切得细。

粮食霉烂发臭，鱼和肉腐烂，都不吃。食物颜色难看，不吃。气味难闻，不吃。烹调不当，不吃。不到该当吃食的时候，不吃。不是按一定方法砍割的肉，不吃。没有一定调味的酱醋，不吃。

席上肉虽然多，吃它不超过主食。

只有酒不限量，却不至于醉。

买来的酒和肉干不吃。

吃完了，姜不撤除，但吃得不多。

10.9　参与国家祭祀典礼，不把祭肉留到第二天。别的祭肉留存不超过三天。若是存放过了三天，便不吃了。

10.10　吃饭的时候不交谈，睡觉的时候不说话。

10.11　虽然是糙米饭小菜汤，也一定得先祭一祭，而且祭的时候还一定恭恭敬敬，好像斋戒了的一样。

10.12　坐席摆的方向不合礼制，不坐。

10.13　行乡饮酒礼后，要等老年人都出去了，自己这才出去。

10.14　本地方人迎神驱鬼，穿着朝服站在东边的台阶上。

place where he commonly sits. But there is no objection to his rice being of the finest quality, nor to his meat being finely minced. Rice affected by the weather or turned he must not eat, nor fish that is not sound, nor meat that is high. He must not eat anything discoloured or that smells bad. He must not eat what is overcooked nor what is undercooked, nor anything that is out of season. He must not eat what has been crookedly cut, nor any dish that lacks its proper seasoning. The meat that he eats must at the very most not be enough to make his breath smell of meat rather than of rice. As regards wine, no limit is laid down; but he must not be disorderly. He may not drink wine bought at a shop or eat dried meat from the market. He need not refrain from such articles of food as have ginger sprinkled over them; but he must not eat much of such dishes.[11]

After a sacrifice in the ducal palace, the flesh must not be kept overnight. No sacrificial flesh may be kept beyond the third day. If it is kept beyond the third day, it may no longer be eaten. While it is being eaten, there must be no conversation, nor any word spoken while lying down after the repast. Any article of food, whether coarse rice, vegetables, broth or melon, that has been used as an offering must be handled with due solemnity.

10.9 He must not sit on a mat that is not straight.

10.10 When the men of his village are drinking wine he leaves the feast directly the village-elders have left. When the men of his village hold their Expulsion Rite[12], he puts on his Court dress and stands on the eastern steps[13].

【原文】

10.15　问人于他邦，再拜而送之。

10.16　康子馈药，拜而受之。曰："丘未达，不敢尝。"

10.17　厩焚。子退朝，曰："伤人乎？"不问马。

10.18　君赐食，必正席先尝之。君赐腥，必熟而荐之。君赐生，必畜之。

侍食于君，君祭，先饭。

10.19　疾，君视之，东首，加朝服，拖绅。

10.20　君命召，不俟驾行矣。

10.21　入太庙，每事问。

10.22　朋友死，无所归，曰："于我殡。"

10.23　朋友之馈，虽车马，非祭肉，不拜。

10.24　寝不尸，居不客。

【今译】

10.15　托人给在外国的朋友问好送礼，便向受托者拜两次送行。

10.16　季康子给孔子送药，孔子拜而接受，却说道："我对这药性不很了解，不敢试服。"

10.17　孔子的马棚失了火。孔子从朝廷回来，道："伤了人吗？"不问到马。

10.18　国君赐以熟食，孔子一定摆正坐位先尝一尝。国君赐以生肉，一定煮熟了，先[给祖宗]进供。国君赐以活物，一定养着它。

同国君一道吃饭，当他举行饭前祭礼的时候，自己先吃饭[不吃菜]。

10.19　孔子病了，国君来探问，他便脑袋朝东，把上朝的礼服披在身上，拖着大带。

10.20　国君呼唤，孔子不等待车辆驾好马，立即先步行。

10.21　见八佾篇第三。

10.22　朋友死亡，没有负责收殓的人，孔子便道："丧葬由我来料理。"

10.23　朋友的赠品，即使是车马，只要不是祭肉，孔子在接受的时候，不行礼。

10.24　孔子睡觉不像死尸一样[直躺着]，平日坐着，也不像接见客人或者自己做客人一样[跪着两膝在席上]。

10.11 When sending a messenger to enquire after someone in another country, he prostrates himself twice while speeding the messenger on his way. When Kang[14] sent him some medicine he prostrated himself and accepted it; but said, "As I am not acquainted with its properties, I cannot venture to taste it."

10.12 When the stables were burnt down, on returning from Court, he said, "Was anyone hurt?" He did not ask about the horses.

10.13 When his prince sends him a present of food, he must straighten his mat and be the first to taste what has been sent. When what his prince sends is a present of uncooked meat, he must cook it and make a sacrificial offering. When his prince sends a live animal, he must rear it. When he is waiting upon his prince at meal-times, while his prince is making the sacrificial offering, he (the gentleman) tastes the dishes. If he is ill and his prince comes to see him, he has himself laid with his head to the East with his Court robes thrown over him and his sash drawn across the bed. When the prince commands his presence he goes straight to the palace without waiting for his carriage to be yoked.

10.14 On entering the Ancestral Temple, he asks about every detail.

10.15 If a friend dies and there are no relatives to fall back on, he says,"The funeral is my affair." On receiving a present from a friend, even a carriage and horses, he does not prostrate himself. He does so only in the case of sacrificial meat being sent.

10.16 In bed he avoids lying in the posture of a corpse.[15] When at home

【原文】

10.25　见齐衰者，虽狎，必变。见冕者与瞽者，虽亵，必以貌。

凶服者式之，式负版者。

有盛馔，必变色而作。

迅雷风烈必变。

10.26　升车，必正立，执绥。

车中，不内顾，不疾言，不亲指。

10.27　色斯举矣，翔而后集。曰："山梁雌雉，时哉时哉！"子路共之，三嗅而作。

【今译】

10.25　孔子看见穿齐衰孝服的人，就是极亲密的，也一定改变态度[表示同情]。看见戴着礼帽和瞎了眼睛的人，即使常相见，也一定有礼貌。

在车中遇着拿了送死人衣物的人，便把身体微微地向前一俯，手伏着车前的横木[表示同情]。遇见背负国家图籍的人，也手伏车前横木。

一有丰富的菜肴，一定神色变动，站立起来。

遇见疾雷、大风，一定改变态度。

10.26　孔子上车，一定先端正地站好，拉着扶手带[登车]。

在车中，不向内回顾，不很快地说话，不用手指指画画。

10.27　[孔子在山谷中行走，看见几只野鸡。]孔子的脸色一动，野鸡便飞向天空，盘旋一阵，又都停在一处。孔子道："这些山梁上的雌雉，得其时呀！得其时呀！"子路向它们拱拱手，它们又振一振翅膀飞去了。

he does not use ritual attitudes. When appearing before[16] anyone in mourning, however well he knows him, he must put on an altered expression, and when appearing before anyone in sacrificial garb, or a blind man, even informally, he must be sure to adopt the appropriate attitude. On meeting anyone in deep mourning he must bow across the bar of his chariot; he also bows to people carrying planks.[17] When confronted with a particularly choice dainty at a banquet, his countenance should change and he should rise to his feet. Upon hearing a sudden clap of thunder or a violent gust of wind, he must change countenance.

10.17 When mounting a carriage, he must stand facing it squarely and holding the mounting-cord. When riding he confines his gaze[18], does not speak rapidly or point with his hands[19].

10.18 (The gentleman) Rises and goes at the first sign, and does not "settle till he has hovered"[20]. (A song) says:

The hen-pheasant of the hill-bridge,
Knows how to bide its time, to bide its time!
When Zilu made it an offering,
It sniffed three times before it rose.[21]

先进篇第十一

【原文】

11.1　子曰："先进于礼乐，野人也；后进于礼乐，君子也。如用之，则吾从先进。"

11.2　子曰："从我于陈、蔡者，皆不及门也。"

11.3　德行：颜渊，闵子骞，冉伯牛，仲弓。言语：宰我，子贡。政事：冉有，季路。文学：子游，子夏。

11.4　子曰："回也非助我者也，于吾言无所不说。"

11.5　子曰："孝哉闵子骞！人不间于其父母昆弟之言。"

11.6　南容三复"白圭"，孔子以其兄之子妻之。

11.7　季康子问："弟子孰为好学？"孔子对曰："有颜回者好学，不

【今译】

11.1　孔子说："先学习礼乐而后做官的是未曾有过爵禄的一般人，先有了官位而后学习礼乐的是卿大夫的子弟。如果要我选用人才，我主张选用先学习礼乐的人。"

11.2　孔子说："跟着我在陈国、蔡国之间忍饥受饿的人，都不在我这里了。"

11.3　[孔子的学生各有所长。]德行好的：颜渊，闵子骞，冉伯牛，仲弓。会说话的：宰我，子贡。能办理政事的：冉有，季路。熟悉古代文献的：子游，子夏。

11.4　孔子说："颜回不是对我有所帮助的人，他对我的话没有不喜欢的。"

11.5　孔子说："闵子骞真是孝顺呀！别人对于他爹娘兄弟称赞他的言语并无异议。"

11.6　南容把"白圭之玷，尚可磨也；斯言之玷，不可为也"的几句诗读了又读，孔子便把自己的侄女嫁给他。

11.7　季康子问道："你学生中谁用功？"孔子答道："有一个叫颜回

BOOK XI

11.1 The Master said, "'Only common people wait till they are advanced in ritual and music [before taking office]. A gentleman can afford to get up his ritual and music later on.' Even if I accepted this saying, I should still be on the side of those who get on with their studies first."

11.2A The Master said, "My adherents in Chen and Cai were none of them in public service."

11.2B Those who worked by moral power were Yan Hui, Min Ziqian, Ran Geng and Ran Yong. Those who spoke well were Zai Yu and Zigong. Those who surpassed in handling public business were Ran Qiu and Zilu; in culture and learning, Ziyou and Zixia.[1]

11.3 The Master said, "Hui was not any help to me; he accepted everything I said."

11.4 The Master said, "Min Ziqian is indeed a very good son. No one can take exception to what his parents or brothers have said of him."[2]

11.5 Nan Rong in reciting the Yi Song repeated the verse about the sceptre of white jade three times. (In consequence of which) Master Kong gave him his elder brother's daughter to marry.[3]

11.6 Kang of the Ji Family asked which of the disciples had a love of learning. Master Kong replied, "There was Yan Hui. He was fond of

【原文】

幸短命死矣，今也则亡。”

11.8　颜渊死，颜路请子之车以为之椁。子曰：“才不才，亦各言其子也。鲤也死，有棺而无椁。吾不徒行以为之椁。以吾从大夫之后，不可徒行也。”

11.9　颜渊死。子曰：“噫！天丧予！天丧予！”

11.10　颜渊死，子哭之恸。从者曰：“子恸矣！”曰：“有恸乎？非夫人之为恸而谁为？”

11.11　颜渊死，门人欲厚葬之。子曰：“不可。”

门人厚葬之。子曰：“回也视予犹父也，予不得视犹子也。非我也，夫二三子也。”

11.12　季路问事鬼神。子曰：“未能事人，焉能事鬼？”

曰：“敢问死。”曰：“未知生，焉知死？”

【今译】

的用功，不幸短命死了，现在就再没有这样的人了。”

11.8　颜渊死了，他父亲颜路请求孔子卖掉车子来替颜渊办外椁。孔子道：“不管有才能或者没有才能，但总是自己的儿子。我的儿子鲤死了，也只有内棺，没有外椁。我不能［卖掉车子］步行来替他买椁。因为我也曾做过大夫，是不可以步行的。”

11.9　颜渊死了，孔子道：“咳！天老爷要我的命呀！天老爷要我的命呀！”

11.10　颜渊死了，孔子哭得很伤心。跟着孔子的人道：“您太伤心了！”孔子道：“真的太伤心了吗？我不为这样的人伤心，还为什么人伤心呢！”

11.11　颜渊死了，孔子的学生们想要很丰厚地埋葬他。孔子道：“不可以。”

学生们仍然很丰厚地埋葬了他。孔子道：“颜回呀！你看待我好像看待父亲，我却不能够像对待儿子一般地看待你。这不是我的主意呀，是你那班同学干的呀。”

11.12　子路问服事鬼神的方法。孔子道：“活人还不能服事，怎么能去服事死人？”

子路又道：“我大胆地请问死是怎么回事？”孔子道：“生的道理还没有弄明白，怎么能够懂得死？”

learning, but unfortunately his allotted span was a short one, and he died. Now there is none."

11.7 When Yan Hui died, his father Yan Lu begged for the Master's carriage, that he might use it to make the enclosure[4] for the coffin. The Master said, "Gifted or not gifted,[5] you have spoken of your son and I will now speak of mine. When Li[6] died he had a coffin, but no enclosure. I did not go on foot in order that he might have an enclosure; for I rank next to the Great Officers[7] and am not permitted to go on foot."

11.8 When Yan Hui died, the Master said, "Alas, Heaven has bereft me! Heaven has bereft me!"

11.9 When Yan Hui died the Master wailed without restraint. His followers said, "Master, you are wailing without restraint!" He said, "Am I doing so? Well, if any man's death could justify abandoned wailing, it would surely be this man's!"

11.10 When Yan Hui died, the disciples wanted to give him a grand burial. The Master said it would be wrong to do so; nevertheless they gave him a grand burial. The Master said, "Hui dealt with me as though I were his father. But I have failed to deal with him as though he were my son.[8] The fault however is not mine. It is yours, my friends!"

11.11 Zilu asked how one should serve ghosts and spirits. The Master said, "Till you have learnt to serve men, how can you serve ghosts?" Zilu then ventured upon a question about the dead. The Master said, "Till you know about the living, how are you to know about the dead?"

【原文】

11.13　闵子侍侧，訚訚如也；子路，行行如也；冉有、子贡，侃侃如也。子乐。"若由也，不得其死然。"

11.14　鲁人为长府。闵子骞曰："仍旧贯，如之何？何必改作？"子曰："夫人不言，言必有中。"

11.15　子曰："由之瑟奚为于丘之门？"门人不敬子路。子曰："由也升堂矣，未入于室也。"

11.16　子贡问："师与商也孰贤？"子曰："师也过，商也不及。"

曰："然则师愈与？"子曰："过犹不及。"

11.17　季氏富于周公，而求也为之聚敛而附益之。子曰："非吾徒也。小子鸣鼓而攻之，可也。"

【今译】

11.13　闵子骞站在孔子身旁，恭敬而正直的样子；子路很刚强的样子；冉有、子贡温和而快乐的样子。孔子高兴起来了。[不过，又道：]"像仲由吧，怕得不到好死。"

11.14　鲁国翻修叫长府的金库。闵子骞道："照着老样子下去怎么样？为什么一定要翻造呢？"孔子道："这个人平日不大开口，一开口一定中肯。"

11.15　孔子道："仲由弹瑟，为什么在我这里弹呢？"因此孔子的学生们瞧不起子路。孔子道："由么，学问已经不错了，只是还不够精深罢了。"

11.16　子贡问孔子："颛孙师（子张）和卜商（子夏）两个人，谁强一些？"孔子道："师呢，有些过分；商呢，有些赶不上。"

子贡道："那么，师强一些吗？"孔子道："过分和赶不上同样不好。"

11.17　季氏比周公还有钱，冉求却又替他搜括，增加更多的财富。孔子道："冉求不是我们的人，你们学生很可以大张旗鼓地来攻击他。"

11.12A When Min Ziqian stood by the Master's side in attendance upon him his attitude was one of polite restraint. That of Zilu was one of impatient energy; that of Ran Qiu and of Zigong was genial and affable. The Master was pleased.

11.12B [The Master said,] "A man like You[9] never dies in his bed."

11.13 When the men of Lu were dealing with the question of the Long Treasury, Min Ziqian said, "What about restoring it on the old lines? I see no necessity for rebuilding it on a new plan."[10] The Master said, "That man is no talker; but when he does say anything, he invariably hits the mark."

11.14 The Master said, "You's zithern has no right to be in my house at all." Whereupon the disciples ceased to respect Zilu. The Master said, "The truth about You is that he has got as far as the guest-hall, but has not yet entered the inner rooms."

11.15 Zigong asked which was the better, Shi or Shang.[11] The Master said, "Shi goes too far and Shang does not go far enough." Zigong said, "If that is so, then Shi excels. " The Master said, "To go too far is as bad as not to go far enough."

11.16 The head of the Ji Family was richer than the Duke of Zhou; but Qiu[12] when entrusted with the task of collecting his revenues for him, added to them and increased the yield. The Master said, "He is no follower of mine. My little ones, you may beat the drum and set upon him.

【原文】

11.18　柴也愚，参也鲁，师也辟，由也喭。

11.19　子曰："回也其庶乎，屡空。赐不受命，而货殖焉，亿则屡中。"

11.20　子张问善人之道。子曰："不践迹，亦不入于室。"

11.21　子曰："论笃是与，君子者乎？色庄者乎？"

11.22　子路问："闻斯行诸？"子曰："有父兄在，如之何其闻斯行之？"

冉有问："闻斯行诸？"子曰："闻斯行之。"

公西华曰："由也问闻斯行诸，子曰，'有父兄在'；求也问闻斯行诸，子曰，'闻斯行之'。赤也惑，敢问。"子曰："求也退，故进之；由也

【今译】

11.18　高柴愚笨，曾参迟钝，颛孙师偏激，仲由鲁莽。

11.19　孔子说："颜回的学问道德差不多了吧，可是常常穷得没有办法。端木赐不安本分，去囤积投机，猜测行情，竟每每猜对了。"

11.20　子张问怎样才是善人。孔子道："善人不踩着别人的脚印走，学问道德也难以到家。"

11.21　孔子说："总是推许言论笃实的人，这种笃实的人是真正的君子呢？还是神情上伪装庄重的人呢？"

11.22　子路问："听到就干起来吗？"孔子道："有爸爸哥哥活着，怎么能听到就干起来？"

冉有问："听到就干起来吗？"孔子道："听到就干起来。"

公西华道："仲由问听到就干起来吗，您说'有爸爸哥哥活着[不能这样做]'；冉求问听到就干起来吗，您说'听到就干起来'。[两个人问题相同，而您的答复相反，]我有些糊涂，大胆地来问问。"孔子道："冉求平日做事退缩，所以我给他壮胆；仲由的胆量却有两个

I give you leave."

11.17 [The Master said,] Chai[13] is stupid, Shen[14] is dull-witted, Shi[15] is too formal; You, too free and easy.[16]

11.18 The Master said, "Hui comes very near to it.[17] He is often empty.Ci (Zigong) was discontented with his lot and has taken steps to enrich himself. In his calculations he often hits the mark."

11.19 Zizhang asked about the Way of the good people. The Master said, "He who does not tread in the tracks[18] cannot expect to find his way into the Inner Room."

11.20 The Master said (of someone), "That his conversation is sound one may grant. But whether he is indeed a true gentleman or merely one who adopts outward airs of solemnity, it is not so easy to say."

11.21 Zilu asked, "When one hears a maxim, should one at once seek occasion to put it into practice? "The Master said, "Your father and elder brother are alive. How can you whenever you hear a maxim at once put it into practice?" Ran Qiu asked, "When one hears a maxim, should one at once seek occasion to put it into practice? " The Master said, "When one hears it, one should at once put it into practice."

Gongxi Hua said, "When You asked, 'When one hears a maxim, should one at once put it into practice?'You said, 'You have a father and elder brother alive.' But when Qiu asked, 'When one hears a maxim, should one at once put it into practice,'you said,'When you hear it, put it into practice.'I am perplexed, and would venture to ask how this was." The

【原文】

兼人，故退之。”

11.23　子畏于匡，颜渊后。子曰：“吾以女为死矣。”曰：“子在，回何敢死？”

11.24　季子然问：“仲由、冉求可谓大臣与？”子曰：“吾以子为异之问，曾由与求之问。所谓大臣者，以道事君，不可则止。今由与求也，可谓具臣矣。”

曰：“然则从之者与？”子曰：“弑父与君，亦不从也。”

11.25　子路使子羔为费宰。子曰：“贼夫人之子。”

子路曰：“有民人焉，有社稷焉，何必读书，然后为学？”

子曰：“是故恶夫佞者。”

11.26 子路、曾皙、冉有、公西华侍坐。子曰：“以吾一日长乎尔，毋吾以也。居则曰：‘不吾知也！’如或知尔，则何以哉？”子路率

【今译】

人的大，勇于作为，所以我要压压他。”

11.23　孔子在匡被囚禁了之后，颜渊最后才来。孔子道：“我以为你是死了。”颜渊道：“您还活着，我怎么敢死呢？”

11.24　季子然问：“仲由和冉求可以说是大臣吗？”孔子道：“我以为你是问别的人，竟问由和求呀。我们所说的大臣，他用最合于仁义的内容和方式来对待君主，如果这样行不通，宁肯辞职不干。如今由和求这两个人，可以说是具有相当才能的臣属了。”

季子然又道：“那么，他们会一切顺从上级吗？”孔子道：“杀父亲、杀君主的事情，他们也不会顺从的。”

11.25　子路叫子羔去做费县县长。孔子道：“这是害了别人的儿子！”

子路道：“那地方有老百姓，有土地和五谷，为什么定要读书才叫做学问呢？”

孔子道：“所以我讨厌强嘴利舌的人。”

11.26　子路、曾皙、冉有、公西华四个人陪着孔子坐着。孔子说道：“因为我比你们年纪都大，[老了，]没有人用我了。你们平日说：‘人家不了解我呀！’假若有人了解你们，[打算请你们出去，]那

Master said, "Qiu is backward; so I urged him on. You is fanatical about Goodness; so I held him back."

11.22 When the Master was trapped in Kuang, Yan Hui fell behind. The Master said, "I thought you were dead." Hui said, "While you are alive how should I dare to die?"

11.23 Ji Ziran[19] asked whether Zilu and Ran Qiu could be called great ministers. The Master said, "I thought you were going to ask some really interesting question; and it is after all only a question about You and Qiu! What I call a great minister is one who will only serve his prince while he can do so without infringement of the Way, and as soon as this is impossible, resigns. But in the present case, so far as concerns You and Qiu, I should merely call them stop-gap ministers." Ji Ziran said, "So you think they would merely do what they were told? " The Master said, "If called upon to slay their father or their prince, even *they* would refuse."

11.24 Zilu got Gao Chai made Warden of Mi.[20] The Master said, "You are doing an ill turn to another man's son." Zilu said, "What he will take charge of at Mi will be the peasants and the Holy Ground and Millet.[21] Surely 'learning consists in other things besides reading books[22].'" The Master said, "It is remarks of that kind that make me hate glib people."[23]

11.25 Once when Zilu, Zeng Xi, Ran Qiu and Gongxi Hua were seated in attendance upon the Master, he said, "You consider me as a somewhat older man than yourselves. Forget for a moment that I am so. At present you are out of office and feel that your merits are not recognized. Now

【原文】

尔而对曰："千乘之国，摄乎大国之间，加之以师旅，因之以饥馑；由也为之，比及三年，可使有勇，且知方也。"夫子哂之。"求！尔何如？"对曰："方六七十，如五六十，求也为之，比及三年，可使足民。如其礼乐，以俟君子。""赤！尔何如？"对曰："非曰能之，愿学焉。宗庙之事，如会同，端章甫，愿为小相焉。""点！尔何如？"鼓瑟希，铿尔，舍瑟而作，对曰："异乎三子者之撰。"子曰："何伤乎？亦各言其志也。"曰："莫春者，春服既成，冠者五六人，童子六七人，浴乎沂，风乎舞雩，咏而归。"夫子喟然叹曰："吾与点也！"

【今译】

你们怎么办呢？"子路不假思索地答道："一千辆兵车的国家，局促地处于几个大国的中间，外面有军队侵犯它，国内又加以灾荒。我去治理，等到三年光景，可以使人人有勇气，而且懂得大道理。"孔子微微一笑。又问："冉求！你怎么样？"答道："国土纵横各六七十里或者五六十里的小国家，我去治理，等到三年光景，可以使人人富足。至于修明礼乐，那只有等待贤人君子了。"又问："公西赤！你怎么样？"答道："不是说我已经很有本领了，我愿意这样学习：祭祀的工作或者同外国盟会，我愿意穿着礼服，戴着礼帽，做一个小司仪者。"又问："曾点！你怎么样？"他弹瑟正近尾声，铿的一声把瑟放下，站了起来答道："我的志向和他们三位所讲的不同。"孔子道："那有什么妨碍呢？正是要各人说出自己的志向呵！"曾皙便道："暮春三月，春天衣服都穿定了，我陪同五六位成年人，六七个小孩，在沂水旁边洗洗澡，在舞雩台上吹吹风，一路唱歌，一路走回来。"孔子长叹一声道："我

supposing someone were to recognize your merits, what employment would you choose?" Zilu promptly and confidently replied, "Give me a country of a thousand war-chariots, hemmed in by powerful enemies, or even invaded by hostile armies,with drought and famine to boot; in the space of three years I could endow the people with courage and teach them in what direction[24] right conduct lies."

Our Master smiled at him. "What about you, Qiu ?" he said. Qiu replied saying, "Give me a domain of sixty to seventy or say fifty to sixty (leagues), and in the space of three years I could bring it about that the common people should lack for nothing. But as to rites and music,[25] I should have to leave them to a real gentleman."

"What about you, Chi?"

(Gongxi Hua) Answered saying, "I do not say I could do this; but I should like at any rate to be trained for it. In ceremonies at the Ancestral Temple or at a conference or general gathering[26] of the feudal princes I should like, clad in the Straight Gown and Emblematic Cap, to play the part of junior assistant."

"Dian,[27] what about you?"

The notes of the zithern he was softly fingering died away; he put it down, rose and replied saying, "I fear my words will not be so well chosen as those of the other three."[28] The Master said, "What harm is there in that? All that matters is that each should name his desire."

Zeng Xi said, "At the end of spring, when the making of the Spring Clothes[29] has been completed, to go with five or six newly-capped youths and six or seven uncapped boys, perform the lustration in the river Yi, take the air at the Rain Dance altars, and then go home singing." The Master heaved a deep sigh and said, "I am with Dian."

When the three others went away, Zeng Xi remained behind and said,

【原文】

三子者出，曾皙后。曾皙曰："夫三子者之言何如?"子曰："亦各言其志也已矣。"曰："夫子何哂由也?"曰："为国以礼，其言不让，是故哂之。""唯求则非邦也与?""安见方六七十如五六十而非邦也者?""唯赤则非邦也与?""宗庙会同，非诸侯而何?赤也为之小，孰能为之大?"

【今译】

同意曾点的主张呀!"子路、冉有、公西华三人都出来了，曾皙后走。曾皙问道："那三位同学的话怎样?"孔子道："也不过各人说说自己的志向罢了。"曾皙又道："您为什么对仲由微笑呢?"孔子道："治理国家应该讲求礼让，可是他的话却一点不谦虚，所以笑笑他。""难道冉求所讲的就不是国家吗?"孔子道："怎样见得横纵各六七十里或者五六十里的土地就不够是一个国家呢?""公西赤所讲的不是国家吗?"孔子道："有宗庙，有国际间的盟会，不是国家是什么?[我笑仲由的不是说他不能治理国家，关键不在是不是国家，而是笑他说话的内容和态度不够谦虚。譬如公西赤，他是个十分懂得礼仪的人，但他只说愿意学着做一个小司仪者。]如果他只做一小司仪者，又有谁来做大司仪者呢?"

"What about the sayings of those three people?" The Master said, "After all, it was agreed that each should tell his wish; and that is just what they did."

Zeng said, "Why did you smile at You?"

The Master said, "Because it is upon observance of ritual that the governance of a State depends; and his words were lacking in the virtue of cession.[30] That is why I smiled at him. "

"I suppose you were contrasting him with Qiu, who (by domain) certainly did not mean kingdom?"

"Where have you ever seen 'a domain of sixty to seventy or fifty to sixty leagues' that was not a kingdom?"

"I suppose, then, you were contrasting him with Chi, who was certainly not asking for a kingdom."

"The business of the Ancestral Temple and such things as conferences and general gatherings can only be undertaken by feudal princes. But if Chi were taking a minor part, what prince is there who is capable of playing a major one?"[31]

颜渊篇第十二

【原文】

12.1 颜渊问仁。子曰:“克己复礼为仁。一日克己复礼，天下归仁焉。为仁由己，而由人乎哉?”

颜渊曰:“请问其目。”子曰:“非礼勿视，非礼勿听，非礼勿言，非礼勿动。”

颜渊曰:“回虽不敏，请事斯语矣。”

12.2 仲弓问仁。子曰:“出门如见大宾，使民如承大祭。己所不欲，勿施于人。在邦无怨，在家无怨。”

仲弓曰:“雍虽不敏，请事斯语矣。”

12.3 司马牛问仁。子曰:“仁者，其言也讱。”

曰:“其言也讱，斯谓之仁已乎?”子曰:“为之难，言之得无讱乎?”

【今译】

12.1 颜渊问仁德。孔子道:“抑制自己，使言语行动都合于礼，就是仁。一旦这样做到了，天下的人都会称许你是仁人。实践仁德，全凭自己，还凭别人吗?”

颜渊道:“请问行动的纲领。”孔子道:“不合礼的事不看，不合礼的话不听，不合礼的话不说，不合礼的事不做。”

颜渊道:“我虽然迟钝，也要实行您这话。”

12.2 仲弓问仁德。孔子道:“出门[工作]好像去接待贵宾，役使百姓好像去承当大祀典[都得严肃认真，小心谨慎]。自己所不喜欢的事物，就不强加于别人。在工作岗位上不对工作有怨恨，就是不在工作岗位上也没有怨恨。”

仲弓道:“我虽然迟钝，也要实行您这话。”

12.3 司马牛问仁德。孔子道:“仁人，他的言语迟钝。”

司马牛道:“言语迟钝，这就叫做仁了吗?”孔子道:“做起来不容易，说话能够不迟钝吗?”

BOOK XII

12.1 Yan Hui asked about Goodness. The Master said, "He who can himself submit to ritual is Good. If (a ruler) could for one day 'himself submit to ritual,' everyone under Heaven would respond to his Goodness. For Goodness is something that must have its source in the ruler himself; it cannot be got from others."

Yan Hui said, "I beg to ask for the more detailed items of this (submission to ritual)." The Master said, "To look at nothing in defiance of ritual, to listen to nothing in defiance of ritual, to speak of nothing in defiance of ritual, never to stir hand or foot in defiance of ritual." Yan Hui said, "I know that I am not clever; but this is a saying that, with your permission, I shall try to put into practice."[1]

12.2 Ran Yong asked about Goodness[2]. The Master said, "Behave when away from home[3] as though you were in the presence of an important guest. Deal with the common people as though you were officiating at an important sacrifice. Do not do to others what you would not like yourself. Then there will be no feelings of opposition to you, whether it is the affairs of a State that you are handling or the affairs of a Family."

Ran Yong said, "I know that I am not clever; but this is a saying that, with your permission, I shall try to put into practice."

12.3 Sima Niu[4] asked about Goodness. The Master said, "The Good (*ren* 仁) man is chary (*ren* 讱) of speech." Sima Niu said, "So that is what is meant by Goodness — to be chary of speech?" The Master said, "Seeing that the doing of it is so difficult, how can one be otherwise than

【原文】

12.4　司马牛问君子。子曰:“君子不忧不惧。”

曰:“不忧不惧，斯谓之君子已乎?”子曰:“内省不疚，夫何忧何惧?”

12.5　司马牛忧曰:“人皆有兄弟，我独亡。”子夏曰:“商闻之矣:死生有命，富贵在天。君子敬而无失，与人恭而有礼。四海之内，皆兄弟也——君子何患乎无兄弟也?”

12.6　子张问明。子曰:“浸润之谮,肤受之愬，不行焉，可谓明也已矣。浸润之谮，肤受之愬，不行焉，可谓远也已矣。”

12.7　子贡问政。子曰:“足食，足兵，民信之矣。”

子贡曰:“必不得已而去，于斯三者何先?”曰:“去兵。”

子贡曰:“必不得已而去，于斯二者何先?”曰:“去食。自古皆有

【今译】

12.4　司马牛问怎样去做一个君子。孔子道:“君子不忧愁，不恐惧。”

司马牛道:“不忧愁，不恐惧，这样就可以叫做君子了吗?”孔子道:“自己问心无愧，那有什么可以忧愁和恐惧的呢?”

12.5　司马牛忧愁地说道:“别人都有好兄弟，单单我没有。”子夏说:“我听说过:死生听之命运，富贵由天安排。君子只是对待工作严肃认真，不出差错，对待别人词色恭谨，合乎礼节。天下之大，到处都是好兄弟——君子又何必着急没有好兄弟呢?”

12.6　子张问怎样才叫做见事明白。孔子道:“点滴而来、日积月累的谗言和肌肤所受、急迫切身的诬告都在你这里行不通，那你可以说是看得明白的了。点滴而来、日积月累的谗言和肌肤所受、急迫切身的诬告也都在你这里行不通，那你可以说是看得远的了。”

12.7　子贡问怎样去治理政事。孔子道:“充足粮食，充足军备，百姓对政府就有信心了。”

子贡道:“如果迫于不得已，在粮食、军备和人民的信心三者之中一定要去掉一项，先去掉哪一项?”孔子道:“去掉军备。”

子贡道:“如果迫于不得已，在粮食和人民的信心两者之中一定要去掉一项，先去掉哪一项?”孔子道:“去掉粮食。[没有粮食，不过死

chary of talking about it?"[5]

12.4 Sima Niu asked about the meaning of the term Gentleman. The Master said, "The Gentleman neither grieves nor fears." Sima Niu said, "So that is what is meant by being a gentleman — neither to grieve nor to fear?" The Master said, "On looking within himself he finds no taint; so why should he either grieve or fear?"

12.5 Sima Niu grieved, saying, "Everyone else has brothers; I alone have none."[6] Zixia said, "I have heard this saying, 'Death and life are the decree of Heaven; wealth and rank depend upon the will of Heaven. If a gentleman attends to business and does not idle away his time, if he behaves with courtesy to others and observes the rules of ritual, then all within the Four Seas[7] are his brothers.' How can any true gentleman grieve that he is without brothers?"

12.6 Zizhang asked the meaning of the term "illumined." The Master said, "He who is influenced neither by the soaking in of slander nor by the assault of denunciation may indeed be called illumined. He who is influenced neither by the soaking in of slander nor by the assault of denunciation may indeed be called 'aloof .'"

12.7 Zigong asked about government. The Master said, "Sufficient food, sufficient weapons, and the confidence of the common people." Zigong said, "Suppose you had no choice but to dispense with one of these three, which would you forgo?" The Master said, "Weapons." Zigong said, "Suppose you were forced to dispense with one of the two that were left, which would you forgo?" The Master said, "Food. For from of old death

【原文】

死，民无信不立。”

12.8 棘子成曰:“君子质而已矣,何以文为?”子贡曰:“惜乎,夫子之说君子也!驷不及舌。文犹质也,质犹文也。虎豹之鞟犹犬羊之鞟。”

12.9 哀公问于有若曰:“年饥，用不足，如之何?”

有若对曰:“盍彻乎?”

曰:“二，吾犹不足，如之何其彻也?”

对曰:“百姓足，君孰与不足?百姓不足，君孰与足?”

12.10 子张问崇德辨惑。子曰:“主忠信，徙义，崇德也。爱之欲其生，恶之欲其死。既欲其生，又欲其死，是惑也。‘诚不以富，

【今译】

亡，但]自古以来谁都免不了死亡。如果人民对政府缺乏信心，国家是站不起来的。”

12.8 棘子成道:“君子只要有好的本质便够了，要那些文采[那些仪节、那些形式]干什么?”子贡道:“先生这样地谈论君子，可惜说错了。一言既出，驷马难追。本质和文采，是同等重要的。假若把虎豹和犬羊两类兽皮拔去有文采的毛，那这两类皮革就很少区别了。”

12.9 鲁哀公向有若问道:“年成不好，国家用度不够，应该怎么办?”

有若答道:“为什么不实行十分抽一的税率呢?”

哀公道:“十分抽二，我还不够，怎么能十分抽一呢?”

答道:“如果百姓的用度够，您怎么会不够?如果百姓的用度不够，您又怎么会够?”

12.10 子张问如何去提高品德，辨别迷惑。孔子道:“以忠诚信实为主，唯义是从，这就可以提高品德。爱一个人，希望他长寿；厌恶起来，恨不得他马上死去。既要他长寿，又要他短命，这便是迷惑。这样，的确对自己毫无好处，只是使人奇怪罢了。”

has been the lot of all men; but a people that no longer trusts its rulers is lost indeed."

12.8 Ji Zicheng[8] said, "A gentleman is a gentleman in virtue of the stuff he is made of. Culture cannot make gentlemen." Zigong said, "I am sorry, Sir, that you should have said that. For the saying goes that 'When a gentleman has spoken, a team of four horses cannot overtake his words.'

"Culture is just as important as inborn qualities; and inborn qualities, no less important than culture. Remove the hairs from the skin of a tiger or panther, and what is left looks just like the hairless hide of a dog or sheep."[9]

12.9 Duke Ai enquired of Master You, saying, "It is a year of dearth, and the State has not enough for its needs. What am I to do?" Master You replied, saying, "Have you not got your tithes?" The Duke said, "Even with two-tenths instead of one, I still should not have enough. What is the use of talking to me about tithes?" Master You said, "When the Hundred Families[10] enjoy plenty, the prince necessarily shares in that plenty. But when the Hundred Families have not enough for their needs, the prince cannot expect to have enough for his needs."

12.10 Zizhang asked what was meant by "piling up moral force"and "deciding when in two minds." The Master said, "By 'piling up moral force' is meant taking loyalty and good faith as one's guiding principles, and migrating to places where right prevails.[11] Again, to love a thing means wanting it to live, to hate a thing means wanting it to perish. But suppose I want something to live and at the same time want it to perish; that is 'being in two minds.'

【原文】

亦祇以异。'"

12.11　齐景公问政于孔子。孔子对曰:"君君，臣臣，父父，子子。"公曰:"善哉!信如君不君，臣不臣，父不父，子不子，虽有粟，吾得而食诸?"

12.12　子曰:"片言可以折狱者，其由也与?"

子路无宿诺。

12.13　子曰:"听讼，吾犹人也。必也使无讼乎?"

12.14　子张问政。子曰:"居之无倦，行之以忠。"

12.15　子曰:"博学于文，约之以礼，亦可以弗畔矣夫!"

12.16　子曰:"君子成人之美，不成人之恶。小人反是。"

12.17　季康子问政于孔子。孔子对曰:"政者，正也。子帅以

【今译】

12.11　齐景公向孔子问政治。孔子答道:"君要像个君，臣要像个臣，父亲要像父亲，儿子要像儿子。"景公道:"对呀!若是君不像君，臣不像臣，父不像父，子不像子，即使粮食很多，我能吃得着吗?"

12.12　孔子说:"根据一方面的语言就可以判决案件的，大概只有仲由吧!"

子路从不拖延诺言。

12.13　孔子说:"审理诉讼，我同别人差不多。一定要使诉讼的事件完全消灭才好。"

12.14　子张问政治。孔子道:"在位不要疲倦懈怠，执行政令要忠心。"

12.15　见雍也篇第六。

12.16　孔子说:"君子成全别人的好事，不促成别人的坏事。小人却和这相反。"

12.17　季康子向孔子问政治。孔子答道:"政字的意思就是端

"Not for her wealth, oh no!
But merely for a change[12]."

12.11 Duke Jing of Qi[13] asked Master Kong about government. Master Kong replied saying, "Let the prince be a prince, the minister a minister, the father a father and the son a son." The Duke said, "How true! For indeed when the prince is not a prince, the minister not a minister, the father not a father, the son not a son, one may have a dish of millet in front of one and yet not know if one will live to eat it."[14]

12.12 The Master said, "Talk about 'deciding a lawsuit with half a word'—You is the man for that." Zilu never slept over a promise.

12.13 The Master said, "I could try a civil suit as well as anyone. But better still to bring it about that there were no civil suits!"

12.14 Zizhang asked about public business. The Master said, "Ponder over it untiringly at home; carry it out loyally when the time comes." (Literally, "Home it untiringly, carry it out loyally.")

12.15 Repetition of 6. 25.

12.16 The Master said, "The gentleman calls attention to the good points in others; he does not call attention to their defects. The small man does just the reverse of this."

12.17 Ji Kang asked Master Kong about the art of ruling. Master Kong

【原文】

正，孰敢不正?”

12.18　季康子患盗，问于孔子。孔子对曰:“苟子之不欲，虽赏之不窃。”

12.19　季康子问政于孔子曰:“如杀无道，以就有道，何如?”孔子对曰:“子为政，焉用杀?子欲善而民善矣。君子之德风，小人之德草。草上之风，必偃。”

12.20　子张问:“士何如斯可谓之达矣?”子曰:“何哉，尔所谓达者?”子张对曰:“在邦必闻，在家必闻。”子曰:“是闻也，非达也。夫达也者，质直而好义，察言而观色，虑以下人。在邦必达，在家必达。夫闻也者，色取仁而行违，居之不疑。在邦必闻，在家必闻。”

【今译】

正。您自己带头端正，谁敢不端正呢?”

12.18　季康子苦于盗贼太多，向孔子求教。孔子答道:“假若您不贪求太多的财货，就是奖励偷抢，他们也不会干。”

12.19　季康子向孔子请教政治，说道:“假若杀掉坏人来亲近好人，怎么样?”孔子答道:“您治理政治，为什么要杀戮?您想把国家搞好，百姓就会好起来。领导人的作风好比风，老百姓的作风好比草。风向哪边吹，草向哪边倒。”

12.20　子张问:“读书人要怎样做才可以叫达了?”孔子道:“你所说的达是什么意思?”子张答道:“做国家的官时一定有名望，在大夫家工作时一定有名望。”孔子道:“这个叫闻，不叫达。怎样才是达呢?品质正直，遇事讲理，善于分析别人的言语，观察别人的颜色，从思想上愿意对别人退让。这种人，做国家的官时固然事事行得通，在大夫家一定事事行得通。至于闻，表面上似乎爱好仁德，实际行为却不如此，可是自己竟以仁人自居而不加疑惑。这种人，做官的时候一定会骗取名望，居家的时候也一定会骗取名望。”

said, "Ruling(*zheng* 政) is straightening(*zheng* 正). If you lead along a straight way, who will dare go by a crooked one?"

12.18 Ji Kang was troubled by burglars. He asked Master Kong what he should do. Master Kong replied saying, "If only you were free from desire, they would not steal even if you paid them to."[15]

12.19 Ji Kang asked Master Kong about government, saying, "Suppose I were to slay those who have not the Way in order to help on those who have the Way, what would you think of it?" Master Kong replied saying, "You are there to rule, not to slay. If you desire what is good, the people will at once be good. The essence of the gentleman is that of wind; the essence of small people is that of grass. And when a wind passes over the grass, it cannot choose but bend."

12.20 Zizhang asked what a knight must be like if he is to be called "influential[16]." The Master said, "That depends on what you mean by 'influential.'" Zizhang replied saying, "If employed by the State, certain to win fame, if employed by a Ruling Family, certain to win fame." The Master said, "That describes being famous; it does not describe being influential. In order to be influential a man must be by nature straightforward and a lover of right. He must examine men's words and observe their expressions, and bear in mind the necessity of deferring to others.[17] Such a one, whether employed by the State or by a Ruling Family, will certainly be 'influential'; whereas the man who wins fame may merely have obtained, by his outward airs, a reputation for Goodness which his conduct quite belies. Anyone who makes his claims with sufficient self-assurance is certain to win fame in a State, certain to win fame in a

【原文】

12.21 樊迟从游于舞雩之下，曰:“敢问崇德，修慝，辨惑。”子曰:“善哉问! 先事后得，非崇德与?攻其恶，无攻人之恶，非修慝与?一朝之忿，忘其身，以及其亲，非惑与?”

12.22 樊迟问仁。子曰:“爱人。”问知。子曰:“知人。”

樊迟未达。子曰:“举直错诸枉，能使枉者直。”

樊迟退，见子夏曰:“乡也吾见于夫子而问知，子曰:‘举直错诸枉，能使枉者直’，何谓也?”

子夏曰:“富哉言乎! 舜有天下，选于众，举皋陶，不仁者远矣。汤

【今译】

12.21 樊迟陪侍孔子在舞雩台下游逛，说道:“请问怎样提高自己的品德，怎样消除别人对自己不露面的怨恨，怎样辨别出哪种是糊涂事。”孔子道:“问得好! 首先付出劳动，然后收获，不是提高品德了吗?批判自己的坏处，不去批判别人的坏处，不就消除无形的怨恨了吗?因为偶然的忿怒，便忘记自己，甚至也忘记了爹娘，不是糊涂吗?”

12.22 樊迟问仁。孔子道:“爱人。”又问智。孔子道:“善于鉴别人物。”

樊迟还不透彻了解。孔子道:“把正直人提拔出来，位置在邪恶人之上，能够使邪恶人正直。”

樊迟退了出来，找着子夏，说道:“刚才我去见老师向他问智，他说，‘把正直人提拔出来，位置在邪恶人之上，能够使邪恶人正直’，这是什么意思?”

子夏道:“意义多么丰富的话呀! 舜有了天下，在众人之中挑选，把皋陶提拔出来，坏人就难以存在了。汤有了天下，在众人之中挑选，

Family."

12.21 Once when Fan Chi was taking a walk with the Master under the trees at the Rain Dance altars, he said, "May I venture to ask about 'piling up moral force,' 'repairing shortcomings' and 'deciding when in two minds'?"[18] The Master said, "An excellent question.'The work first; the reward afterwards'; is not that piling up moral force?'Attack the evil that is within yourself; do not attack the evil that is in others.'Is not this 'repairing shortcomings'?

Because of a morning's blind rage
To forget one's own safety
And even endanger one's kith and kin[19]

is that not a case of'divided mind'?"

12.22 Fan Chi asked about the Good (ruler). The Master said, "He loves men." He asked about the wise (ruler). The Master said, "He knows men." Fan Chi did not quite understand.[20] The Master said, "By raising the straight and putting them on top of the crooked, he can make the crooked straight."[21] Fan Chi withdrew, and meeting Zixia said to him, "Just now I was with the Master and asked him about the wise (ruler). He said, 'By raising the straight and putting them on top of the crooked he can make the crooked straight.' What did he mean?"

Zixia said, "Oh, what a wealth of instruction is in those words! When Shun had all that is under Heaven, choosing from among the multitude he raised up Gao Yao, and straightway Wickedness disappeared. When Tang had all that is under Heaven, choosing from among the multitude

【原文】

有天下，选于众，举伊尹，不仁者远矣。”

12.23　子贡问友。子曰：“忠告而善道之，不可则止，毋自辱焉。”

12.24　曾子曰：“君子以文会友，以友辅仁。”

【今译】

把伊尹提拔出来，坏人也就难以存在了。”

12.23　子贡问对待朋友的方法。孔子道：“忠心地劝告他，好好地引导他，他不听从，也就罢了，不要自找侮辱。”

12.24　曾子说：“君子用文章学问来聚会朋友，用朋友来帮助自己培养仁德。”

he raised up Yi Yin; and straightway Wickedness disappeared."

12.23 Zigong asked about friends. The Master said, "Inform them loyally and guide them discreetly. If that fails, then desist. Do not court humiliation."

12.24 Master Zeng said, "The gentleman by his culture collects friends about him, and through these friends promotes Goodness."

子路篇第十三

【原文】

13.1　子路问政。子曰："先之劳之。"请益。曰："无倦。"

13.2　仲弓为季氏宰，问政。子曰："先有司，赦小过，举贤才。"

曰："焉知贤才而举之？"子曰："举尔所知；尔所不知，人其舍诸？"

13.3　子路曰："卫君待子而为政，子将奚先？"

子曰："必也正名乎？"

子路曰："有是哉，子之迂也！奚其正？"

子曰："野哉，由也！君子于其所不知，盖阙如也。名不正，则言不顺；言不顺，则事不成；事不成，则礼乐不兴；礼乐不兴，则刑罚

【今译】

13.1　子路问政治。孔子道："自己给百姓带头，然后让他们勤劳地工作。"子路请求多讲一点。孔子又道："永远不要懈怠。"

13.2　仲弓做了季氏的总管，向孔子问政治。孔子道："给工作人员带头，不计较人家的小错误，提拔优秀人才。"

仲弓道："怎样去识别优秀人才把他们提拔出来呢？"孔子道："提拔你所知道的；那些你所不知道的，别人难道会埋没他们吗？"

13.3　子路对孔子说："卫君等着您去治理国政，您准备首先干什么？"

孔子道："那一定是纠正名分上的用词不当吧！"

子路道："您的迂腐竟到如此地步吗！这又何必纠正？"

孔子道："你怎么这样卤莽！君子对于他所不懂的，大概采取保留态度[你怎么能乱说呢]？用词不当，言语就不能顺理成章；言语不顺理成章，工作就不可能搞好；工作搞不好，国家的礼乐制度也就举办不起来；礼乐制度举办不起来，刑罚也就不会得当；刑罚不得当，百

BOOK XIII

13.1 Zilu asked about government. The Master said, "Lead them; encourage them!" Zilu asked for a further maxim. The Master said, "Untiringly."

13.2 Ran Yong, having become steward of the Ji Family, asked about government. The Master said, "Get as much as possible done first by your subordinates.[1] Pardon small offences. Promote men of superior capacity." Ran Yong said, "How does one know a man of superior capacity, in order to promote him?" The Master said, "Promote those you know, and those whom you do not know other people will certainly not neglect."

13.3 Zilu said, "If the prince of Wei were waiting for you to come and administer his country for him, what would be your first measure?" The Master said, "It would certainly be to correct language." Zilu said, "Can I have heard you aright? Surely what you say has nothing to do with the matter. Why should language be corrected?" The Master said, "You! How boorish you are! A gentleman, when things he does not understand are mentioned, should maintain an attitude of reserve. If language is incorrect, then what is said does not concord with what was meant; and if what is said does not concord with what was meant, what is to be done cannot be effected. If what is to be done cannot be effected, then rites and music will not flourish. If rites and music do not flourish, then mutilations and lesser punishments will go astray. And if mutilations and lesser punishments go astray, then the people have nowhere to put hand

【原文】

不中；刑罚不中，则民无所措手足。故君子名之必可言也，言之必可行也。君子于其言，无所苟而已矣。”

13.4　樊迟请学稼。子曰:“吾不如老农。”请学为圃。曰:“吾不如老圃。”

樊迟出。子曰:“小人哉，樊须也! 上好礼，则民莫敢不敬；上好义，则民莫敢不服；上好信，则民莫敢不用情。夫如是，则四方之民襁负其子而至矣，焉用稼?”

13.5　子曰:“诵《诗》三百，授之以政，不达；使于四方，不能专对；虽多，亦奚以为?”

13.6　子曰:“其身正，不令而行；其身不正，虽令不从。”

13.7　子曰:“鲁卫之政，兄弟也。”

【今译】

姓就会[惶惶不安，]连手脚都不晓得摆在哪里才好。所以君子用一个词，一定[有它一定的理由，]可以说得出来；而顺理成章的话也一定行得通。君子对于措词说话要没有一点马虎的地方才罢了。”

13.4　樊迟请求学种庄稼。孔子道:“我不如老农民。”又请求学种菜蔬。孔子道:“我不如老菜农。”

樊迟退了出来。孔子道:“樊迟真是小人! 统治者讲究礼节，百姓就没有人敢不尊敬；统治者行为正当，百姓就没有人敢不服从；统治者诚恳信实，百姓就没有人敢不说真话。做到这样，四方的百姓都会背负着小儿女来投奔，为什么要自己种庄稼呢?”

13.5　孔子说:“熟读《诗经》三百篇，交给他以政治任务，却办不通；叫他出使外国，又不能独立地去谈判酬酢；纵是读得多，有什么用处呢?”

13.6　孔子说:“统治者本身行为正当，不发命令，事情也行得通。他本身行为不正当，纵三令五申，百姓也不会信从。”

13.7　孔子说:“鲁国的政治和卫国的政治，像兄弟一般[地相差不远]。”

or foot.

"Therefore the gentleman uses only such language as is proper for speech, and only speaks of what it would be proper to carry into effect. The gentleman, in what he says, leaves nothing to mere chance."[2]

13.4 Fan Chi asked the Master to teach him about farming. The Master said, "You had much better consult some old farmer." He asked to be taught about gardening. The Master said, "You had much better go to some old vegetable-gardener." When Fan Chi had gone out, the Master said, "Fan is no gentleman! If those above them love ritual, then among the common people none will dare to be disrespectful. If those above them love right, then among the common people none will dare to be disobedient. If those above them love good faith, then among the common people none will dare depart from the facts[3]. If a gentleman is like that, the common people will flock to him from all sides with their babies strapped to their backs. What need has he to practise farming?"[4]

13.5 The Master said, "A man may be able to recite the three hundred *Songs*; but, if when given a post in the government, he cannot turn his merits to account, or when sent on a mission to far parts he cannot answer particular questions,[5] however extensive his knowledge may be, of what use is it to him?"

13.6 The Master said, "If the ruler himself is upright, all will go well even though he does not give orders. But if he himself is not upright, even though he gives orders, they will not be obeyed."

13.7 The Master said, "In their politics Lu and Wei are still brothers."[6]

【原文】

13.8 子谓卫公子荆:"善居室。始有,曰:'苟合矣。'少有,曰:'苟完矣。'富有,曰:'苟美矣。'"

13.9 子适卫,冉有仆。子曰:"庶矣哉!"

冉有曰:"既庶矣,又何加焉?"曰:"富之。"

曰:"既富矣,又何加焉?"曰:"教之。"

13.10 子曰:"苟有用我者,期月而已可也,三年有成。"

13.11 子曰:"'善人为邦百年,亦可以胜残去杀矣。'诚哉是言也!"

13.12 子曰:"如有王者,必世而后仁。"

13.13 子曰:"苟正其身矣,于从政乎何有?不能正其身,如正人何?"

【今译】

13.8 孔子谈到卫国的公子荆,说:"他善于居家过日子,刚有一点,便说道:'差不多够了。'增加了一点,又说道:'差不多完备了。'多有一点,便说道:'差不多富丽堂皇了。'"

13.9 孔子到卫国,冉有替他驾车子。孔子道:"好稠密的人口!"

冉有道:"人口已经众多了,又该怎么办呢?"孔子道:"使他们富裕起来。"

冉有道:"已经富裕了,又该怎么办呢?"孔子道:"教育他们。"

13.10 孔子说:"假若有用我主持国家政事的,一年便差不多了,三年便会很有成绩。"

13.11 孔子说:"'善人治理国政连续到一百年,也可以克服残暴免除虐杀了。'这句话真说得对呀!"

13.12 孔子说:"假若有王者兴起,一定需要三十年才能使仁政大行。"

13.13 孔子说:"假若端正了自己,治理国政有什么困难呢?连本身都不能端正,怎么端正别人呢?"

13.8 The Master said of the Wei grandee Jing[7], "He dwelt as a man should dwell in his house. When things began to prosper with him, he said, 'Now they[8] will begin to be a little more suitable.' When he was better off still, he said, 'Now they will be fairly complete.' When he was really rich, he said, 'Now I shall be able to make them quite beautiful.'"

13.9 When the Master was going to Wei, Ran Qiu drove him. The Master said, "What a dense population!" Ran Qiu said, "When the people have multiplied, what next should be done for them?" The Master said, "Enrich them." Ran Qiu said, "When one has enriched them, what next should be done for them?" The Master said, "Instruct them."

13.10 The Master said, "If only someone were to make use of me, even for a single year, I could do a great deal; and in three years I could finish off the whole work."

13.11 The Master said, "'Only if the right sort of people had charge of a country for a hundred years would it become really possible to stop cruelty and do away with slaughter.' How true the saying is!"

13.12 The Master said, "If a Kingly Man[9] were to arise, within a single generation Goodness would prevail."

13.13 The Master said, "Once a man has contrived to put himself aright, he will find no difficulty at all in filling any government post. But if he cannot put himself aright, how can he hope to succeed in putting others right?"[10]

【原文】

13.14　冉子退朝。子曰:"何晏也?"对曰:"有政。"子曰:"其事也。如有政,虽不吾以,吾其与闻之。"

13.15　定公问:"一言而可以兴邦,有诸?"

孔子对曰:"言不可以若是其几也。人之言曰:'为君难,为臣不易。'如知为君之难也,不几乎一言而兴邦乎?"

曰:"一言而丧邦,有诸?"

孔子对曰:"言不可以若是其几也。人之言曰:'予无乐乎为君,唯其言而莫予违也。'如其善而莫之违也,不亦善乎?如不善而莫之违也,不几乎一言而丧邦乎?"

13.16　叶公问政。子曰:"近者说,远者来。"

13.17　子夏为莒父宰,问政。子曰:"无欲速,无见小利。欲速,则不达;见小利,则大事不成。"

【今译】

13.14　冉有从办公的地方回来。孔子道:"为什么今天回得这样晚呢?"答道:"有政务。"孔子道:"那只是事务罢了。若是有政务,虽然不用我了,我也会知道的。"

13.15　鲁定公问:"一句话兴盛国家,有这事么?"

孔子答道:"说话不可以像这样地简单机械。不过,大家都说:'做君上很难,做臣子不容易。'假若知道做君上的艰难,[自然会谨慎认真地干去,]不近于一句话便兴盛国家么?"

定公又道:"一句话丧失国家,有这事么?"

孔子答道:"说话不可以像这样地简单机械。不过,大家都说:'我做国君没有别的快乐,只是我说什么话都没有人违抗我。'假若说的话正确而没有人违抗,不也好么?假若说的话不正确而也没有人违抗,不近于一句话便丧失国家么?"

13.16　叶公问政治。孔子道:"境内的人使他高兴,境外的人使他来投奔。"

13.17　子夏做了莒父的县长,问政治。孔子道:"不要图快,不要顾小利。图快,反而不能达到目的;顾小利,就办不成大事。"

13.14 Once when Master Ran came back from Court[11], the Master said, "Why are you so late?" He replied, saying, "There were affairs of State." The Master said, "You must mean private business. If there had been affairs of State, although I am not used[12], I too should have been bound to hear of them."

13.15 Duke Ding asked if there were any one phrase that sufficed to save a country. Master Kong replied saying, "No phrase could ever be like that.[13] But here is one that comes near to it. There is a saying among men: 'It is hard to be a prince and not easy to be a minister.' A ruler who really understood that it was 'hard to be a prince' would have come fairly near to saving his country by a single phrase."

Duke Ding said, "Is there any one phrase that could ruin a country?" Master Kong said, "No phrase could ever be like that. But here is one that comes near to it. There is a saying among men: 'What pleasure is there in being a prince, unless one can say whatever one chooses, and no one dares to disagree?' So long as what he says is good, it is of course good also that he should not be opposed. But if what he says is bad, will it not come very near to his ruining his country by a single phrase?"

13.16 The "Duke" of She asked about government[14]. The Master said, "When the near approve and the distant approach."

13.17 When Zixia was Warden of Jufu[15], he asked for advice about government. The Master said, "Do not try to hurry things. Ignore minor considerations. If you hurry things, your personality will not come into play.[16] If you let yourself be distracted by minor considerations, nothing

【原文】

13.18　叶公语孔子曰："吾党有直躬者，其父攘羊，而子证之。"孔子曰："吾党之直者异于是：父为子隐，子为父隐。——直在其中矣。"

13.19　樊迟问仁。子曰："居处恭，执事敬，与人忠。虽之夷狄，不可弃也。"

13.20　子贡问曰："何如斯可谓之士矣？"子曰："行己有耻，使于四方，不辱君命，可谓士矣。"

曰："敢问其次。"曰："宗族称孝焉，乡党称悌焉。"

曰："敢问其次。"曰："言必信，行必果，硁硁然小人哉！——抑

【今译】

13.18　叶公告诉孔子道："我那里有个坦白直率的人，他父亲偷了羊，他便告发。"孔子道："我们那里坦白直率的人和你们的不同：父亲替儿子隐瞒，儿子替父亲隐瞒——直率就在这里面。"

13.19　樊迟问仁。孔子道："平日容貌态度端正庄严，工作严肃认真，对别人忠心诚意。这几种品德，纵到外国去，也是不能废弃的。"

13.20　子贡问道："怎样才可以叫做'士'？"孔子道："自己行为保持羞耻之心，出使外国，很好地完成君主的使命，可以叫做'士'了。"

子贡道："请问次一等的。"孔子道："宗族称赞他孝顺父母，乡里称赞他恭敬尊长。"

子贡又道："请问再次一等的。"孔子道："言语一定信实，行为一定坚决，这是不问是非黑白而只管自己贯彻言行的小人呀！但也可以

important will ever get finished."

13.18 The "Duke" of She addressed Master Kong saying, "In my country there was a man called Upright Gong[17]. His father appropriated a sheep, and Gong bore witness against him." Master Kong said, "In my country the upright men are of quite another sort. A father will screen his son, and a son his father — which incidentally does involve a sort of uprightness."

13.19 Fan Chi asked about Goodness. The Master said, "In private life, courteous; in public life, diligent; in relationships, loyal. This is a maxim that no matter where you may be, even amid the barbarians of the east or north, may never be set aside."

13.20 Zigong asked, "What must a man be like in order that he may be called a true knight (of the Way)?" The Master said, "He who

> In the furtherance of his own interests
> Is held back by scruples,
> Who as an envoy to far lands
> Does not disgrace his prince's commission

may be called a true knight."

Zigong said, "May I venture to ask who would rank next?" The Master said, "He whom his relatives commend for filial piety, his fellow-villagers, for deference to his elders." Zigong said, "May I venture to ask who would rank next?" The Master said, "He who always stands by his word, who undertakes nothing that he does not bring to achievement.

【原文】

亦可以为次矣。”

曰:“今之从政者何如?”子曰:“噫!斗筲之人，何足算也?”

13.21 子曰:“不得中行而与之，必也狂狷乎?狂者进取，狷者有所不为也。”

13.22 子曰:“南人有言曰:‘人而无恒，不可以作巫医。’善夫!”

“不恒其德，或承之羞。”子曰:“不占而已矣。”

13.23 子曰:“君子和而不同，小人同而不和。”

13.24 子贡问曰:“乡人皆好之，何如?”子曰:“未可也。”

“乡人皆恶之，何如?”子曰:“未可也;不如乡人之善者好之，其不善者恶之。”

【今译】

说是再次一等的‘士’了。”

子贡道:“现在的执政诸公怎么样?”孔子道:“咳!这班器识狭小的人算得什么?”

13.21 孔子说:“得不到言行合乎中庸的人和他相交，那一定要交到激进的人和狷介的人吧!激进者一意向前,狷介者也不肯做坏事。”

13.22 孔子说:“南方人有句话说，‘人假若没有恒心，连巫医都做不了。’这句话很好呀!”

《易经》恒卦的爻辞说:“三心二意，翻云覆雨，总有人招致羞耻。”孔子又说:“这话的意思是叫无恒心的人不必去占卦罢了。”

13.23 孔子说:“君子用自己的正确意见来纠正别人的错误意见，使一切都做到恰到好处，却不肯盲从附和。小人只是盲从附和，却不肯表示自己的不同意见。”

13.24 子贡问道:“满乡村的人都喜欢他，这个人怎么样?”孔子道:“还不行。”

子贡便又道:“满乡村的人都厌恶他,这个人怎么样?”孔子道:“还不行。最好是满乡村的好人都喜欢他，满乡村的坏人都厌恶他。”

Such a one may be in the humblest[18] possible circumstances, but all the same we must give him the next place."

Zigong said, "What would you say of those who are now conducting the government?" The Master said, "Ugh! A set of peck-measures,[19] not worth taking into account."

13.21 The Master said, "If I cannot get men who steer a middle course to associate with, I would far rather have the impetuous and hasty[20]. For the impetuous at any rate assert themselves; and the hasty have this at least to be said for them, that there are things they leave undone."

13.22 The Master said, "The men of the south have a saying, 'Without stability[21] a man will not even make a good *shaman* or witch-doctor.'[22] Well said!" Of the maxim: If you do not stabilize an act of *de*, you will get evil by it (instead of good), the Master said, "They (i.e. soothsayers) do not simply read the omens."

13.23 The Master said, "The true gentleman is conciliatory but not accommodating. Common people are accommodating but not conciliatory[23]."

13.24 Zigong asked, saying, "What would you feel about a man who was loved by all his fellow-villagers?" The Master said, "That is not enough."

"What would you feel about a man who was hated by all his fellow-villagers?" The Master said, "That is not enough. Best of all would be that the good people in his village loved him and the bad hated him."

【原文】

13.25　子曰:“君子易事而难说也。说之不以道，不说也；及其使人也，器之。小人难事而易说也。说之虽不以道，说也；及其使人也，求备焉。”

13.26　子曰:“君子泰而不骄，小人骄而不泰。”

13.27　子曰:“刚、毅、木、讷近仁。”

13.28　子路问曰:“何如斯可谓之士矣?”子曰:“切切偲偲，怡怡如也，可谓士矣。朋友切切偲偲，兄弟怡怡。”

13.29　子曰:“善人教民七年，亦可以即戎矣。”

13.30　子曰:“以不教民战，是谓弃之。”

【今译】

13.25　孔子说:“在君子底下工作很容易，讨他的欢喜却难。不用正当的方式去讨他的欢喜，他不会欢喜的；等到他使用人的时候，却衡量各人的才德去分配任务。在小人底下工作很难，讨他的欢喜却容易。用不正当的方式去讨他的欢喜，他会欢喜的；等到他使用人的时候，便会百般挑剔，求全责备。”

13.26　孔子说:“君子安详舒泰，却不骄傲凌人；小人骄傲凌人，却不安详舒泰。”

13.27　孔子说:“刚强，果决，朴质，而言语不轻易出口，有这四种品德的人近于仁德。”

13.28　子路问道:“怎么样才可以叫做‘士’了呢?”孔子道:“互相批评，和睦共处，可以叫做‘士’了。朋友之间，互相批评；兄弟之间，和睦共处。”

13.29　孔子说:“善人教导人民达七年之久，也能够叫他们作战了。”

13.30　孔子道:“用未经受过训练的人民去作战，这等于糟踏生命。”

13.25 The Master said, "The true gentleman is easy to serve, yet difficult to please. For if you try to please him in any manner inconsistent with the Way, he refuses to be pleased; but in using the services of others he only expects of them what they are capable of performing. Common people are difficult to serve, but easy to please. Even though you try to please them in a manner inconsistent with the Way, they will still be pleased; but in using the services of others they expect them (irrespective of their capacities) to do any work that comes along."

13.26 The Master said, "The gentleman is dignified, but never haughty; common people are haughty, but never dignified."

13.27 The Master said, "Imperturbable, resolute, treelike,[24] slow to speak — such a one is near to Goodness."

13.28 Zilu asked, "What must a man be like, that he may be called a true knight of the Way?" The Master said, "He must be critical and exacting, but at the same time indulgent. Then he may be called a true knight.Critical and exacting with regard to the conduct of his friends; indulgent towards his brothers."

13.29, 13.30 The Master said, "Only when men of the right sort[25] have instructed a people for seven years ought there to be any talk of engaging them in warfare." The Master said, "To lead into battle a people that has not first been instructed is to betray them."

宪问篇第十四

【原文】

14.1　宪问耻。子曰:“邦有道，谷；邦无道，谷，耻也。”

“克、伐、怨、欲不行焉，可以为仁矣?”子曰:“可以为难矣，仁则吾不知也。”

14.2　子曰:“士而怀居，不足以为士矣。”

14.3　子曰:“邦有道，危言危行；邦无道，危行言孙。”

14.4　子曰:“有德者必有言，有言者不必有德。仁者必有勇，勇者不必有仁。”

14.5　南宫适问于孔子曰:“羿善射，奡荡舟，俱不得其死然。禹

【今译】

14.1　原宪问如何叫耻辱。孔子道:“国家政治清明，做官领薪俸；国家政治黑暗，做官领薪俸，这就是耻辱。”

原宪又道:“好胜、自夸、怨恨和贪心四种毛病都不曾表现过，这可以说是仁人了吗?”孔子道:“可以说是难能可贵的了，若说是仁人，那我不能同意。”

14.2　孔子说:“读书人而留恋安逸，便不配做读书人了。”

14.3　孔子说:“政治清明，言语正直，行为正直；政治黑暗，行为正直，言语谦顺。”

14.4　孔子说:“有道德的人一定有名言，但有名言的人不一定有道德。仁人一定勇敢，但勇敢的人不一定仁。”

14.5　南宫适向孔子问道:“羿擅长射箭，奡擅长水战，都没有得

BOOK XIV

14.1 Yuan Si asked about compunction.[1] The Master said, "When a country is ruled according to the Way, (the gentleman) accepts rewards. But when a country is not ruled according to the Way, he shows compunction in regard to rewards."

14.2 Of the saying "He upon whom neither love of mastery, vanity, resentment nor covetousness have any hold may be called Good," the Master said, "Such a one has done what is difficult; but whether he should be called Good I do not know."

14.3 The Master said, "The knight of the Way who thinks only of sitting quietly at home is not worthy to be called a knight."[2]

14.4 The Master said, "When the Way prevails in the land, be bold in speech and bold in action. When the Way does not prevail, be bold in action but conciliatory in speech."

14.5 The Master said, "One who has accumulated moral power (*de*) will certainly also possess eloquence; but he who has eloquence does not necessarily possess moral power. A Good Man will certainly also possess courage; but a brave man is not necessarily Good."

14.6 Nangong Kuo[3] asked Master Kong, saying, "Yi[4] was a mighty archer and Ao shook the boat[5]; yet both of them came to a bad end.[6] Whereas Yu and Ji, who devoted themselves to agriculture, came into possession

【原文】

稷躬稼而有天下。”夫子不答。

南宫适出。子曰:“君子哉若人!尚德哉若人!”

14.6 子曰:“君子而不仁者有矣夫,未有小人而仁者也。”

14.7 子曰:“爱之,能勿劳乎?忠焉,能勿诲乎?”

14.8 子曰:“为命,裨谌草创之,世叔讨论之,行人子羽修饰之,东里子产润色之。”

14.9 或问子产。子曰:“惠人也。”

问子西。曰:“彼哉!彼哉!”

问管仲。曰:“人也。夺伯氏骈邑三百,饭疏食,没齿无怨言。”

14.10 子曰:“贫而无怨难,富而无骄易。”

【今译】

到好死。禹和稷自己下地种田,却得到了天下。[怎样解释这些历史?]”孔子没有答复。

南宫适退了出来。孔子道:“这个人,好一个君子!这个人,多么尊尚道德!”

14.6 孔子说:“君子之中不仁的人有的吧,小人之中却不会有仁人。”

14.7 孔子说:“爱他,能不叫他劳苦吗?忠于他,能够不教诲他吗?”

14.8 孔子说:“郑国外交辞令的创制,裨谌拟稿,世叔提意见,外交官子羽修改,子产作文词上的加工。”

14.9 有人向孔子问子产是怎样的人物。孔子道:“是宽厚慈惠的人。”

又问到子西。孔子道:“他呀,他呀!”

又问到管仲。孔子道:“他是人才。剥夺了伯氏骈邑三百户的采地,使伯氏只能吃粗粮,到死没有怨恨的话。”

14.10 孔子说:“贫穷却没有怨恨,很难;富贵却不骄傲,倒容易做到。”

of all that is under Heaven."[7]

At the time our Master made no reply, but when Nangong had withdrawn he said, "He is a true gentleman indeed, is that man! He has a right apprisal of 'virtue's power'(*de*),[8] has that man!"

14.7 The Master said, "It is possible to be a true gentleman and yet lack Goodness. But there has never yet existed a Good man who was not a gentleman."

14.8 The Master said, "How can he be said truly to love,[9] who exacts no effort from the objects of his love? How can he be said to be truly loyal, who refrains from admonishing the object of his loyalty?"

14.9 The Master said, "When a ducal mandate was being prepared Bi Chen[10] first made a rough draft, Shi Shu checked and revised it, Ziyu the Receiver of Envoys amended and embellished it; Zichan of Dongli gave it amplitude and colour."

14.10, 14.11 Someone asked about Zichan. The Master said, "A kindly[11] man!" Asked about Zixi[12] he said, "That man! That man!" Asked about Guan Zhong he said, "This is the sort of man he was: he could seize the fief of Pian with its three hundred villages from its owner, the head of the Bo Family; yet Bo, though he 'lived on coarse food'[13] to the end of his days, never uttered a single word of resentment."[14] The Master said, "To be poor and not resent it[15] is far harder than to be rich, yet not presumptuous."

14.12 The Master said, "Meng Gongchuo would have done well enough

【原文】

14.11　子曰:“孟公绰为赵魏老则优，不可以为滕薛大夫。”

14.12　子路问成人。子曰:“若臧武仲之知，公绰之不欲，卞庄子之勇，冉求之艺，文之以礼乐，亦可以为成人矣。”曰:“今之成人者何必然?见利思义，见危授命，久要不忘平生之言，亦可以为成人矣。”

14.13　子问公叔文子于公明贾曰:“信乎，夫子不言，不笑，不取乎?”

公明贾对曰:“以告者过也。夫子时然后言，人不厌其言；乐然后笑，人不厌其笑；义然后取，人不厌其取。”

子曰:“其然?岂其然乎?”

14.14　子曰:“臧武仲以防求为后于鲁，虽曰不要君，吾不信也。”

【今译】

14.11　孔子说:“孟公绰，若是叫他做晋国诸卿赵氏、魏氏的家臣，那是力有余裕的，却没有才能来做滕、薛这样小国的大夫。”

14.12　子路问怎样才是全人。孔子道:“智慧像臧武仲，清心寡欲像孟公绰，勇敢像卞庄子，多才多艺像冉求，再用礼乐来成就他的文采，也可以说是全人了。”等了一会，又道:“现在的全人哪里一定要这样?看见利益便能想起该得不该得，遇到危险便肯付出生命，经过长久的穷困日子都不忘记平日的诺言，也可以说是全人了。”

14.13　孔子向公明贾问到公叔文子，说:“他老人家不言语，不笑，不取，是真的吗?”

公明贾答道:“这是传话的人说错了。他老人家到应说话的时候才说话，别人不厌恶他的话；高兴了才笑，别人不厌恶他的笑；应该取才取，别人不厌恶他的取。”

孔子道:“如此的吗?难道真是如此的吗?”

14.14　孔子说:“臧武仲[逃到齐国之前，]凭借着他的采邑防城请求立其子弟嗣为鲁国卿大夫，纵然有人说他不是要挟，我是不相信的。”

as Comptroller of the Zhao or Wei families; but he was not fit to be a State minister even in Teng or Xue[16]."

14.13 Zilu asked what was meant by "the perfect man." The Master said, "If anyone had the wisdom of Zang Wuzhong[17], the uncovetousness of Meng Gongchuo, the valour of Zhuangzi of Bian[18], and the dexterity of Ran Qiu, and had graced these virtues by the cultivation of ritual and music, then indeed I think we might call him 'a perfect man.'"

He said, "But perhaps to-day we need not ask all this of the perfect man. One who, when he sees a chance of gain, stops to think whether to pursue it would be right; when he sees that (his prince) is in danger, is ready to lay down his life; when the fulfilment of an old promise is exacted, stands by what he said long ago — him indeed I think we might call 'a perfect man.'"

14.14 The Master asked Gongming Jia[19] about Gongshu Wen[20], saying, "Is it a fact that your master neither 'spoke nor laughed nor took'?" Gongming Jia replied saying, "The people who told you this were exaggerating. My master never spoke till the time came to do so; with the result that people never felt that they had had too much of his talk. He never laughed unless he was delighted; so people never felt they had had too much of his laughter. He never took[21] unless it was right to do so, so that people never felt he had done too much taking." The Master said, "Was that so? Can that really have been so?"

14.15 The Master said, "Zang Wuzhong occupied the fief of Fang and then demanded from (the Duke of) Lu that (his brother) Wei should be allowed to take the fief over from him. It is said that he applied no pres-

【原文】

14.15　子曰:“晋文公谲而不正，齐桓公正而不谲。”

14.16　子路曰:“桓公杀公子纠，召忽死之，管仲不死。”曰:“未仁乎?”子曰:“桓公九合诸侯，不以兵车，管仲之力也。如其仁，如其仁。”

14.17　子贡曰:“管仲非仁者与?桓公杀公子纠，不能死，又相之。”子曰:“管仲相桓公，霸诸侯，一匡天下，民到于今受其赐。微管仲，吾其被发左衽矣。岂若匹夫匹妇之为谅也，自经于沟渎而莫之知也?”

14.18　公叔文子之臣大夫僎与文子同升诸公。子闻之，曰:“可以为‘文’矣。”

【今译】

14.15　孔子说:“晋文公诡诈好耍手段，作风不正派；齐桓公作风正派，不用诡诈，不耍手段。”

14.16　子路道:“齐桓公杀了他哥哥公子纠，[公子纠的师傅]召忽因此自杀，[但是他的另一师傅]管仲却活着。”接着又道:“管仲该不是有仁德的吧?”孔子道:“齐桓公多次地主持诸侯间的盟会，停止了战争，都是管仲的力量。这就是管仲的仁德，这就是管仲的仁德。”

14.17　子贡道:“管仲不是仁人吧?桓公杀掉了公子纠，他不但不以身殉难，还去辅相他。”孔子道:“管仲辅相桓公，称霸诸侯，使天下一切都得到匡正，人民到今天还受到他的好处。假若没有管仲，我们都会披散着头发，衣襟向左边开[沦为落后民族]了。他难道要像普通老百姓一样守着小节小信，在山沟中自杀，还没有人知道吗?”

14.18　公叔文子的家臣大夫僎，[由于文子的推荐，]和文子一道做了国家的大臣。孔子知道这事，便道:“这便可以谥为‘文’了。”

sure upon his prince; but I do not believe it."[22]

14.16 The Master said, "Duke Wen of Jin could rise to an emergency, but failed to carry out the plain dictates of ritual. Duke Huan of Qi carried out the dictates of ritual, but failed when it came to an emergency."[23]

14.17 Zilu said, "When Duke Huan put to death (his brother) Prince Jiu, Shao Hu gave his life in an attempt to save the prince; but Guan Zhong did not.[24] Must one not say that he fell short of Goodness?" The Master said, "That Duke Huan was able to convene the rulers of all the States without resorting to the use of his war-chariots was due to Guan Zhong. But as to his[25] Goodness, as to his Goodness!"

14.18 Zigong said, "I fear Guan Zhong was not Good. When Duke Huan put to death his brother Prince Jiu, Guan Zhong so far from dying on Jiu's behalf became Duke Huan's Prime Minister." The Master said, "Through having Guan Zhong as his Minister Duke Huan became leader of the feudal princes, uniting and reducing to good order all that is under Heaven; so that even to-day the people are benefiting by what he then did for them. Were it not for Guan Zhong we might now be wearing our hair loose and folding our clothes to the left![26] We must not expect from him what ordinary men and women regard as 'true constancy'— to go off and strangle oneself in some ditch or drain, and no one the wiser."

14.19 Gongshu Wen, when summoned to office by the Duke(of Wei), brought with him and presented to the Duke his retainer Xun, the same Xun who became a State officer. The Master hearing of it[27] said, "With good reason was he accorded the title Wen."

【原文】

14.19　子言卫灵公之无道也，康子曰："夫如是，奚而不丧?"孔子曰："仲叔圉治宾客，祝鮀治宗庙，王孙贾治军旅。夫如是，奚其丧?"

14.20　子曰："其言之不怍，则为之也难。"

14.21　陈成子弑简公。孔子沐浴而朝，告于哀公曰："陈恒弑其君，请讨之。"公曰："告夫三子!"

孔子曰："以吾从大夫之后，不敢不告也。君曰'告夫三子'者!"

之三子告，不可。孔子曰："以吾从大夫之后，不敢不告也。"

14.22　子路问事君。子曰："勿欺也，而犯之。"

14.23　子曰："君子上达，小人下达。"

14.24　子曰："古之学者为己，今之学者为人。"

【今译】

14.19　孔子讲到卫灵公的昏乱，康子道："既然这样，为什么不败亡?"孔子道："他有仲叔圉接待宾客，祝鮀管理祭祀，王孙贾统率军队，像这样，怎么会败亡?"

14.20　孔子说："那个人大言不惭，他实行就不容易。"

14.21　陈恒杀了齐简公。孔子斋戒沐浴而后朝见鲁哀公，报告道："陈恒杀了他的君主，请您出兵讨伐他。"哀公道："你向季孙、仲孙、孟孙三人去报告吧!"

孔子[退了出来,]道："因为我曾忝为大夫，不敢不来报告，但是君上却对我说：'给那三人报告吧!'"

孔子又去报告三位大臣，[三位]不肯出兵。孔子道："因为我曾忝为大夫，不敢不报告。"

14.22　子路问怎样服侍人君。孔子道："不要[阳奉阴违地]欺骗他，却可以[当面]触犯他。"

14.23　孔子说："君子通达于仁义，小人通达于财利。"

14.24　孔子说："古代学者的目的在修养自己的学问道德，现代学者的目的却在装饰自己，给别人看。"

14.20 The Master referred to Duke Ling of Wei as being no follower of the true Way. Kang[28] said, "How is it then that he does not come to grief?" Master Kong said, "He has Zhongshu Yu[29] to deal with foreign envoys and guests, the priest Tuo to regulate the ceremonies in his ancestral temple and Wangsun Jia to command his armies. Why then should he come to grief?"

14.21 The Master said, "Do not be too ready to speak of it[30], lest the doing of it should prove to be beyond your powers."

14.22 When Chen Heng assassinated Duke Jian of Qi, Master Kong washed his head and limbs,[31] went to Court and informed Duke Ai of Lu, saying, "Chen Heng has slain his prince. I petition that steps should be taken to punish him." The Duke said, "You had better inform the Three." Master Kong said, "As I rank next to the Great Officers, I could not do otherwise than lay this information before you. And now your Highness says 'Inform the Three?'"He then went to the Three and informed them. They refused his petition. Master Kong said, "As I rank next to the Great Officers, I could not do otherwise than lay this petition before you."

14.23 Zilu asked him how to serve a prince. The Master said, "Never oppose him by subterfuges."

14.24 The Master said, "The gentleman can influence those who are above him; the small man can only influence those who are below him."

14.25 The Master said, "In old days men studied for the sake of self-improvement; nowadays men study in order to impress other people."

【原文】

14.25　蘧伯玉使人于孔子。孔子与之坐而问焉，曰："夫子何为？"对曰："夫子欲寡其过而未能也。"

使者出。子曰："使乎！使乎！"

14.26　子曰："不在其位，不谋其政。"

曾子曰："君子思不出其位。"

14.27　子曰："君子耻其言而过其行。"

14.28　子曰："君子道者三，我无能焉：仁者不忧，知者不惑，勇者不惧。"子贡曰："夫子自道也。"

14.29　子贡方人。子曰："赐也贤乎哉？夫我则不暇。"

14.30　子曰："不患人之不己知，患其不能也。"

14.31　子曰："不逆诈，不亿不信，抑亦先觉者，是贤乎！"

【今译】

14.25　蘧伯玉派一位使者访问孔子。孔子给他坐位，而后问道："他老人家干些什么？"使者答道："他老人家想减少过错却还没能做到。"

使者辞了出来。孔子道："好一位使者！好一位使者！"

14.26　见泰伯篇第八。

曾子说："君子所思虑的不超出自己的工作岗位。"

14.27　孔子说："说得多，做得少，君子以为耻。"

14.28　孔子说："君子所行的三件事，我一件也没能做到：仁德的人不忧虑，智慧的人不迷惑，勇敢的人不惧怕。"子贡道："这正是他老人家对自己的叙述哩。"

14.29　子贡讥评别人。孔子对他道："你就够好了吗？我却没有这闲工夫。"

14.30　孔子说："不着急别人不知道我，只着急自己没有能力。"

14.31　孔子说："不预先怀疑别人的欺诈，也不无根据地猜测别人的不老实，却能及早发觉，这样的人是一位贤者吧！"

14.26 Qu Boyu[32] sent a messenger to Master Kong. Master Kong bade the man be seated and asked of him saying, "What is your master doing?" He replied, saying, "My master is trying to diminish the number of his failings;[33] but he has not hitherto been successful." When the messenger had gone away, the Master said, "What a messenger, what a messenger!"

14.27, 14.28 When the Master said, "He who holds no rank in a State does not discuss its policies," Master Zeng said, "A true gentleman, even in his thoughts, never departs from what is suitable to his rank."[34]

14.29 The Master said, "A gentleman is ashamed to let his words outrun his deeds."

14.30 The Master said, "The Ways of the true gentleman are three. I myself have met with success in none of them. For he that is really Good is never unhappy, he that is really wise is never perplexed, he that is really brave is never afraid." Zigong said, "That, Master, is your own Way[35]!"

14.31 Zigong was always criticizing other people. The Master said, "It is fortunate for Ci that he is so perfect himself as to have time to spare for this. I myself have none."

14.32 The Master said, "(A gentleman) Does not grieve that people do not recognize his merits; he grieves at his own incapacities."

14.33 The Master said, "Is it the man who 'does not count beforehand upon the falsity of others nor reckon upon promises not being kept,' or

【原文】

14.32　微生亩谓孔子曰:“丘何为是栖栖者与?无乃为佞乎?”孔子曰:“非敢为佞也，疾固也。”

14.33　子曰:“骥不称其力，称其德也。”

14.34　或曰:“以德报怨，何如?”子曰:“何以报德?以直报怨，以德报德。”

14.35　子曰:“莫我知也夫!”子贡曰:“何为其莫知子也?”子曰:“不怨天，不尤人，下学而上达。知我者其天乎!”

14.36　公伯寮愬子路于季孙。子服景伯以告，曰:“夫子固有惑志于公伯寮，吾力犹能肆诸市朝。”

子曰:“道之将行也与，命也；道之将废也与，命也。公伯寮其如命何!”

【今译】

14.32　微生亩对孔子道:“你为什么这样忙忙碌碌的呢?不是要逞你的口才么?”孔子道:“我不是敢逞口才，而是讨厌那种顽固不通的人。”

14.33　孔子说:“称千里马叫做骥，并不是赞美它的气力，而是赞美他的品质。”

14.34　有人对孔子道:“拿恩惠来报答怨恨，怎么样?”孔子道:“拿什么来酬答恩惠呢?拿公平正直来报答怨恨，拿恩惠来酬答恩惠。”

14.35　孔子叹道:“没有人知道我呀!”子贡道:“为什么没有人知道您呢?”孔子道:“不怨恨天，不责备人，学习一些平常的知识，却透彻了解很高的道理。知道我的，只是天吧!”

14.36　公伯寮向季孙毁谤子路。子服景伯告诉孔子，并且说:“他老人家已经被公伯寮所迷惑了，可是我的力量还能把他的尸首在街头示众。”

孔子道:“我的主张将实现吗，听之于命运；我的主张将永不实现吗，也听之于命运。公伯寮能把我的命运怎样呢!”

he who is conscious beforehand of deceit, that is the true sage?"[36]

14.34 Weisheng Mu said to Master Kong, "Qiu,[37] what is your object in going round perching now here, now there? Is it not simply to show off the fact that you are a clever talker?" Master Kong said, "I have no desire to be thought a clever talker; but I do not approve of obstinacy."[38]

14.35 The Master said, "The horse Ji[39] was not famed for its strength but for its inner qualities(*de*)."

14.36 Someone said, "What about the saying 'Meet resentment with inner power(*de*)'?"[40] The Master said, "In that case, how is one to meet inner power? Rather, meet resentment with upright dealing and meet inner power with inner power."

14.37 The Master said, "The truth is, no one knows me!"[41] Zigong said, "What is the reason that you are not known?" The Master said, "I do not 'accuse Heaven, nor do I lay the blame on men.'

"But the studies[42] of men here below are felt on high, and perhaps after all I am known; not here, but in Heaven!"

14.38 Gongbo Liao spoke against Zilu to the Ji Family. Zifu Jingbo[43] informed the Master saying, "I fear my master's[44] mind has been greatly unsettled by this. But in the case of Gongbo Liao, I believe my influence is still great enough to have his carcase exposed in the market-place."The Master said, "If it is the will of Heaven that the Way shall prevail, then the Way will prevail. But if it is the will of Heaven that the Way should perish, then it must perish. What can Gongbo Liao do against Heaven's

【原文】

14.37　子曰："贤者辟世，其次辟地，其次辟色，其次辟言。"

子曰："作者七人矣。"

14.38　子路宿于石门。晨门曰："奚自？"子路曰："自孔氏。"曰："是知其不可而为之者与？"

14.39　子击磬于卫，有荷蒉而过孔氏之门者，曰："有心哉，击磬乎！"既而曰："鄙哉！硁硁乎！莫己知也，斯己而已矣。深则厉，浅则揭。"

子曰："果哉！末之难矣。"

14.40　子张曰："《书》云：'高宗谅阴，三年不言。'何谓也？"子曰："何必高宗，古之人皆然。君薨，百官总己以听于冢宰三年。"

【今译】

14.37　孔子说："有些贤者逃避恶浊社会而隐居，次一等的择地而处，再次一等的避免不好的脸色，再次一等的回避恶言。"

孔子又说："像这样的人已经有七位了。"

14.38　子路在石门住了一宵，[第二天清早进城，]司门者道："从哪儿来？"子路道："从孔家来。"司门者道："就是那位知道做不到却定要去做的人吗？"

14.39　孔子在卫国，一天正敲着磬，有一个挑着草筐子的汉子恰在门前走过，便说道："这个敲磬是有深意的呀！"等一会又说道："磬声硁硁的，可鄙呀！[它好像在说，没有人知道我呀！]没有人知道自己，这就罢休好了。水深，索性连衣裳走过去；水浅，无妨撩起衣裳走过去。"

孔子道："好坚决！没有办法说服他了。"

14.40　子张道："《尚书》说：'殷高宗守孝，住在凶庐，三年不言语。'这是什么意思？"孔子道："不仅仅高宗，古人都是这样：国君死了，继承的君王三年不问政治，各部门的官员听命于宰相。"

will?"

14.39 The Master said, "Best of all, to withdraw from one's generation; next to withdraw to another land; next to leave because of a look; next best to leave because of a word."[45]

14.40 The Master said, "The makers[46] were seven…"

14.41 Zilu was spending the night at the Stone Gates.[47] The gate-keeper said, "Where are you from?" Zilu said, "From Master Kong's." The man said, "He's the one who 'knows it's no use, but keeps on doing it,' is that not so?"

14.42 The Master was playing the stone-chimes, during the time when he was in Wei. A man carrying a basket passed the house where he and his disciples had established themselves. He said, "How passionately he beats his chimes!" When the tune was over, he said, "How petty and small-minded! A man whose talents no one recognizes has but one course open to him — to mind his own business! 'If the water is deep, use the stepping-stones; if it is shallow, then hold up your skirts.'"[48] The Master said, "That is indeed[49] an easy way out!"

14.43 Zizhang said, "The *Books* says, 'When Gao Zong was in the Shed of Constancy[50], he did not speak for three years.' What does this mean?" The Master said, "Not Gao Zong in particular. All the men of old did this. Whenever a prince died, the ministers (of the last prince) all continued in their offices, taking their orders from the Prime Minister; and this lasted for three years."

【原文】

14.41 子曰:“上好礼，则民易使也。”

14.42 子路问君子。子曰:“修己以敬。”

曰:“如斯而已乎?”曰: “修己以安人。”

曰:“如斯而已乎?”曰:“修己以安百姓。修己以安百姓，尧舜其犹病诸?”

14.43 原壤夷俟。子曰:“幼而不孙悌，长而无述焉，老而不死，是为贼。”以杖叩其胫。

14.44 阙党童子将命。或问之曰:“益者与?”子曰:“吾见其居于位也，见其与先生并行也。非求益者也，欲速成者也。”

【今译】

14.41 孔子说:“在上位的人若遇事依礼而行，就容易使百姓听从指挥。”

14.42 子路问怎样才能算是一个君子。孔子道:“修养自己来严肃认真地对待工作。”

子路道:“这样就够了吗?”孔子道:“修养自己来使上层人物安乐。”

子路道:“这样就够了吗?”孔子道:“修养自己来使所有老百姓安乐。修养自己来使所有老百姓安乐，尧舜大概还没有完全做到哩!”

14.43 原壤两腿像八字一样张开坐在地上，等着孔子。孔子骂道:“你幼小时候不懂礼节，长大了毫无贡献，老了还白吃粮食，真是个害人精。”说完，用拐杖敲了敲他的小腿。

14.44 阙党的一个童子来向孔子传达信息。有人问孔子道:“这小孩是肯求上进的人吗?”孔子道:“我看见他[大模大样地]坐在位上，又看见他同长辈并肩而行。这不是个肯求上进的人，只是一个想走捷径的人。”

14.44 The Master said, "So long as the ruler loves ritual,[51] the people will be easy to handle."

14.45 Zilu asked about the qualities of a true gentleman. The Master said, "He cultivates in himself the capacity to be diligent in his tasks." Zilu said, "Can he not go further than that?" The Master said, "He cultivates in himself the capacity to ease the lot of other people[52]." Zilu said, "Can he not go further than that?" The Master said, "He cultivates in himself the capacity to ease the lot of the whole populace. If he can do that, could even Yao or Shun find cause to criticize him?"

14.46 Yuan Rang sat waiting for the Master in a sprawling position.[53] The Master said, "Those who when young show no respect to their elders achieve nothing worth mentioning when they grow up. And merely to live on, getting older and older, is to be a useless pest."

And he struck him across the shins with his stick.

14.47 A boy from the village of Que used to come with messages. Someone asked about him, saying, "Is he improving himself [54]?" The Master said, "Judging by the way he sits in grown-up people's places and walks alongside of people older than himself, I should say he was bent upon getting on quickly rather than upon improving himself."

卫灵公篇第十五

【原文】

15.1　卫灵公问陈于孔子。孔子对曰:“俎豆之事，则尝闻之矣；军旅之事，未之学也。”明日遂行。

15.2　在陈绝粮，从者病，莫能兴。子路愠见曰:“君子亦有穷乎?”子曰:“君子固穷，小人穷斯滥矣。”

15.3　子曰:“赐也，女以予为多学而识之者与?”对曰:“然。非与?”曰:“非也，予一以贯之。”

15.4　子曰:“由!知德者鲜矣。”

15.5　子曰:“无为而治者其舜也与?夫何为哉?恭己正南面而已矣。”

15.6　子张问行。子曰:“言忠信，行笃敬，虽蛮貊之邦，行矣。

【今译】

15.1　卫灵公向孔子问军队陈列之法。孔子答道:“礼仪的事情，我曾经听到过；军队的事情，从来没有学过。”第二天便离开卫国。

15.2　孔子在陈国断绝了粮食，跟随的人都饿病了，爬不起床来。子路很不高兴地来见孔子，说道:“君子也有穷得毫无办法的时候吗?”孔子道:“君子虽然穷，还是坚持着；小人一穷便无所不为了。”

15.3　孔子道:“赐!你以为我是多多地学习又能够记得住的吗?”子贡答道:“对呀，难道不是这样吗?”孔子道:“不是的，我有一个基本观念来贯串它。”

15.4　孔子对子路道:“由!懂得‘德’的人可少啦。”

15.5　孔子说:“自己从容安静而使天下太平的人大概只有舜吧?他干了什么呢?庄严端正地坐朝廷罢了。”

15.6　子张问如何才能使自己到处行得通。孔子道:“言语忠诚老实，行为忠厚严肃，纵到了别的部族国家，也行得通。言语欺诈无

BOOK XV

15.1 Duke Ling of Wei asked Master Kong about the marshalling of troops. Master Kong replied saying, "About the ordering of ritual vessels I have some knowledge; but warfare is a thing I have never studied." Next day he resumed his travels. In Chen supplies fell short and his followers became so weak that they could not drag themselves on to their feet. Zilu came to the Master and said indignantly, "Is it right that even gentlemen should be reduced to such straits?" The Master said, "A gentleman can withstand hardships; it is only the small man who, when submitted to them, is swept off his feet[1]."

15.2 The Master said, "Ci,[2] I believe you look upon me as one whose aim is simply to learn and retain in mind as many things as possible." He replied, "That is what I thought. Is it not so?" The Master said, "No; I have one (thread) upon which I string them all."

15.3 The Master said, "You,[3] those who understand moral force (*de*) are few."

15.4 The Master said, "Among those that 'ruled by inactivity'[4] surely Shun may be counted. For what action did he take? He merely placed himself gravely and reverently with his face due south; that was all."

15.5 Zizhang asked about getting on with people. The Master said, "Be loyal and true to your every word, serious and careful in all you do; and you will get on well enough, even though you find yourself among barbar-

【原文】

言不忠信，行不笃敬，虽州里，行乎哉？立则见其参于前也，在舆则见其倚于衡也，夫然后行。”子张书诸绅。

15.7　子曰：“直哉史鱼！邦有道，如矢；邦无道，如矢。君子哉蘧伯玉！邦有道，则仕；邦无道，则可卷而怀之。”

15.8　子曰：“可与言而不与之言，失人；不可与言而与之言，失言。知者不失人，亦不失言。”

15.9　子曰：“志士仁人，无求生以害仁，有杀身以成仁。”

15.10　子贡问为仁。子曰：“工欲善其事，必先利其器。居是邦

【今译】

信，行为刻薄轻浮，就是在本乡本土，能行得通吗？站立的时候，就[仿佛]看见‘忠诚老实忠厚严肃’几个字在我们面前；在车箱里，也[仿佛]看见它刻在前面的横木上；[时时刻刻记着它，]这才能使自己到处行得通。”子张把这些话写在大带上。

15.7　孔子说：“好一个刚直不屈的史鱼！政治清明也像箭一样直，政治黑暗也像箭一样直。好一个君子蘧伯玉！政治清明就出来做官，政治黑暗就可以把自己的本领收藏起来。”

15.8　孔子说：“可以同他谈，却不同他谈，这是错过人才；不可以同他谈，却同他谈，这是浪费言语。聪明人既不错过人才，也不浪费言语。”

15.9　孔子说：“志士仁人，不贪生怕死因而损害仁德，只勇于牺牲来成全仁德。”

15.10　子贡问怎样去培养仁德。孔子道：“工人要搞好他的工作，一定先要搞好他的工具。我们住在一个国家，就要敬奉那些大官

ians. But if you are disloyal and untrustworthy in your speech, frivolous and careless in your acts, even though you are among your own neighbours, how can you hope to get on well? When standing,[5] see these principles ranged before you; in your carriage, see them resting on the yoke. Then you may be sure that you will get on." Zizhang accordingly inscribed the maxim upon his sash.

15.6 The Master said, "Straight and upright indeed was the recorder Yu![6] When the Way prevailed in the land he was (straight) as an arrow; when the Way ceased to prevail, he was (straight) as an arrow. A gentleman indeed is Qu Boyu.[7] When the Way prevailed in his land, he served the State; but when the Way ceased to prevail, he knew how to 'wrap it[8] up and hide it in the folds of his dress.'"

15.7 The Master said, "Not to talk to[9] one who could be talked to, is to waste a man. To talk to those who cannot be talked to, is to waste one's words. 'He who is truly wise never wastes a man'; but on the other hand, he never wastes his words."

15.8 The Master said, "Neither the knight who has truly the heart of a knight nor the man of good stock who has the qualities that belong to good stock[10] will ever seek life at the expense of Goodness; and it may be that he has to give his life in order to achieve Goodness."

15.9 Zigong asked how to become Good. The Master said, "A craftsman, if he means to do good work, must first sharpen his tools. In whatever State you dwell

【原文】

也，事其大夫之贤者，友其士之仁者。”

15.11　颜渊问为邦。子曰：“行夏之时，乘殷之辂，服周之冕，乐则《韶》《舞》。放郑声，远佞人。郑声淫，佞人殆。”

15.12　子曰：“人无远虑，必有近忧。”

15.13　子曰：“已矣乎！吾未见好德如好色者也。”

15.14　子曰：“臧文仲其窃位者与！知柳下惠之贤而不与立也。”

15.15　子曰：“躬自厚而薄责于人，则远怨矣。”

15.16　子曰：“不曰‘如之何，如之何’者，吾末如之何也已矣。”

【今译】

中的贤人，结交那些士人中的仁人。”

15.11　颜渊问怎样去治理国家。孔子道：“用夏朝的历法，坐殷朝的车子，戴周朝的礼帽，音乐就用《韶》和《武》。舍弃郑国的乐曲，斥退小人。郑国的乐曲靡曼淫秽，小人危险。”

15.12　孔子说：“一个人没有长远的考虑，一定会有眼前的忧患。”

15.13　孔子说：“完了吧！我从没见过像喜欢美貌一般地喜欢美德的人哩！”

15.14　孔子说：“臧文仲大概是个做官不管事的人，他明知柳下惠贤良，却不给他官位。”

15.15　孔子说：“多责备自己，而少责备别人，怨恨自然不会来了。”

15.16　孔子说：“[一个人]不想想‘怎么办，怎么办’的，对这种人，我也不知道怎么办了。”

Take service with such of its officers as are
worthy,
Make friends with such of its knights as are
Good."

15.10 Yan Hui asked about the making of a State. The Master said, "One would go by the seasons of Xia;[11] as State-coach for the ruler one would use that of Yin,[12] and as head-gear of ceremony wear the Zhou hat.[13] For music one would take as model the Succession Dance, and would do away altogether with the tunes of Zheng[14]; one would also keep clever talkers at a distance. For the tunes of Zheng are licentious and clever talkers are dangerous."

15.11 The Master said, "He who will not worry about what is far off will soon find something worse than worry close at hand."

15.12 The Master said, "In vain have I looked for one whose desire to build up his moral power was as strong as sexual desire."

15.13 The Master said, "Surely one would not be wrong in calling Zang Wenzhong a stealer of other men's ranks? He knew that Liuxia Hui was the best man for the post, yet would not have him as his colleague."

15.14 The Master said, "To demand much from oneself and little from others is the way (for a ruler) to banish discontent."

15.15 The Master said, "If a man does not continually ask himself 'What am I to do about this, what am I to do about this?' there is no possibility

【原文】

15.17 子曰:“群居终日,言不及义,好行小慧,难矣哉!”

15.18 子曰:“君子义以为质,礼以行之,孙以出之,信以成之。君子哉!”

15.19 子曰:“君子病无能焉,不病人之不己知也。”

15.20 子曰:“君子疾没世而名不称焉。”

15.21 子曰:“君子求诸己,小人求诸人。”

15.22 子曰:“君子矜而不争,群而不党。”

15.23 子曰:“君子不以言举人,不以人废言。”

【今译】

15.17 孔子说:“同大家整天在一块,不说一句有道理的话,只喜欢卖弄小聪明,这种人真难教导!”

15.18 孔子说:“君子[对于事业],以合宜为原则,依礼节实行它,用谦逊的言语说出它,用诚实的态度完成它。真个是位君子呀!”

15.19 孔子说:“君子只惭愧自己没有能力,不怨恨别人不知道自己。”

15.20 孔子说:“到死而名声不被人家称述,君子引以为恨。”

15.21 孔子说:“君子要求自己,小人要求别人。”

15.22 孔子说:“君子庄矜而不争执,合群而不闹宗派。”

15.23 孔子说:“君子不因为人家一句话[说得好]便提拔他,不因为他是坏人而鄙弃他的好话。”

of my doing anything about him."

15.16 The master said, "Those who are capable of spending a whole day together without ever once discussing questions of right or wrong, but who content themselves with performing petty acts of clemency, are indeed difficult[15]."

15.17 The Master said, "The gentleman who takes the right as his material to work upon and ritual as the guide in putting what is right into practice, who is modest in setting out his projects and faithful in carrying them to their conclusion, he indeed is a true gentleman."

15.18 The Master said, "A gentleman is distressed by his own lack of capacity; he is never distressed at the failure of others to recognize his merits."

15.19 The Master said, "A gentleman has reason to be distressed if he ends his days without making a reputation for himself."[16]

15.20 The Master said, "The demands that a gentleman makes are upon himself; those that a small man makes are upon others."[17]

15.21 The Master said, "A gentleman is proud, but not quarrelsome, allies himself with individuals, but not with parties."

15.22 The Master said, "A gentleman does not

Accept men because of what they say,

【原文】

15.24 子贡问曰:"有一言而可以终身行之者乎?"子曰:"其'恕'乎!己所不欲,勿施于人。"

15.25 子曰:"吾之于人也,谁毁谁誉?如有所誉者,其有所试矣。斯民也,三代之所以直道而行也。"

15.26 子曰:"吾犹及史之阙文也。有马者借人乘之,今亡矣夫!"

15.27 子曰:"巧言乱德。小不忍,则乱大谋。"

15.28 子曰:"众恶之,必察焉;众好之,必察焉。"

15.29 子曰:"人能弘道,非道弘人。"

15.30 子曰:"过而不改,是谓过矣。"

【今译】

15.24 子贡问道:"有没有一句可以终身奉行的话呢?"孔子道:"大概是'恕'吧!自己所不想要的任何事物,就不要加给别人。"

15.25 孔子说:"我对于别人,诋毁了谁?称赞了谁?假若我有所称赞,必然是曾经考验过他的。夏、商、周三代的人都如此,所以三代能直道而行。"

15.26 孔子说:"我还能够看到史书存疑的地方。有马的人[自己不会训练,]先给别人使用,这种精神,今天也没有了吧!"

15.27 孔子说:"花言巧语足以败坏道德。小事情不忍耐,便会败坏大事情。"

15.28 孔子说:"大家厌恶他,一定要去考察;大家喜爱他,也一定要去考察。"

15.29 孔子说:"人能够把道廓大,不是用道来廓大人。"

15.30 孔子说:"有错误而不改正,那个错误便真叫做错误了。"

Nor reject sayings, because the speaker is
what he is."

15.23 Zigong asked saying, "Is there any single saying that one can act upon all day and every day? " The Master said, "Perhaps the saying about consideration: 'Never do to others what you would not like them to do to you.'"

15.24 The Master said, "In speaking of the men of the day I have always refrained from praise and blame alike. But if there is indeed anyone whom I have praised, there is a means by which he may be tested. For the common people here round us are just such stuff as the three dynasties[18] worked upon in the days when they followed the Straight Way."

15.25 The Master said, "I can still remember the days when a scribe left blank spaces[19], and when someone using a horse (for the first time) hired a man to drive it.[20] But that is all over now!"

15.26 The Master said, "Clever talk can confound the workings of moral force, just as small impatiences can confound great projects."

15.27 The Master said, "When everyone dislikes a man, enquiry is necessary; when everyone likes a man, enquiry is necessary."

15.28 The Master said, "A man can enlarge his Way; but there is no Way that can enlarge a man[21]."

15.29 The Master said, "To have faults and to be making no effort to

【原文】

15.31　子曰:“吾尝终日不食，终夜不寝，以思，无益，不如学也。”

15.32　子曰:“君子谋道不谋食。耕也，馁在其中矣；学也，禄在其中矣。君子忧道不忧贫。”

15.33　子曰:“知及之，仁不能守之；虽得之，必失之。知及之，仁能守之。不庄以涖之，则民不敬。知及之，仁能守之，庄以涖之，动之不以礼，未善也。”

15.34　子曰:“君子不可小知而可大受也，小人不可大受而可小知也。”

15.35　子曰:“民之于仁也，甚于水火。水火，吾见蹈而死者

【今译】

15.31　孔子说:“我曾经整天不吃，整晚不睡，去想，没有益处，不如去学习。”

15.32　孔子说:“君子用心力于学术，不用心力于衣食。耕田，也常常饿着肚皮；学习，常常得到俸禄。君子只着急得不到道，不着急得不到财。”

15.33　孔子说:“聪明才智足以得到它，仁德不能保持它；就是得到，一定会丧失。聪明才智足以得到它，仁德能保持它，不用严肃态度来治理百姓，百姓也不会认真[地生活和工作]。聪明才智足以得到它，仁德能保持它，能用严肃的态度来治理百姓，假若不合理合法地动员百姓，是不够好的。”

15.34　孔子道:“君子不可以用小事情考验他，却可以接受重大任务；小人不可以接受重大任务，却可以用小事情考验他。”

15.35　孔子说:“百姓需要仁德，更急于需要水火。往水火里去，

amend them is to have faults indeed!"[22]

15.30 The Master said, "I once spent a whole day without food and a whole night without sleep, in order to meditate. It was no use. It is better to learn."[23]

15.31 The Master said, "A gentleman, in his plans, thinks of the Way; he does not think how he is going to make a living. Even farming sometimes entails times of shortage; and even learning may incidentally lead to high pay. But a gentleman's anxieties concern the progress of the Way; he has no anxiety concerning poverty."

15.32 The Master said, "He whose wisdom brings him into power, needs Goodness to secure that power. Else, though he get it, he will certainly lose it. He whose wisdom brings him into power and who has Goodness whereby to secure that power, if he has not dignity wherewith to approach the common people, they will not respect him. He whose wisdom has brought him into power, who has Goodness whereby to secure that power and dignity wherewith to approach the common people, if he handle them contrary to the prescriptions of ritual, is still a bad ruler."[24]

15.33 The Master said, "It is wrong for a gentleman to have knowledge of menial matters[25] and proper that he should be entrusted with great responsibilities. It is wrong for a small man to be entrusted with great responsibilities, but proper that he should have a knowledge of menial matters."

15.34 The Master said, "Goodness is more to the people than water and fire. I have seen men lose their lives when 'treading upon' water and fire; but

【原文】

矣，未见蹈仁而死者也。”

15.36　子曰：“当仁，不让于师。”

15.37　子曰：“君子贞而不谅。”

15.38　子曰：“事君，敬其事而后其食。”

15.39　子曰：“有教无类。”

15.40　子曰：“道不同，不相为谋。”

15.41　子曰：“辞达而已矣。”

15.42　师冕见，及阶，子曰：“阶也。”及席，子曰：“席也。”皆坐，子告之曰：“某在斯，某在斯。”

师冕出。子张问曰：“与师言之道与？”子曰：“然；固相师之道也。”

【今译】

我看见因而死了的，却从没有看见践履仁德因而死了的。”

15.36　孔子说：“面临着仁德，就是老师，也不同他谦让。”

15.37　孔子说：“君子讲大信，却不讲小信。”

15.38　孔子说：“对待君上，认真工作，把拿俸禄的事放在后面。”

15.39　孔子说：“人人我都教育，没有[贫富、地域等等]区别。”

15.40　孔子说：“主张不同，不互相商议。”

15.41　孔子说：“言辞，足以达意便罢了。”

15.42　师冕来见孔子，走到阶沿，孔子道：“这是阶沿啦。”走到坐席旁，孔子道：“这是坐席啦。”都坐定了，孔子告诉他说：“某人在这里，某人在这里。”

师冕辞了出来。子张问道：“这是同瞎子讲话的方式吗？”孔子道：“对的；这本来是帮助瞎子的方式。”

I have never seen anyone lose his life through 'treading upon' Goodness."[26]

15.35 The Master said, "When it comes to Goodness one need not avoid competing with one's teacher."

15.36 The Master said, "From a gentleman consistency is expected, but not blind fidelity."

15.37 The Master said, "In serving one's prince one should be

Intent upon the task,
Not bent upon the pay."

15.38 The Master said, "There is a difference[27] in instruction but none in kind."

15.39 The Master said, "With those who follow a different Way it is useless to take counsel."

15.40 The Master said, "In official speeches[28] all that matters is to get one's meaning through."

15.41 The Music-master Mian came to see him. When he reached the steps, the Master said, "Here are the steps."[29] When he reached the mat, the Master said, "Here is the mat." When everyone was seated the Master informed him saying, "So-and-so is here; so-and-so is there." When the Music-master Mian had gone, Zizhang asked saying, "Is that the recognized way to talk to a Music-master?" The Master said, "Yes, certainly it is the recognized way to help a Music-master."

季氏篇第十六

【原文】

16.1　季氏将伐颛臾。冉有、季路见于孔子曰:“季氏将有事于颛臾。”

孔子曰:“求!无乃尔是过与?夫颛臾，昔者先王以为东蒙主，且在邦域之中矣，是社稷之臣也。何以伐为?”

冉有曰:“夫子欲之，吾二臣者皆不欲也。”

孔子曰:“求!周任有言曰:‘陈力就列，不能者止。’危而不持，颠而不扶，则将焉用彼相矣?且尔言过矣，虎兕出于柙，龟玉毁于椟中，是谁之过与?”

冉有曰:“今夫颛臾，固而近于费。今不取，后世必为子孙忧。”

孔子曰:“求!君子疾夫舍曰欲之而必为之辞。丘也闻有国有家

【今译】

16.1　季氏准备攻打颛臾。冉有、子路两人谒见孔子，说道:“季氏准备对颛臾使用兵力。”

孔子道:“冉求!这难道不应该责备你吗?颛臾，上代的君王曾经授权他主持东蒙山的祭祀，而且它的国境早在我们最初被封时的疆土之中，这正是和鲁国共安危存亡的藩属，为什么要去攻打它呢?”

冉有道:“季孙要这么干，我们两人本来都是不同意的。”

孔子道:“冉求!周任有句话说:‘能够贡献自己的力量，这再任职;如果不行，就该辞职。’譬如瞎子遇到危险，不去扶持;将要摔倒了，不去搀扶，那又何必用助手呢?你的话是错了。老虎犀牛从槛里逃了出来，龟壳美玉在匣子里毁坏了，这是谁的责任呢?”

冉有道:“颛臾，城墙既然坚牢，而且离季孙的采邑费地很近。现今不把它占领，日子久了，一定会给子孙留下祸害。”

孔子道:“冉求!君子就讨厌[那种态度，]不说自己贪心无厌，却一定另找藉口。我听说过:无论是诸侯或者大夫，不必着急财富不多，

BOOK XVI

16.1 1The Head of the Ji Family decided to attack Zhuanyu[1]. 2Ran Qiu and Zilu[2] came to see Master Kong and said to him, "The Head of the Ji Family has decided to take steps with regard to Zhuanyu."3 Master Kong said, "Qiu, I fear you must be held responsible for this crime. 4 Zhuanyu was long ago appointed by the Former Kings[3] to preside over the sacrifices to Mount Dongmeng. Moreover, it lies within the boundaries of our State, and its ruler is a servant of our own Holy Ground and Millet. How can such an attack be justified?"

5 Ran Qiu said, "It is our employer who desires it. Neither of us two ministers desires it." 6 Master Kong said, "Qiu, among the sayings of Zhou Ren[4] there is one which runs:'He who can bring his powers into play steps into the ranks[5]; he who cannot, stays behind.' Of what use to anyone are such counsellors as you, who see your master tottering, but do not give him a hand, see him falling, but do not prop him up? 7 Moreover, your plea is a false one. For if a tiger or wild buffalo escapes from its cage or a precious ornament of tortoise-shell or jade gets broken in its box, whose fault is it[6]?"

8 Ran Qiu said, "The present situation is this: Zhuanyu is strongly fortified and is close to Mi[7]. If he does not take it now, in days to come it will certainly give trouble to his sons or grandsons." 9 Master Kong said, "Qiu, a true gentleman, having once denied that he is in favour of a course, thinks it wrong to make any attempt to condone that course. 10 Concerning the head of a State or Family I have heard the saying:

He is not concerned lest his people should

【原文】

者，不患寡而患不均，不患贫而患不安。盖均无贫，和无寡，安无倾。夫如是，故远人不服，则修文德以来之。既来之，则安之。今由与求也，相夫子，远人不服，而不能来也；邦分崩离析，而不能守也；而谋动干戈于邦内。吾恐季孙之忧，不在颛臾，而在萧墙之内也。”

16.2　孔子曰:“天下有道，则礼乐征伐自天子出；天下无道，则礼乐征伐自诸侯出。自诸侯出，盖十世希不失矣；自大夫出，五世希

【今译】

只须着急财富不均；不必着急人民太少，只须着急境内不安。若是财富平均，便无所谓贫穷；境内和平团结，便不会觉得人少；境内平安，便不会倾危。做到这样，远方的人还不归服，便再修仁义礼乐的政教来招致他们。他们来了，就得使他们安心。如今仲由和冉求两人辅相季孙，远方之人不归服，却不能招致；国家支离破碎，却不能保全；反而想在国境以内使用兵力。我恐怕季孙的忧愁不在颛臾，却在鲁君哩。”

16.2　孔子说:“天下太平，制礼作乐以及出兵都决定于天子；天下昏乱，制礼作乐以及出兵便决定于诸侯。决定于诸侯，大概传到十代，很少还能继续的；决定于大夫，传到五代，很少还能继续的；若

be poor,
But only lest what they have should be ill-apportioned.
He is not concerned lest they should be few,
But only lest they should be divided against one another.

And indeed, if all is well-apportioned, there will be no poverty; if they are not divided against one another, there will be no lack of men. 11If such a state of affairs exists, yet the people of far-off lands still do not submit, then the ruler must attract them by enhancing the prestige (*de*) of his culture; and when they have been duly attracted,[8] he contents them. And where there is contentment there will be no upheavals.

"12To-day with you two, You and Qiu, acting as counsellors to your master, the people of far lands do not submit to him, and he is not able to attract them. The State itself is divided and tottering, disrupted and cleft, but he can do nothing to save it and is now planning to wield buckler and axe within the borders of his own land. I am afraid that the troubles of the Ji Family are due not to what is happening in Zhuanyu, but to what is going on behind the screenwall of his own gate[9]."

16.2 Master Kong said, "When the Way prevails under Heaven all orders concerning ritual, music and punitive expeditions are issued by the Son of Heaven himself. When the Way does not prevail, such orders are issued by the feudal princes; and when this happens, it is to be observed that ten generations rarely pass before the dynasty falls. If such orders are issued by State Ministers, five generations rarely pass before they lose their power. When the retainers of great Houses seize a country's

【原文】

不失矣；陪臣执国命，三世希不失矣。天下有道，则政不在大夫。天下有道，则庶人不议。”

16.3　孔子曰：“禄之去公室五世矣，政逮于大夫四世矣，故夫三桓之子孙微矣。”

16.4　孔子曰：“益者三友，损者三友。友直，友谅，友多闻，益矣。友便辟，友善柔，友便佞，损矣。”

16.5　孔子曰：“益者三乐，损者三乐。乐节礼乐，乐道人之善，乐多贤友，益矣。乐骄乐，乐佚游，乐晏乐，损矣。”

16.6　孔子曰：“侍于君子有三愆：言未及之而言谓之躁，言及

【今译】

是大夫的家臣把持国家政权，传到三代，很少还能继续的。天下太平，国家的最高政治权力就不会掌握在大夫之手。天下太平，老百姓就不会议论纷纷。”

16.3　孔子说：“国家政权离开了鲁君，[从鲁君来说，]已经五代了；政权到了大夫之手，[从季氏来说，]已经四代了，所以桓公的三房子孙现在也衰微了。”

16.4　孔子说：“有益的朋友三种，有害的朋友三种。同正直的人交友，同信实的人交友，同见闻广博的人交友，便有益了。同谄媚奉承的人交友，同当面恭维背面毁谤的人交友，同夸夸其谈的人交友，便有害了。”

16.5　孔子说：“有益的快乐三种，有害的快乐三种。以得到礼乐的调节为快乐，以宣扬别人的好处为快乐，以交了不少有益的朋友为快乐，便有益了。以骄傲为快乐，以游荡忘返为快乐，以饮食荒淫为快乐，便有害了。”

16.6　孔子说：“陪着君子说话容易犯三种过失：没轮到他说话，

commission,[10] three generations rarely pass before they lose their power. When the Way prevails under Heaven, policy is not decided by Ministers; when the Way prevails under Heaven, commoners[11] do not discuss public affairs."

16.3 Master Kong said, "Power over the exchequer was lost by the Ducal House[12] five generations ago, and government has been in the hands of Ministers[13] for four generations. Small wonder that the descendants of the Three Huan[14] are fast losing their power!"

16.4 Master Kong said, "There are three sorts of friends that are profitable, and three sorts that are harmful. Friendship with the upright, with the true-to-death and with those who have heard much is profitable. Friendship with the obsequious, friendship with those who are good at accommodating their principles, friendship with those who are clever at talk is harmful."

16.5 Master Kong said, "There are three sorts of pleasure that are profitable, and three sorts of pleasure that are harmful. The pleasure got from the due ordering of ritual and music, the pleasure got from discussing the good points in the conduct of others, the pleasure of having many wise friends is profitable. But pleasure got from profligate enjoyments, pleasure got from idle gadding about, pleasure got from comfort and ease is harmful."

16.6 Master Kong said, "There are three mistakes that are liable to be made when waiting upon a gentleman. To speak before being called upon to do so;this is called forwardness. Not to speak when called upon to do

【原文】

之而不言谓之隐，未见颜色而言谓之瞽。”

16.7　孔子曰：“君子有三戒：少之时，血气未定，戒之在色；及其壮也，血气方刚，戒之在斗；及其老也，血气既衰，戒之在得。”

16.8　孔子曰：“君子有三畏：畏天命，畏大人，畏圣人之言。小人不知天命而不畏也，狎大人，侮圣人之言。”

16.9　孔子曰：“生而知之者上也，学而知之者次也；困而学之，又其次也；困而不学，民斯为下矣。”

16.10　孔子曰：“君子有九思：视思明，听思聪，色思温，貌思恭，言思忠，事思敬，疑思问，忿思难，见得思义。”

【今译】

却先说，叫做急躁；该说话了，却不说，叫做隐瞒；不看看君子的脸色便贸然开口，叫做瞎眼睛。”

16.7　孔子说：“君子有三件事情应该警惕戒备：年轻的时候，血气未定，便要警戒，莫迷恋女色；等到壮大了，血气正旺盛，便要警戒，莫好胜喜斗；等到年老了，血气已经衰弱，便要警戒，莫贪求无厌。”

16.8　孔子说：“君子害怕的有三件事：怕天命，怕王公大人，怕圣人的言语。小人不懂得天命，因而不怕它；轻视王公大人，轻侮圣人的言语。”

16.9　孔子说：“生来就知道的是上等，学习然后知道的是次一等；实践中遇见困难，再去学它，又是再次一等；遇见困难而不学，老百姓就是这种最下等的了。”

16.10　孔子说：“君子有九种考虑：看的时候，考虑看明白了没有；听的时候，考虑听清楚了没有；脸上的颜色，考虑温和么；容貌态度，考虑庄矜么；说的言语，考虑忠诚老实么；对待工作，考虑严肃认真么；遇到疑问，考虑怎样向人家请教；将发怒了，考虑有什么后患；看见可得的，考虑是否应该得。”

so; this is called secretiveness. To speak without first noting the expression of his face; this is called 'blindness.'"

16.7 Master Kong said, "There are three things against which a gentleman is on his guard. In his youth, before his blood and vital humours have settled down, he is on his guard against lust. Having reached his prime, when the blood and vital humours have finally hardened, he is on his guard against strife. Having reached old age, when the blood and vital humours are already decaying, he is on his guard against avarice."

16.8 Master Kong said, "There are three things that a gentleman fears: he fears the will of Heaven, he fears great men, he fears the words of the Divine Sages. The small man does not know the will of Heaven and so does not fear it. He treats great men with contempt, and scoffs at the words of the Divine Sages."

16.9 Master Kong said, "Highest are those who are born wise. Next are those who become wise by learning. After them come those who have to toil painfully in order to acquire learning. Finally, to the lowest class of the common people belong those who toil painfully without ever managing to learn."

16.10 Master Kong said, "The gentleman has nine cares. In seeing he is careful to see clearly, in hearing he is careful to hear distinctly, in his looks he is careful to be kindly; in his manner to be respectful, in his words to be loyal, in his work to be diligent. When in doubt he is careful to ask for information; when angry he has a care for the consequences; and when he sees a chance of gain, he thinks carefully whether the pur-

【原文】

16.11　孔子曰:“见善如不及，见不善如探汤。吾见其人矣，吾闻其语矣。隐居以求其志，行义以达其道。吾闻其语矣，未见其人也。”

16.12　齐景公有马千驷，死之日，民无德而称焉。伯夷叔齐饿于首阳之下，民到于今称之。其斯之谓与?

16.13　陈亢问于伯鱼曰:“子亦有异闻乎?”

对曰:“未也。尝独立，鲤趋而过庭。曰:‘学《诗》乎?’对曰:‘未也。’‘不学《诗》，无以言。’鲤退而学《诗》。他日，又独立，鲤趋而过庭。曰:‘学礼乎?’对曰:‘未也。’‘不学礼，无以立。’鲤退而学礼。闻斯二者。”

陈亢退而喜曰:“问一得三:闻《诗》，闻礼，又闻君子之远其子也。”

【今译】

16.11　孔子说:“看见善良，努力追求，好像赶不上似的;遇见邪恶，使劲避开，好像将伸手到沸水里。我看见这样的人，也听过这样的话。避世隐居求保全他的意志，依义而行来贯彻他的主张。我听过这样的话，却没有见过这样的人。”

16.12　齐景公有马四千匹，死了以后，谁都不觉得他有什么好行为可以称述。伯夷、叔齐两人饿死在首阳山下，大家到现在还称颂他们。那就是这个意思吧!

16.13　陈亢向孔子的儿子伯鱼问道:“您在老师那儿，也得着与众不同的传授吗?”

答道:“没有。他曾经一个人站在庭中，我恭敬地走过。他问我道:‘学《诗》没有?’我道:‘没有。’他便道:‘不学《诗》就不会说话。’我退回便学《诗》。过了几天，他又一个人站在庭中，我又恭敬地走过。他问道:‘学礼没有?’我答:‘没有。’他道:‘不学礼，便没有立足社会的依据。’我退回便学礼。只听到这两件。”

陈亢回去非常高兴地道:“我问一件事，知道了三件事。知道《诗》，知道礼，又知道君子对他儿子的态度。”

suit of it would be consonant with the Right."

16.11, 16.12 Master Kong said, "'When they see what is good, they grasp at it as though they feared it would elude them. When they see what is not good, they test it cautiously, as though putting a finger into hot water.' I have heard this saying; I have even seen such men.'It is by dwelling in seclusion that they seek the fulfilment of their aims; it is by deeds of righteousness that they extend the influence of their Way.' I have heard this saying; but I have never seen such men. 'Duke Jing of Qi had a thousand teams of horses; but on the day of his death the people could think of no good deed for which to praise him.[15] Boyi and Shuqi starved at the foot of Mount Shouyang; yet the people sing their praises down to this very day.' Does not this saying illustrate the other[16]?"

16.13 Ziqin questioned Boyu[17] saying, "As his son[18] you must after all surely have heard something different from what the rest of us hear." Boyu replied saying, "No. Once when he was standing alone and I was hurrying [19] past him across the court-yard, he said, 'Have you studied the *Songs*?' I replied saying, 'No.' (He said) 'If you do not study the *Songs*, you will find yourself at a loss in conversation.' So I retired and studied the *Songs*. Another day he was again standing alone, and as I hurried across the courtyard, he said, 'Have you studied the rituals?' I replied saying, 'No.' (He said) 'If you do not study the rituals, you will find yourself at a loss how to take your stand[20].' So I retired and studied the rituals. These two things I heard from him."

Ziqin came away delighted, saying, "I asked about one point, but got information about three. I learnt about the *Songs*, about the rituals, and also learnt that a gentleman keeps his son at a distance."[21]

【原文】

16.14　邦君之妻，君称之曰夫人，夫人自称曰小童；邦人称之曰君夫人，称诸异邦曰寡小君；异邦人称之亦曰君夫人。

【今译】

16.14　国君的妻子，国君称她为夫人，她自称为小童；国内的人称她为君夫人，但对外国人便称她为寡小君；外国人也称她为君夫人。

16.14 The wife of the ruler of a State is referred to by the ruler as "That person." She refers to herself as "Little boy." The people of the country call her "That person of the prince's." When speaking of her to people of another State the ruler calls her "This lonely one's little prince." But people of another State likewise call her "That person of the prince's."[22]

阳货篇第十七

【原文】

17.1　阳货欲见孔子，孔子不见，归孔子豚。孔子时其亡也，而往拜之。遇诸涂。谓孔子曰："来！予与尔言。"曰："怀其宝而迷其邦，可谓仁乎？"曰："不可。——好从事而亟失时，可谓知乎？"曰："不可。——日月逝矣，岁不我与。"孔子曰："诺；吾将仕矣。"

17.2　子曰："性相近也，习相远也。"

17.3　子曰："唯上知与下愚不移。"

17.4　子之武城，闻弦歌之声。夫子莞尔而笑，曰："割鸡焉用牛刀？"

子游对曰："昔者偃也闻诸夫子曰：'君子学道则爱人，小人学道则易使也。'"

子曰："二三子！偃之言是也。前言戏之耳。"

【今译】

17.1　阳货想要孔子来拜会他，孔子不去，他便送孔子一个[蒸熟了的]小猪[使孔子到他家来道谢]。孔子探听他不在家的时候，去拜谢。两人在路上碰着了。他叫着孔子道："来！我同你说话。"[孔子走了过去。]他又道："自己有一身的本领，却听任着国家的事情糊里糊涂，可以叫做仁爱吗？"[孔子没吭声。]他便自己接口道："不可以；——一个人喜欢做官，却屡屡错过机会，可以叫做聪明吗？"[孔子仍然没吭声。]他又自己接口道："不可以；——时光一去，就不再回来了呀。"孔子这才说道："好吧；我打算做官了。"

17.2　孔子说："人性情本相近，因为习染不同，便相距悬远。"

17.3　孔子说："只有上等的智者和下等的愚人是改变不了的。"

17.4　孔子到了[子游做县长的]武城，听到了弹琴瑟唱诗歌的声音。孔子微微笑着，说道："宰鸡，何必用宰牛的刀？[治理这个小地方，用得着教育吗？]"

子游答道："以前我听老师说过，做官的学习了，就会有仁爱之心；老百姓学习了，就容易听指挥，听使唤。[教育总是有用的。]"

孔子便向学生们道："你们听着！言偃的这话是正确的。我刚才那句话不过同他开玩笑罢了。"

BOOK XVII

17.1 Yang Huo[1] wanted to see Master Kong; but Master Kong would not see him. He sent Master Kong a sucking pig. Master Kong, choosing a time when he knew Yang Huo would not be at home, went to tender acknowledgment; but met him in the road. He spoke to Master Kong, saying, "Come here, I have something to say to you." What he said was "Can one who hides his jewel[2] in his bosom and lets his country continue to go astray be called Good?" "Certainly not." "Can one who longs to take part in affairs, yet time after time misses the opportunity to do so—can such a one be called wise?" "Certainly not." "The days and months go by, the years do not wait upon our bidding." Master Kong said, "All right;[3] I am going to serve."

17.2 The Master said, "By nature, near together; by practice far apart."[4]

17.3 The Master said, "It is only the very wisest and the very stupidest who cannot change."

17.4 When the Master went to the walled town of Wu[5], he heard the sound of stringed instruments and singing. Our Master said with a gentle smile, "To kill a chicken one does not use an ox-cleaver."[6] Ziyou replied saying, "I remember once hearing you say, 'A gentleman who has studied the Way will be all the tenderer towards his fellow-men; a commoner who has studied the Way will be all the easier to employ.'" The Master said, "My disciples, what he says is quite true. What I said just now was only meant as a joke."

【原文】

17.5　公山弗扰以费畔，召，子欲往。

子路不说，曰:“末之也，已，何必公山氏之之也?”

子曰:“夫召我者，而岂徒哉?如有用我者，吾其为东周乎?”

17.6　子张问仁于孔子。孔子曰:“能行五者于天下为仁矣。”

“请问之。”曰:“恭，宽，信，敏，惠。恭则不侮，宽则得众，信则人任焉，敏则有功，惠则足以使人。”

17.7　佛肸召，子欲往。

子路曰:“昔者由也闻诸夫子曰:‘亲于其身为不善者，君子不入也。’佛肸以中牟畔，子之往也，如之何?”

子曰:“然。有是言也。不曰坚乎，磨而不磷；不曰白乎，涅而不缁。吾岂匏瓜也哉?焉能系而不食?”

17.8　子曰:“由也!女闻六言六蔽矣乎?”对曰:“未也。”

【今译】

17.5　公山弗扰盘踞在费邑图谋造反，叫孔子去，孔子准备去。

子路很不高兴，说道:“没有地方去便算了，为什么一定要去公山氏那里呢?”

孔子道:“那个叫我去的人，难道是白白召我吗?假若有人用我，我将使周文王武王之道在东方复兴。”

17.6　子张向孔子问仁。孔子道:“能够处处实行五种品德，便是仁人了。”

子张道:“请问哪五种。”孔子道:“庄重，宽厚，诚实，勤敏，慈惠。庄重就不致遭受侮辱，宽厚就会得到大众的拥护，诚实就会得到别人的任用，勤敏就会工作效率高、贡献大，慈惠就能够使唤人。”

17.7　佛肸叫孔子，孔子打算去。

子路道:“从前我听老师说过，‘亲自做坏事的人那里，君子是不去的。’如今佛肸盘踞中牟谋反，您却要去，怎么说得过去呢?”

孔子道:“对，我有过这话。但是，你不知道吗?最坚固的东西，磨也磨不薄；最白的东西，染也染不黑。我难道是匏瓜吗?哪里能够只是被悬挂着而不给人吃食呢?”

17.8　孔子说:“仲由!你听过有六种品德便会有六种弊病吗?”子路答道:“没有。”

17.5 Gongshan Furao,[7] when he was holding the castle of Mi in revolt (against the Ji Family), sent for the Master, who would have liked to go; but Zilu did not approve of this and said to the Master, "After having refused in so many cases, why go to Gongshan of all people?" The Master said, "It cannot be for nothing[8] that he has sent for me. If anyone were to use me, I believe I could make a 'Zhou in the east[9].'"

17.6 Zizhang asked Master Kong about Goodness. Master Kong said, "He who could put the Five into practice everywhere under Heaven would be Good." Zizhang begged to hear what these were. The Master said, "Courtesy, breadth, good faith, diligence and clemency. 'He who is courteous is not scorned, he who is broad wins the multitude, he who is of good faith is trusted by the people, he who is diligent succeeds in all he undertakes, he who is clement can get service from the people.'"[10]

17.7 Bi Xi[11] summoned the Master, and he would have liked to go. But Zilu said, "I remember your once saying, 'Into the house of one who is in his own person doing what is evil, the gentleman will not enter.' Bi Xi is holding Zhongmou[12] in revolt. How can you think of going to him?" The Master said, "It is true that there is such a saying. But is it not also said that there are things 'so hard that no grinding will ever wear them down,' that there are things 'so white that no steeping will ever make them black'? Am I indeed to be forever like the bitter gourd that is only fit to hang up,[13] but not to eat[14]?"

17.8 The Master said, "You, have you ever been told of the Six Sayings about the Six Degenerations?" Zilu replied, "No, never."(The Master

【原文】

“居！吾语女。好仁不好学，其蔽也愚；好知不好学，其蔽也荡；好信不好学，其蔽也贼；好直不好学，其蔽也绞；好勇不好学，其蔽也乱；好刚不好学，其蔽也狂。”

17.9　子曰：“小子何莫学夫诗？诗，可以兴，可以观，可以群，可以怨。迩之事父，远之事君；多识于鸟兽草木之名。”

17.10　子谓伯鱼曰：“女为《周南》、《召南》矣乎？人而不为《周南》、《召南》，其犹正墙面而立也与？”

17.11　子曰：“礼云礼云，玉帛云乎哉？乐云乐云，钟鼓云乎哉？”

17.12　子曰：“色厉而内荏，譬诸小人，其犹穿窬之盗也与？”

【今译】

孔子道：“坐下！我告诉你。爱仁德，却不爱学问，那种弊病就是容易被人愚弄；爱耍聪明，却不爱学问，那种弊病就是放荡而无基础；爱诚实，却不爱学问，那种弊病就是[容易被人利用，反而]害了自己；爱直率，却不爱学问，那种弊病就是说话尖刻，刺痛人心；爱勇敢，却不爱学问，那种弊病就是捣乱闯祸；爱刚强，却不爱学问，那种弊病就是胆大妄为。”

17.9　孔子说：“学生们为什么没有人研究诗？读诗，可以培养联想力，可以提高观察力，可以锻炼合群性，可以学得讽刺方法。近呢，可以运用其中道理来事奉父母；远呢，可以用来服事君上；而且可以多多认识鸟兽草木的名称。”

17.10　孔子对伯鱼说道：“你研究过《周南》和《召南》了吗？人假若不研究《周南》和《召南》，那会像面正对着墙壁而站着吧！”

17.11　孔子说：“礼呀礼呀，仅是指玉帛等等礼物而说的吗？乐呀乐呀，仅是指钟鼓等等乐器而说的吗？”

17.12　孔子说：“颜色严厉，内心怯弱，若用坏人作比喻，怕像个挖洞跳墙的小偷吧！”

said,) "Come, then; I will tell you. Love of Goodness without love of learning[15] degenerates into silliness. Love of wisdom without love of learning degenerates into utter lack of principle. Love of keeping promises without love of learning degenerates into villainy[16]. Love of uprightness without love of learning degenerates into harshness. Love of courage without love of learning degenerates into turbulence[17]. Love of courage without love of learning degenerates into mere recklessness."

17.9 The Master said, "Little ones, why is it that none of you study the *Songs*? For the *Songs* will help you to incite people's emotions, to observe their feelings, to keep company, to express your grievances. They may be used at home in the service of one's father; abroad, in the service of one's prince. Moreover, they will widen your acquaintance with the names[18] of birds, beasts, plants and trees."

17.10 The Master addressed Boyu saying, "Have you done the *Zhou Nan* and the *Shao Nan*[19] yet? He who has not even done the *Zhou Nan* and the *Shao Nan* is as though he stood with his face pressed against a wall!"

17.11 The Master said, "Ritual, ritual! Does it mean no more than presents of jade and silk? Music, music! Does it mean no more than bells and drums?"

17.12 The Master said, "To assume an outward air of fierceness when inwardly trembling is (to take a comparison from low walks of life) as dishonest as to sneak into places where one has no right to be, by boring a hole or climbing through a gap."

【原文】

17.13 子曰:“乡愿，德之贼也。”

17.14 子曰:“道听而涂说，德之弃也。”

17.15 子曰:“鄙夫可与事君也与哉?其未得之也，患得之。既得之，患失之。苟患失之，无所不至矣。”

17.16 子曰:“古者民有三疾，今也或是之亡也。古之狂也肆，今之狂也荡；古之矜也廉，今之矜也忿戾；古之愚也直，今之愚也诈而已矣。”

17.17 子曰:“巧言令色，鲜矣仁。”

17.18 子曰:“恶紫之夺朱也，恶郑声之乱雅乐也，恶利口之覆邦家者。”

17.19 子曰:“予欲无言。”子贡曰:“子如不言，则小子何述焉?”

【今译】

17.13 孔子说:“没有真是非的好好先生是足以败坏道德的小人。”

17.14 孔子说:“听到道路传言就四处传播，这是应该革除的作风。”

17.15 孔子说:“鄙夫，难道能同他共事吗?当他没有得到职位的时候，生怕得不着；已经得着了，又怕失去。假若生怕失去，会无所不用其极了。”

17.16 孔子说:“古代的人民还有三种[可贵的]毛病，现在呢，或许都没有了。古代的狂人肆意直言，现在的狂人便放荡无羁了；古代自己矜持的人还有些不能触犯的地方，现在自己矜持的人却只是一味老羞成怒，无理取闹罢了；古代的愚人还直率，现在的愚人却只是欺诈耍手段罢了。”

17.17 见学而篇第一。

17.18 孔子说:“紫色夺去了大红色的光彩和地位，可憎恶；郑国的乐曲破坏了典雅的乐曲，可憎恶；强嘴利舌颠覆国家，可憎恶。”

17.19 孔子说:“我想不说话了。”子贡道:“您假若不说话，那

17.13 The Master said, "The 'honest villager' spoils true virtue(*de*)."

17.14 The Master said, "To tell in the lane what you have heard on the highroad is to throw merit (*de*) away."

17.15 The Master said, "How could one ever possibly serve one's prince alongside of such low-down creatures? Before they have got office, they think about nothing but how to get it; and when they have got it, all they care about is to avoid losing it. And so soon as they see themselves in the slightest danger of losing it, there is no length to which they will not go."

17.16 In old days the common people had three faults, part[20] of which they have now lost. In old days the impetuous were merely impatient of small restraints; now they are utterly insubordinate. In old days the proud were stiff and formal; now they are touchy and quarrelsome. In old days simpletons were at any rate straightforward; but now "simple-mindedness" exists only as a device of the impostor.

17.17 The Master said, "Clever talk and a pretentious manner are seldom found in the Good."

17.18 The Master said, "I hate to see roan killing red, I hate to see the tunes of Zheng corrupting Court music, I hate to see sharp mouths over-turning kingdoms and clans."

17.19 The Master said, "I would much rather not have to talk." Zigong said, "If our Master did not talk, what should we little ones have to hand

【原文】

子曰："天何言哉?四时行焉，百物生焉，天何言哉?"

17.20　孺悲欲见孔子，孔子辞以疾。将命者出户，取瑟而歌，使之闻之。

17.21　宰我问："三年之丧，期已久矣。君子三年不为礼，礼必坏；三年不为乐，乐必崩。旧谷既没，新谷既升，钻燧改火，期可已矣。"

子曰："食夫稻，衣夫锦，于女安乎?"

曰："安。"

"女安，则为之!夫君子之居丧，食旨不甘，闻乐不乐，居处不安，故不为也。今女安，则为之!"

宰我出。子曰："予之不仁也!子生三年，然后免于父母之怀。夫三年之丧，天下之通丧也。予也有三年之爱于其父母乎!"

【今译】

我们传述什么呢?"孔子道："天说了什么呢?四季照样运行，百物照样生长，天说了什么呢?"

17.20　孺悲来，要会晤孔子，孔子托言有病，拒绝接待。传命的人刚出房门，孔子便把瑟拿下来弹，并且唱着歌，故意使孺悲听到。

17.21　宰我问道："父母死了，守孝三年，为期也太久了。君子有三年不去习礼仪，礼仪一定会废弃掉；三年不去奏音乐，音乐一定会失传。陈谷既已吃完了，新谷又已登场；打火用的燧木又经过了一个轮回，一年也就可以了。"

孔子道："[父母死了，不到三年，]你便吃那个白米饭，穿那个花缎衣，你心里安不安呢?"

宰我道："安。"

孔子便抢着道："你安，你就去干吧!君子的守孝，吃美味不晓得甜，听音乐不觉得快乐，住在家里不以为舒适，才不这样干。如今你既然觉得心安，便去干好了。"

宰我退了出来。孔子道："宰予真不仁呀!儿女生下地来，三年以后才能完全脱离父母的怀抱。替父母守孝三年，天下都是如此的。宰予难道就没有从他父母那里得着三年怀抱的爱护吗?"

down about him?" The Master said, "Heaven does not speak; yet the four seasons run their course thereby,[21] the hundred creatures, each after its kind, are born thereby. Heaven does no speaking!"

17.20 Ru Bei[22] wanted to see Master Kong. Master Kong excused himself on the ground of ill-health. But when the man who had brought the message was going out through the door he took up his zithern and sang, taking good care that the messenger should hear.

17.21 Zai Yu asked about the three years' mourning,[23] and said he thought a year would be quite long enough: "If gentlemen suspend their practice of the rites[24] for three years, the rites will certainly decay; if for three years they make no music, music will certainly be destroyed.[25] (In a year) The old crops have already vanished, the new crops have come up, the whirling drills have made new fire. Surely a year would be enough?"

The Master said, "Would you then (after a year) feel at ease in eating good rice and wearing silk brocades?" Zai Yu said, "Quite at ease." (The Master said,) "If you would really feel at ease, then do so. But when a true gentleman is in mourning, if he eats dainties, he does not relish them; if he hears music, it does not please him; if he sits in his ordinary seat, he is not comfortable. That is why he abstains from these things. But if you would really feel at ease, there is no need for you to abstain."

When Zai Yu had gone out, the Master said, "How inhuman[26] Yu is! Only when a child is three years old does it leave its parents' arms. The three years' mourning is the universal mourning everywhere under Heaven.[27] And Yu—was he not the darling of his father and mother for three years?"

【原文】

17.22 子曰:“饱食终日，无所用心，难矣哉!不有博弈者乎?为之，犹贤乎已。”

17.23 子路曰:“君子尚勇乎!”子曰:“君子义以为上，君子有勇而无义为乱，小人有勇而无义为盗。”

17.24 子贡曰:“君子亦有恶乎?”子曰:“有恶：恶称人之恶者，恶居下流而讪上者，恶勇而无礼者，恶果敢而窒者。”

曰:“赐也亦有恶乎?”“恶徼以为知者，恶不孙以为勇者，恶讦以为直者。”

17.25 子曰:“唯女子与小人为难养也，近之则不孙，远之则怨。”

17.26 子曰:“年四十而见恶焉，其终也已。”

【今译】

17.22 孔子说:“整天吃饱了饭，什么事也不做，不行的呀!不是有掷彩下弈的游戏吗?干干也比闲着好。”

17.23 子路问道:“君子尊贵勇敢不?”孔子道:“君子认为义是最可尊贵的，君子只有勇，没有义，就会捣乱造反；小人只有勇，没有义，就会做土匪强盗。”

17.24 子贡道:“君子也有憎恨的事吗?”孔子道:“有憎恨的事：憎恨一味传播别人的坏处的人，憎恨在下位而毁谤上级的人，憎恨勇敢却不懂礼节的人，憎恨勇于贯彻自己的主张，却顽固不通、执拗到底的人。”

孔子又道:“赐，你也有憎恶的事吗?”子贡随即答道:“我憎恨偷袭别人的成绩却作为自己的聪明的人，憎恨毫不谦虚却自以为勇敢的人，憎恨揭发别人阴私却自以为直率的人。”

17.25 孔子道:“只有女子和小人是难得同他们共处的，亲近了，他会无礼；疏远了，他会怨恨。”

17.26 孔子说:“到了四十岁还被厌恶，他这一生也就完了。”

17.22 The Master said, "Those who do nothing all day but cram themselves with food and never use their minds are difficult. Are there not games such as draughts? To play them would surely be better than doing nothing at all."

17.23 Zilu said, "Is courage to be prized by a gentleman?" The Master said, "A gentleman gives the first place to Right. If a gentleman has courage but neglects Right, he becomes turbulent. If a small man has courage but neglects Right, he becomes a thief."

17.24 Zigong said, "Surely even the gentleman must have his hatreds?" The Master said, "He has his hatreds. He hates those who point out what is hateful in others. He hates those who dwell in low estate[28] revile all who are above them. He hates those who love deeds of daring but neglect ritual. He hates those who are active and venturesome, but are violent in temper. I suppose you also have your hatreds?" Zigong said,[29] "I hate those who mistake cunning for wisdom. I hate those who mistake insubordination for courage. I hate those who mistake tale-bearing for honesty."

17.25 The Master said, "Women and people of low birth are very hard to deal with. If you are friendly with them, they get out of hand, and if you keep your distance, they resent it."

17.26 The Master said, "One who has reached the age of forty and is still disliked will be so till the end."

微子篇第十八

【原文】

18.1　微子去之，箕子为之奴，比干谏而死。孔子曰："殷有三仁焉。"

18.2　柳下惠为士师，三黜。人曰："子未可以去乎？"曰："直道而事人，焉往而不三黜？枉道而事人，何必去父母之邦？"

18.3　齐景公待孔子曰："若季氏，则吾不能；以季孟之间待之。"曰："吾老矣，不能用也。"孔子行。

18.4　齐人归女乐，季桓子受之，三日不朝，孔子行。

18.5　楚狂接舆歌而过孔子曰："凤兮凤兮！何德之衰？往者不可

【今译】

18.1　[纣王昏乱残暴，]微子便离开了他，箕子做了他的奴隶，比干谏劝而被杀。孔子说："殷商末年有三位仁人。"

18.2　柳下惠做法官，多次被撤职。有人对他说："您不可以离开鲁国吗？"他道："正直地工作，到哪里去不多次被撤职？不正直地工作，为什么一定要离开祖国呢？"

18.3　齐景公讲到对待孔子的打算时说："用鲁君对待季氏的模样对待孔子，那我做不到；我要用次于季氏而高于孟氏的待遇来对待他。"不久，又说道："我老了，没有什么作为了。"孔子便离开了齐国。

18.4　齐国送了许多歌姬舞女给鲁国，季桓子接受了，三天不问政事，孔子就离职走了。

18.5　楚国的狂人接舆一面走过孔子的车子，一面唱着歌，道："凤凰呀，凤凰呀！为什么这么倒霉？过去的不能再挽回，未来的还可

BOOK XVIII

18.1 The lord of Wei fled from him[1], the lord of Ji suffered slavery at his hands, Bi Gan rebuked him and was slain. Master Kong said, "In them the Yin had three Good men."

18.2 When Liuxia Hui was Leader of the Knights[2], he was three times dismissed. People said to him, "Surely you would do well to seek service elsewhere?" He said, "If I continue to serve men in honest ways, where can I go and not be three times dismissed? If, on the other hand, I am willing to serve men by crooked ways, what need is there for me to leave the land of my father and mother?"

18.3 Duke Jing of Qi received Master Kong; he said, "To treat him on an equality with the head of the Ji Family is impossible. I will receive him as though he ranked between the head of the Ji and the head of the Meng." (At the interview) He said, "I am old and have no use for you." Whereupon Master Kong left (the land of Qi).[3]

18.4 The people of Qi sent to Lu a present of female musicians,[4] and Ji Huan[5] accepted them. For three days no Court was held, whereupon Master Kong left Lu.

18.5 Jieyu, the madman of Chu, came past Master Kong, singing as he went:

"Oh phoenix, phoenix

【原文】

谏，来者犹可追。已而，已而! 今之从政者殆而!”

孔子下，欲与之言。趋而辟之，不得与之言。

18.6　长沮、桀溺耦而耕，孔子过之，使子路问津焉。长沮曰：“夫执舆者为谁?”子路曰：“为孔丘。”曰：“是鲁孔丘与?”曰：“是也。”曰：“是知津矣。”问于桀溺。桀溺曰：“子为谁?”曰：“为仲由。”曰：“是鲁孔丘之徒与?”对曰：“然。”曰：“滔滔者天下皆是也，而谁以易之?且而与其从辟人之士也，岂若从辟世之士哉?”耰而不辍。子路行以告。夫子怃然曰：“鸟兽不可与同群，吾非斯人之徒与而谁与?天下有道，丘不与易也。”

【今译】

不再着迷。算了吧，算了吧! 现在的执政诸公危乎其危!”

孔子下车，想同他谈谈，他却赶快避开，孔子没法同他谈。

18.6　长沮、桀溺两人一同耕田，孔子在那儿经过，叫子路去问渡口。长沮问子路：“那位驾车子的是谁?”子路道：“是孔丘。”他又道：“是鲁国的那位孔丘吗?”子路道：“是的。”他便道：“他么，早晓得渡口在哪儿了。”去问桀溺。桀溺道：“您是谁?”子路道：“我是仲由。”桀溺道：“您是鲁国孔丘的门徒吗?”答道：“对的。”他便道：“像洪水一样的坏东西到处都是，你们同谁去改革它呢?你与其跟着[孔丘那种]逃避坏人的人，为什么不跟着[我们这些]逃避整个社会的人呢?”说完，仍旧不停地做田里工夫。子路回来报告给孔子。孔子很失望地道：“我们既然不可以同飞禽走兽合群共处，若不同人群打交道，又同什么去打交道呢?如果天下太平，我就不会同你们一道来从事改革了。”

How dwindled is your power!
As to the past, reproof is idle,
But the future may yet be remedied.
Desist, desist!
Great in these days is the peril of those who
fill office."

Master Kong got down,[6] desiring to speak with him; but the madman hastened his step and got away, so that Master Kong did not succeed in speaking to him.

18.6 Changju and Jieni were working as plough-mates together. Master Kong, happening to pass that way, told Zilu to go and ask them where the river could be forded. Changju said, "Who is it for whom you are driving?" Zilu said, "For Kong Qiu." He said, "What, Kong Qiu of Lu?" Zilu said, "Yes, he." Changju said, "In that case he already knows where the ford is[7]." Zilu then asked Jieni. Jieni said, "Who are you?" He said, "I am Zilu." Jieni said, "You are a follower of Kong Qiu of Lu, are you not?" He said, "That is so." Jieni said, "Under Heaven there is none that is not swept along by the same flood. Such is the world and who can change it? As for you, instead of following one who flees from this man and that, you would do better to follow one who shuns this whole generation of men. And with that he went on covering the seed."

Zilu went and told his master, who said ruefully, "One cannot herd with birds and beasts. If I am not to be a man among other men, then what am I to be? If the Way prevailed under Heaven, I should not be trying to alter things."

【原文】

18.7　子路从而后，遇丈人，以杖荷蓧。子路问曰："子见夫子乎？"丈人曰："四体不勤，五谷不分。孰为夫子？"植其杖而芸。子路拱而立。止子路宿，杀鸡为黍而食之，见其二子焉。明日，子路行以告。子曰："隐者也。"使子路反见之。至，则行矣。子路曰："不仕无义。长幼之节，不可废也；君臣之义，如之何其废之？欲洁其身，而乱大伦。君子之仕也，行其义也。道之不行，已知之矣。"

18.8　逸民：伯夷、叔齐、虞仲、夷逸、朱张、柳下惠、少连。子曰："不降其志，不辱其身，伯夷、叔齐与！"谓"柳下惠、少连，

【今译】

18.7　子路跟随着孔子，却远落在后面，碰到一个老头，用拐杖挑着除草用的工具。子路问道："您看见我的老师吗？"老头道："你这人，四肢不劳动，五谷不认识，谁晓得你的老师是什么人？"说完，便扶着拐杖去锄草。子路拱着手恭敬地站着。他便留子路到他家住宿，杀鸡、做饭给子路吃，又叫他两个儿子出来相见。第二天，子路赶上了孔子，报告了这件事。孔子道："这是位隐士。"叫子路回去再看看他。子路到了那里，他却走开了。子路便道："不做官是不对的。长幼间的关系，是不可能废弃的；君臣间的关系，怎么能不管呢？你原想不玷污自身，却不知道这样隐居便是忽视了君臣间的必要关系。君子出来做官，只是尽应尽之责。至于我们的政治主张行不通，早就知道了。"

18.8　古今被遗落的人才有伯夷、叔齐、虞仲、夷逸、朱张、柳下惠、少连。孔子道："不动摇自己意志，不辱没自己身份，是伯夷、叔齐吧！"又说："柳下惠、少连降低自己意志，屈辱自己身份了，

18.7 Once when Zilu was following (the Master) he fell behind and met an old man carrying a basket[8] slung over his staff. Zilu asked him, saying, "Sir, have you seen my master?" The old man said, "You who

With your four limbs do not toil,
Who do not sift the five grains,[9]

who is your master?" And with that he planted his staff in the ground and began weeding, while Zilu stood by with his hands pressed together.[10]

He kept Zilu for the night, killed a fowl, prepared a dish of millet for his supper and introduced him to his two sons. Zilu said, "It is not right to refuse to serve one's country. The laws of age and youth may not be set aside. And how can it be right for a man to set aside the duty that binds minister to prince, or in his desire to maintain his own integrity, to subvert the Great Relationship? A gentleman's service to his country consists in doing such right as he can. That the Way does not prevail, he knows well enough beforehand."

Next day Zilu went on his way and reported what had happened. The Master said, "He is a recluse," and told Zilu to go back and visit him again. But on arriving at the place he found that the old man had gone away.

18.8 Subjects whose services were lost to the State: Boyi, Shuqi, Yuzhong,[11] Yiyi, Zhuzhang, Liuxia Hui, Shaolian. The Master said, "Those of them who 'would neither abate their high resolve nor bring humiliation upon themselves' were, I suppose, Boyi and Shuqi." It means that[12] Liuxia Hui and Shaolian did abate their high resolve and bring humiliation upon themselves. "Their words were consonant with the Relationships, their deeds were consonant with prudence; this and no

【原文】

降志辱身矣，言中伦，行中虑，其斯而已矣”。谓“虞仲、夷逸，隐居放言，身中清，废中权。我则异于是，无可无不可”。

18.9 大师挚适齐，亚饭干适楚，三饭缭适蔡，四饭缺适秦，鼓方叔入于河，播鼗武入于汉，少师阳、击磬襄入于海。

18.10 周公谓鲁公曰:“君子不施其亲，不使大臣怨乎不以。故旧无大故，则不弃也。无求备于一人!”

18.11 周有八士：伯达、伯适、仲突、仲忽、叔夜、叔夏、季随、季騧。

【今译】

可是言语合乎法度，行为经过思虑，那也不过如此罢了。”又说:“虞仲、夷逸逃世隐居，放肆直言。行为廉洁，被废弃也是他的权术。我就和他们这些人不同，没有什么可以，也没有什么不可以。”

18.9 太师挚逃到了齐国，二饭乐师干逃到了楚国，三饭乐师缭逃到了蔡国，四饭乐师缺逃到了秦国，打鼓的方叔入居黄河之滨，摇小鼓的武入居汉水之涯，少师阳和击磬的襄入居海边。

18.10 周公对鲁公说道:“君子不怠慢他的亲族，不让大臣抱怨没被信用。老臣故人没有发生严重过失，就不要抛弃他。不要对某一人求全责备!”

18.11 周朝有八个有教养的人：伯达、伯适、仲突、仲忽、叔夜、叔夏、季随、季騧。

more," means that Yuzhong and Yiyi, on the contrary, "lived in seclusion and refrained from comment. They secured personal integrity; and when set aside maintained due balance.[13] As for me, I am different from any of these. I have no 'thou shalt' or 'thou shalt not.'"

18.9 The Chief Musician Zhi betook himself to Qi; Gan, the leader of the band at the second meal[14], betook himself to Chu, Liao (leader of the band at the third meal) went to Cai, and Que (leader of the band at the fourth meal) went to Qin. The big drummer Fang Shu went within[15] the River, the kettledrummer Wu went within the River Han, the Minor Musician Yang and Xiang, the player of the stonechimes, went within the sea.[16]

18.10 The Duke of Zhou addressed the Duke of Lu, saying, "A gentleman never discards his kinsmen; nor does he ever give occasion to his chief retainers to chafe at not being used. None who have been long in his service does he ever dismiss without grave cause. He does not expect one man to be capable of everything."[17]

18.11 Zhou had its Eight Knights:

Elder-brother Da (d'at)
Elder-brother Shi (g'uât)
Middle-brother Tu (t'ut)
Middle-brother Hu (hut)
Younger-brother Ye (zia)
Younger-brother Xia (g'a)
Youngest-brother Sui (d'uâ)
Youngest-brother Gua (Kuâ)[18]

子张篇第十九

【原文】

19.1 子张曰:“士见危致命,见得思义,祭思敬,丧思哀,其可已矣。”

19.2 子张曰:“执德不弘,信道不笃,焉能为有?焉能为亡?”

19.3 子夏之门人问交于子张。子张曰:“子夏云何?”

对曰:“子夏曰:‘可者与之,其不可者拒之。’”

子张曰:“异乎吾所闻:君子尊贤而容众,嘉善而矜不能。我之大贤与,于人何所不容?我之不贤与,人将拒我,如之何其拒人也?”

【今译】

19.1 子张说:“读书人看见危险便肯豁出生命,看见有所得便考虑是否该得,祭祀时候考虑严肃恭敬,居丧时候考虑悲痛哀伤,那也就可以了。”

19.2 子张说:“对于道德,行为不坚强,信仰不忠实,[这种人,]有他不为多,没他不为少。”

19.3 子夏的学生向子张问怎样去交朋友。子张道:“子夏说了些什么?”

答道:“子夏说,可以交的去交他,不可以交的拒绝他。”

子张道:“我所听到的与此不同:君子尊敬贤人,也接纳普通人;鼓励好人,可怜无能的人。我是非常好的人吗,对什么人不能容纳呢?我是坏人吗,别人会拒绝我,我怎能去拒绝别人呢?”

BOOK XIX

19.1 Zizhang said, "A knight who confronted with danger is ready to lay down his life, who confronted with the chance of gain thinks first of right, who judges sacrifice by the degree of reverence shown and mourning by the degree of grief—such a one is all that can be desired."

19.2 Zizhang said, "He who sides with moral force (*de*) but only to a limited extent,[1] who believes in the Way, but without conviction—how can one count him as with us, how can one count him as not with us?"

19.3 The disciples of Zixia asked Zizhang about intercourse with others. Zizhang said, "What does Zixia tell you?" He replied saying, "Zixia says:

> Go with those with whom it is proper to go;
> Keep at a distance those whom it is proper to
> keep at a distance."

Zizhang said, "That is different from what I have been told:

> A gentleman reverences those that excel, but
> 'finds room'[2] for all;
> He commends the good and pities the
> incapable.

Do I myself greatly excel others? In that case I shall certainly find room for everyone. Am I myself inferior to others? In that case, it would be

【原文】

19.4　子夏曰："虽小道，必有可观者焉；致远恐泥，是以君子不为也。"

19.5　子夏曰："日知其所亡，月无忘其所能，可谓好学也已矣。"

19.6　子夏曰："博学而笃志，切问而近思，仁在其中矣。"

19.7　子夏曰："百工居肆以成其事，君子学以致其道。"

19.8　子夏曰："小人之过也必文。"

19.9　子夏曰："君子有三变：望之俨然，即之也温，听其言也厉。"

【今译】

19.4　子夏说道："就是小技艺，一定有可取的地方；恐怕它妨碍远大事业，所以君子不从事于它。"

19.5　子夏说："每天知道所未知的，每月复习所已能的，可以说是好学了。"

19.6　子夏说："广泛地学习，坚守自己志趣；恳切地发问，多考虑当前的问题，仁德就在这中间了。"

19.7　子夏说："各种工人居住于其制造场所完成他们的工作，君子则用学习获得那个道。"

19.8　子夏说："小人对于错误一定加以掩饰。"

19.9　子夏说："君子有三变：远远望着，庄严可畏；向他靠拢，温和可亲；听他的话，严厉不苟。"

others who would keep me at a distance. So that the question of keeping others at a distance does not arise[3].”

19.4 Zixia said, “Even the minor walks[4] (of knowledge) have an importance of their own. But if pursued too far they tend to prove a hindrance;for which reason a gentleman does not cultivate them.”

19.5 Zixia said, “He who from day to day is conscious of what he still lacks, and from month to month never forgets what he has already learnt, may indeed be called a true lover of learning.”

19.6 Zixia said,

> “One who studies widely and with set purpose,
> Who questions earnestly, then thinks for himself about what he has heard

—such a one will incidentally[5] achieve Goodness.”

19.7 Zixia said, “Just as the hundred[6] apprentices must live in workshops to perfect themselves in their craft, so the gentleman studies, that he may improve himself in the Way.”

19.8 Zixia said, “When the small man goes wrong, it is always on the side of over-elaboration.”

19.9 Zixia said, “A gentleman has three varying aspects: seen from afar, he looks severe, when approached he is found to be mild, when heard

【原文】

19.10　子夏曰："君子信而后劳其民；未信，则以为厉己也。信而后谏；未信，则以为谤己也。"

19.11　子夏曰："大德不逾闲，小德出入可也。"

19.12　子游曰："子夏之门人小子，当洒扫应对进退，则可矣，抑末也。本之则无，如之何？"

子夏闻之，曰："噫！言游过矣！君子之道，孰先传焉？孰后倦焉？譬诸草木，区以别矣。君子之道，焉可诬也？有始有卒者，其惟圣人乎！"

【今译】

19.10　子夏说："君子必须得到信仰以后才去动员百姓；否则百姓会以为你在折磨他们。必须得到信任以后才去进谏，否则君上会以为你在毁谤他。"

19.11　子夏说："人的重大节操不能逾越界限，作风上的小节稍稍放松一点是可以的。"

19.12　子游道："子夏的学生，叫他们做做打扫、接待客人、应对进退的工作，那是可以的；不过这只是末节罢了。探讨他们的学术基础却没有，怎么可以呢？"

子夏听了这话，便道："咳！言游说错了！君子的学术，哪一项先传授呢？哪一项最后讲述呢？学术犹如草木，是要区别为各种各类的。君子的学术，如何可以歪曲？[依照一定的次序去传授而]有始有终的，大概只有圣人吧！"

speaking he turns out to be incisive."

19.10 Zixia said, "A gentleman obtains the confidence of those under him, before putting burdens upon them. If he does so before he has obtained their confidence, they feel that they are being exploited. It is also true that he obtains the confidence (of those above him) before criticizing them. If he does so before he has obtained their confidence, they feel that they are being slandered."

19.11 Zixia said, "So long as in undertakings of great moral import a man does not 'cross the barrier,' in undertakings of little moral import he may 'come out and go in.'"[7]

19.12 Ziyou said, "Zixia's disciples and scholars, so long as it is only a matter of sprinkling and sweeping floors, answering summonses and replying to questions, coming forward and retiring, are all right. But these are minor matters. Set them to anything important, and they would be quite at a loss."

Zixia, hearing of this, said, "Alas, Yan You is wholly mistaken. Of the Way of the True Gentleman it is said:

> If it be transmitted to him before he is ripe,
> By the time he is ripe, he will weary of it.

Disciples may indeed be compared to plants and trees. They have to be separately treated according to their kinds.

"In the Way of the Gentleman there can be no bluff. It is only the Divine Sage who embraces in himself both the first step and the last."

【原文】

19.13　子夏曰："仕而优则学，学而优则仕。"

19.14　子游曰："丧致乎哀而止。"

19.15　子游曰："吾友张也为难能也，然而未仁。"

19.16　曾子曰："堂堂乎张也，难与并为仁矣。"

19.17　曾子曰："吾闻诸夫子：人未有自致者也，必也亲丧乎！"

19.18　曾子曰："吾闻诸夫子：孟庄子之孝也，其他可能也；其不改父之臣与父之政，是难能也。"

19.19　孟氏使阳肤为士师，问于曾子。曾子曰："上失其道，民散久矣。如得其情，则哀矜而勿喜！"

【今译】

19.13　子夏说："做官了，有余力便去学习；学习了，有余力便去做官。"

19.14　子游说："居丧，充分表现了他的悲哀也就够了。"

19.15　子游说："我的朋友子张是难能可贵的了，然而还不能做到仁。"

19.16　曾子说："子张的为人高得不可攀了，难以携带别人一同进入仁德。"

19.17　曾子说："我听老师说过，平常时候，人不可能来自动地充分发挥感情，[如果有，]一定在父母死亡的时候吧！"

19.18　曾子说："我听老师说过：孟庄子的孝，别的都容易做到；而留用他父亲的僚属，保持他父亲的政治设施，是难以做到的。"

19.19　孟氏任命阳肤做法官，阳肤向曾子求教。曾子道："现今在上位的人不依规矩行事，百姓早就离心离德了。你假若能够审出罪犯的真情，便应该同情他，可怜他，切不要自鸣得意！"

19.13 Zixia said, "The energy that a man has left over after doing his duty to the State, he should devote to study; the energy that he has left after studying, he should devote to service of the State."

19.14 Ziyou said, "The ceremonies of mourning should be carried to the extreme that grief dictates, and no further."

19.15 Ziyou said, "My friend Zhang does 'the things that it is hard to be able to do'; but he is not yet Good."

19.16 Master Zeng said, "Zhang is so self-important. It is hard to become Good when working side by side with such a man."

19.17 Master Zeng said, "I once heard the Master say, though a man may never before have shown all that is in him, he is certain to do so when mourning for a father or mother."

19.18 Master Zeng said, "I once heard the Master say, filial piety such as that of Meng Zhuang[8] might in other respects be possible to imitate; but the way in which he changed neither his father's[9] servants nor his father's domestic policy, that would indeed be hard to emulate."

19.19 When the Chief of the Meng Family[10] appointed Yang Fu as Leader of the Knights[11], Yang Fu[12] came for advice to Master Zeng. Master Zeng said, "It is long since those above lost the Way of the Ruler and the common people lost their cohesion. If you find evidence of this, then be sad and show pity rather than be pleased at discovering such evidence."

【原文】

19.20　子贡曰："纣之不善，不如是之甚也。是以君子恶居下流，天下之恶皆归焉。"

19.21　子贡曰："君子之过也，如日月之食焉：过也，人皆见之；更也，人皆仰之。"

19.22　卫公孙朝问于子贡曰："仲尼焉学？"子贡曰："文武之道，未坠于地，在人。贤者识其大者，不贤者识其小者。莫不有文武之道焉。夫子焉不学？而亦何常师之有？"

19.23　叔孙武叔语大夫于朝曰："子贡贤于仲尼。"

子服景伯以告子贡。

子贡曰："譬之宫墙，赐之墙也及肩，窥见室家之好。夫子之墙数仞，不得其门而入，不见宗庙之美，百官之富。得其门者或寡矣。夫子之云，不亦宜乎！"

【今译】

19.20　子贡说："商纣的坏，不像现在传说的这么厉害。所以君子憎恨居于下流，一居下流，天下的什么坏名声都会集中在他身上了。"

19.21　子贡说："君子的过失好比日蚀月蚀：错误的时候，每个人都看得见；更改的时候，每个人都仰望着。"

19.22　卫国的公孙朝向子贡问道："孔仲尼的学问是从哪里学来的？"子贡道："周文王武王之道，并没有失传，散在人间。贤能的人便抓住大处，不贤能的人只抓些末节。没有地方没有文王武王之道。我的老师何处不学，又为什么要有一定的老师，专门的传授呢？"

19.23　叔孙武叔在朝廷中对官员们说："子贡比他老师仲尼要强些。"

子服景伯便把这话告诉子贡。

子贡道："拿房屋的围墙作比喻吧：我家的围墙只有肩膀那么高，谁都可以探望到房屋的美好。我老师的围墙却有几丈高，找不到大门走进去，就看不到他那宗庙的雄伟，房舍的多种多样。能够找着大门的人或许不多吧，那么，武叔他老人家的这话，不也是自然的吗？"

19.20 Zigong said, "The tyrant Zhou cannot really have been as wicked as all this! That is why a gentleman hates to 'dwell on low ground.' He knows that all filth under Heaven tends to accumulate there."

19.21 Zigong said, "The faults of a gentleman are like eclipses of the sun or moon. If he does wrong, everyone sees it. When he corrects his fault, every gaze is turned up towards him."

19.22 Gongsun Chao of Wei[13] asked Zigong, "From whom did Zhongni[14] derive his learning?" Zigong said, "The Way of the kings Wen and Wu has never yet utterly fallen to the ground. Among men,[15] those of great understanding have recorded the major principles of this Way and those of less understanding have recorded the minor principles. So that there is no one who has not access to the Way of Wen and Wu. From whom indeed did our Master *not* learn? But at the same time, what need had he of any fixed and regular teacher?"

19.23 Shusun Wushu[16] talking to some high officers at Court said, "Zigong is a better man than Zhongni." Zifu Jingbo repeated this to Zigong. Zigong said, "Let us take as our comparison the wall round a building. My wall only reaches to the level of a man's shoulder, and it is easy enough to peep over it and see the good points of the house on the other side. But our Master's wall rises many times a man's height, and no one who is not let in by the gate can know the beauty and wealth of the palace that, with its ancestral temple, its hundred ministrants, lies hidden within. But it must be admitted that those who are let in by the gate are few; so that it is small wonder His Excellency should have spoken as he did."

【原文】

19.24　叔孙武叔毁仲尼。子贡曰："无以为也！仲尼不可毁也。他人之贤者，丘陵也，犹可逾也；仲尼，日月也，无得而逾焉。人虽欲自绝，其何伤于日月乎？多见其不知量也。"

19.25　陈子禽谓子贡曰："子为恭也，仲尼岂贤于子乎？"

子贡曰："君子一言以为知，一言以为不知，言不可不慎也。夫子之不可及也，犹天之不可阶而升也。夫子之得邦家者，所谓立之斯立，道之斯行，绥之斯来，动之斯和。其生也荣，其死也哀，如之何其可及也？"

【今译】

19.24　叔孙武叔毁谤仲尼。子贡道："不要这样做！仲尼是毁谤不了的。别人的贤能，好比山邱，还可以超越过去；仲尼，简直是太阳和月亮，不可能超越它。人家纵是要自绝于太阳月亮，那对太阳月亮有什么损害呢？只是表示他不自量罢了。"

19.25　陈子禽对子贡道："您对仲尼是客气吧，是谦让吧，难道他真比您还强吗？"

子贡道："高贵人物由一句话表现他的有知，也由一句话表现他的无知，所以说话不可不谨慎。他老人家的不可以赶得上，犹如青天的不可以用阶梯爬上去。他老人家如果得国而为诸侯，或者得到采邑而为卿大夫，那正如我们所说的一叫百姓人人能立足于社会，百姓自会人人能立足于社会；一引导百姓，百姓自会前进；一安抚百姓，百姓自会从远方来投靠；一动员百姓，百姓自会同心协力。他老人家，生得光荣，死得可惜，怎么能够赶得上呢？"

19.24 Shusun Wushu having spoken disparagingly of Zhongni, Zigong said, "It is no use; Zhongni cannot be disparaged. There may be other good men; but they are merely like hillocks or mounds that can easily be climbed. Zhongni is the sun and moon that cannot be climbed over. If a man should try to cut himself off from them, what harm would it do to the sun and moon? It would only show that he did not know his own measure."

19.25 Ziqin said to Zigong, "This is an affectation of modesty. Zhongni is in no way your superior." Zigong said, "You should be more careful about what you say. A gentleman, thought for a single word he may be set down as wise, for a single word is set down as a fool. It would be as hard to equal our Master as to climb up on a ladder to the sky. Had our Master ever been put in control of a State or of a great Family, it would have been as is described in the words:'He raised them, and they stood, he led them and they went. He steadied them as with a rope, and they came. He stirred them, and they moved harmoniously. His life was glorious, his death bewailed.'[17] How can such a one ever be equalled?"

尧曰篇第二十

【原文】

20.1　尧曰:“咨!尔舜!天之历数在尔躬，允执其中。四海困穷，天禄永终。”

舜亦以命禹。

曰:“予小子履敢用玄牡，敢昭告于皇皇后帝：有罪不敢赦。帝臣不蔽，简在帝心。朕躬有罪，无以万方；万方有罪，罪在朕躬。”

周有大赉，善人是富。“虽有周亲，不如仁人。百姓有过，在予一人。”

【今译】

20.1　尧[让位给舜的时候，]说道:“啧啧!你这位舜!上天的大命已经落到你的身上了，诚实地保持着那正确吧!假若天下的百姓都陷于困苦贫穷，上天给你的禄位也会永远地终止了。”

舜[让位给禹的时候，]也说了这一番话。

[汤]说:“我履谨用黑色牡牛作牺牲，明明白白地告于光明而伟大的天帝：有罪的人[我]不敢擅自去赦免他。您的臣仆[的善恶]我也不隐瞒掩盖，您心里也是早就晓得的。我本人若有罪，就不要牵连天下万方；天下万方若有罪，都归我一个人来承担。”

周朝大封诸侯，使善人都富贵起来。“我虽然有至亲，却不如有仁德之人。百姓如果有罪过，应该由我来担承。”

BOOK XX

20.1 Yao said, "Oh you, Shun!

Upon you in your own person now rests the
heavenly succession;[1]
Faithfully grasp it by the centre.
The Four Seas may run dry;[2]
But this heavenly gift lasts forever."

Shun too, when giving his charge to Yu···(hiatus).

(Tang[3]) Said, "I, your little son Lü, venture to sacrifice a black ox and tell you, oh most august sovereign God, that those who are guilty[4] I dare not spare; but God's servants I will not slay. The decision is in your heart, O God.

"If I in my own person do any wrong, let it never be visited upon the many lands. But if anywhere in the many lands wrong be done, let it be visited upon my person."[5]

When Zhou gave its great largesses,
It was the good who were enriched:
"Although I have my Zhou kinsmen,
They are less to me than the Good Men[6].
If among the many families
There be one that does wrong,

【原文】

谨权量，审法度，修废官，四方之政行焉。兴灭国，继绝世，举逸民，天下之民归心焉。

所重：民、食、丧、祭。

宽则得众，信则民任焉，敏则有功，公则说。

20.2　子张问于孔子曰："何如斯可以从政矣？"

子曰："尊五美，屏四恶，斯可以从政矣。"

子张曰："何谓五美？"

子曰："君子惠而不费，劳而不怨，欲而不贪，泰而不骄，威而不猛。"

子张曰："何谓惠而不费？"

子曰："因民之所利而利之，斯不亦惠而不费乎？择可劳而劳之，

【今译】

检验并审定度量衡，修复已废弃的机关工作，全国的政令就都会通行了。恢复被灭亡的国家，承续已断绝的后代，提拔被遗落的人才，天下的百姓就都会心悦诚服了。

所重视的：人民、粮食、丧礼、祭祀。

宽厚就会得到群众的拥护，勤敏就会有功绩，公平就会使百姓高兴。

20.2　子张向孔子问道："怎样就可以治理政事呢？"

孔子道："尊贵五种美德，排除四种恶政，这就可以治理政事了。"

子张道："五种美德是些什么？"

孔子道："君子给人民以好处，而自己却无所耗费；劳动百姓，百姓却不怨恨；自己欲仁欲义，却不能叫做贪；安泰矜持却不骄傲；威严却不凶猛。"

子张道："给人民以好处，自己却无所耗费，这应该怎么办呢？"

孔子道："就着人民能得利益之处因而使他们有利，这不也是给人民以好处而自己却无所耗费吗？选择可以劳动的[时间、情况和人民]

Let the wrong be visited on me alone."

(King Wu) Paid strict attention to weights and measures, reviewed the statutes and laws, restored disused offices, and gave a policy to all the four quarters of the world. He raised up States that had been destroyed, re-established lines of succession that had been broken, summoned lost subjects back to prominence, and all the common people under Heaven gave their hearts to him. What he cared for most was that the people should have food, and that the rites of mourning and sacrifice should be fulfilled.

He who is broad[7] wins the multitude, he who keeps his word is trusted by the people, he who is diligent succeeds in all he undertakes, he who is just is the joy (of the people).

20.2 Zizhang asked Master Kong, saying, "What must a man do, that he may thereby be fitted to govern the land?" The Master said, "He must pay attention to the Five Lovely Things[8] and put away from him the Four Ugly Things." Zizhang said, "What are they, that you call the Five Lovely Things?" The Master said, "A gentleman 'can be bounteous without extravagance, can get work out of people without arousing resentment, has longings but is never covetous, is proud but never insolent, inspires awe but is never ferocious.'"

Zizhang said, "What is meant by being bounteous without extravagance?" The Master said, "If he gives to the people only such advantages as are really advantageous to them, is he not being bounteous without extravagance? If he imposes upon them only such tasks as they are capable of performing, is he not getting work out of them without arousing resentment? If what he longs for and what he gets is Goodness, who

【原文】

又谁怨?欲仁而得仁，又焉贪?君子无众寡，无小大，无敢慢，斯不亦泰而不骄乎?君子正其衣冠，尊其瞻视，俨然人望而畏之，斯不亦威而不猛乎?”

子张曰:“何谓四恶?”

子曰:“不教而杀谓之虐；不戒视成谓之暴；慢令致期谓之贼；犹之与人也，出纳之吝谓之有司。”

20.3　孔子曰:“不知命，无以为君子也；不知礼，无以立也；不知言，无以知人也。”

【今译】

再去劳动他们，又有谁来怨恨呢?自己需要仁德便得到了仁德，又贪求什么呢?无论人多人少，无论势力大小，君子都不敢怠慢他们，这不也是安泰矜持却不骄傲吗?君子衣冠整齐，目不邪视，庄严地使人望而有所畏惧，这不也是威严却不凶猛吗?”

子张道:“四种恶政又是些什么呢?”

孔子道:“不加教育便加杀戮叫做虐；不加申诫便要成绩叫做暴；起先懈怠，突然限期叫做贼；同是给人以财物，出手悭吝，叫做小家子气。”

20.3　孔子说:“不懂得命运，没有可能作为君子；不懂得礼，没有可能立足于社会；不懂得分辨人家的言语，没有可能认识人。”

can say that he is covetous? A gentleman, irrespective of whether he is dealing with many persons or with few, with the small or with the great, never presumes to slight them. Is not this indeed being 'proud without insolence'? A gentleman sees to it that his clothes and hat are put on straight, and imparts such dignity to his gaze that he imposes on others. No sooner do they see him from afar than they are in awe. Is not this indeed inspiring awe without ferocity?"

Zizhang said, "What are they, that you call the Four Ugly Things?" The Master said, "Putting men to death, without having taught them (the Right); that is called savagery. Expecting the completion of tasks, without giving due warning; that is called oppression. To be dilatory about giving orders, but to expect absolute punctuality, that is called being a tormentor. And similarly, though meaning to let a man have something, to be grudging about bringing it out from within, that is called behaving like a petty functionary."

20.3 The Master said, "He who does not understand the will of Heaven cannot be regarded as a gentleman. He who does not know the rites cannot take his stand. He who does not understand words[9] cannot understand people."

注释 NOTES *

BOOK Ⅰ

1 The "after all"implies "even though one does not hold office."

2 Several of the disciples belonged to other States(e. g. Wei and Qi); but there is no evidence that they came to Lu on account of Confucius. Unless, however, there is here some allusion that escapes us, the phrase must refer to the visits of admirers from abroad, perhaps friends made during the Master's journeys in Henan.

3 See Introduction, p.292.

4 i.e. upon what is fundamental, as opposed to "the twigs," i.e. small arts and accomplishments, which the gentleman leaves to his inferiors.

5 See Introduction, p.292.

6 And so keep in memory.

7 i.e. not when they ought to be working in the fields. Bad rulers, on the contrary, listen to music or go hunting when they ought to be attending to business, continually employ labour on ostentatious building-schemes, etc.

* There are "Notes," "Additional notes" and "Textual notes" in Waley's translation. It is not so convenient for the readers. Thus we abbreviated "Textual notes" and combined "Notes" with "Additional notes."(亚瑟・韦利的译本附有注释、补注以及文本注释，检阅不甚方便。对此我们作了技术处理，略去了考据式的文本注释，将注释和补注合并。)

8 i.e. learn to recite the *Songs*, practise archery, deportment, and the like.

9 i.e. knowledge of ritual, precedents, the correct use on social occasions of verses from the *Songs*, etc.

10 i.e. irresponsible and unreliable in his dealings with others.

11 i.e. of those who still reckon in terms of "profit and loss," and have not taken *ren* (Goodness 仁) as their standard.

12 Cf. Terms, p. 305.

13 See Introduction, p.292.

14 Not, of course, about the details of administration, but about the secret, general maxims which inspire the ruler.

15 See Terms, p.309.

16 i.e. what of it as a motto?

17 *The Book of Songs,* p.46, which describes the elegance of a lover. Zigong interprets it as describing the pains the gentleman has taken to improve his character, and suggests that Confucius prefers the second maxim ("Poor, yet delighting…") because it implies a greater effort of self-improvement.

BOOK II

1 A young grandee of Lu, whose father sent him to study with Confucius. He died in 481B. C.

2 A disciple.

3 Evidently by "disobey" Confucius meant "disobey the rituals." The reply was intended to puzzle the enquirer and made him think.

4 Son of Meng Yi.

5 A disciple; see Introduction, p. 292.

6 See Introduction, p.292.

7 The favourite disciple. His early death is several times referred to in this book.

8 i.e. whether he is fit to be entrusted with office. There is no need to have seen him actually handling practical issues.

9 Literally, "warming up." The business of the teacher is to give fresh life to the Scriptures by reinterpreting them so that they apply to the problems of modern life. All scriptures have been used in this way.

10 i.e. a specialist, a tool used for a special purpose. He need only have general, moral qualifications.

11 Cf. Terms, p.306.

12 For "thinking,"see Terms, p.316.

13 The metaphor is one of weaving or netting. "Strand" (*duan*端) is a sprout, something that sticks out, and so "the loose end of a thread." The moral Way as opposed to the opportunist Way of the World must be followed consistently. It is no use working at it in disconnected patches.

14 Familiar name of the disciple Zilu, see Introduction, p. 291.

15 That knowledge consists in knowing that one does not know is a frequent theme in early Chinese texts. Cf. *Dao De Jing*, ch. LXXI .

16 *The Book of Songs* , p. 213. It puns on Ganlu, the name of a mountain, and *ganlu*（干禄） "seeking princely rewards, preferment."

17 Literally, "leave a gap," a metaphor derived from the language of copyists and scribes.

18 *Zai qi zhong*（在其中） is an idiom (cf. 7.15, 13.18, 15.31,19.6) which can never be translated literally. It is used of results that occur incidentally without being the main object of a certain course of action.

19 Duke of Lu from 494-468 B.C.

20 i.e. Confucius.

21 Head of the three families who were *de facto* rulers of Lu. Died 469 B.C.

22 i.e. what Europeans call the *Book of History*. The passage does not occur in the genuine books. What it meant in its original context no doubt was "Be pious to your ancestors … be generous in rewarding your officers of State." Confucius "reanimates" the ancient text, in order to prove that a virtuous private life makes a real contribution towards the public welfare.

23 See Introduction, p.292.

24 Supposed to have ruled in the 3rd and 2nd millennia B.C.

25 The dynasty which still had a nominal hegemony in the time of Confucius.

26 The fall of Yin took place in the eleventh century B.C. It was on the site of one of their capitals that the famous "Henan oracle-bones" were found.

BOOK Ⅲ

1 One of the Three Families that had usurped most of the powers of the Duke of Lu.

2 Eight teams of dancers. The exact number of performers is in every ritual a matter of extreme importance. The Ji Family's crime consisted in usurping rites which were proper only to the Ducal House; or, possibly, proper only to the Emperor. They were "making the twigs heavy and the trunk light"—the surest way to ruin.

3 "He comes in solemn state…" *The Book of Songs*, p.231. Its use was obviously only appropriate at the Emperor's Court. It would have been out of place at the Duke's palace, and was still more so in the hall

of the Three Families.

4 Where in several States the ruling families had been ousted by usurpers.

5 To the spirit of the mountain, a thing which the Duke alone had the right to do. The offering is said to have consisted of jade objects.

6 Who was in the service of the Ji Family.

7 The mountain must surely know enough of ritual to be aware that no sacrifice but the Duke's could be accepted. The sense is carried on from 4.4.

8 Familiar name of Zixia. An alternative interpretation of Confucius's reply is "In painting, the plain colour (i.e. the white) is put on last," because otherwise it would get soiled. This explanation lands us in all kinds of difficulties, and is based, I think, on a misunderstanding of a passage in the *Zhou Li*, LXXIX (page17; Biot's translation, 2.516), which in reality means: "When birds, beasts and snakes are combined with the symbols of the four seasons and with the five colours in their proper arrangements, and are thus duly displayed, this is called 'skilled work.' In the business of painting (i.e. of decorating the personal possessions of officials with designs appropriate to their rank) plain work comes after (i.e. is not considered so highly).""Plain work" is painted in the appropriate colours, but lacks the birds, beasts and snakes that decorate the appurtenances of the mighty. Confucius uses the same maxim as the *Zhou Li*, but reinterprets it as meaning not "In painting plain work is not so highly esteemed," but "The painting comes after the plain groundwork."The *Zhou Li* commentary tries to force upon "plain work" the impossible sense of "application of white pigment," thus making the last sentence totally disconnected from the context.

9 In Henan, where descendants of the Xia still carried on the sacrifices. Confucius laments that these States had not preserved the docu-

ments and rites of their ancestors. The interrogative particles seem to have been accidentally omitted.

10 i.e. do not worry about "spirits being present" and the like. What matters is the state of mind of the sacrificer. If he is not heart and soul "there," the sacrifice is useless.

11 Commander-in-chief in the State of Wei.

12 This rhymed saying means that it is better to be on good terms with the hearth-god and have a full belly than waste one's food on the Ancestors, who cannot enjoy it. Confucius, who is usually able to reinterpret old maxims in a new, moral sense, finds himself obliged to reject this cynical piece of peasant-lore *in toto*.

13 i.e. we in Lu have all three dynasties, Xia, Yin, and Zhou to look back upon and imitate.

14 Erected in honour of the first Duke of Zhou.

15 A village with which Confucius's family had been connected.

16 The poem *Tian Wen* is supposed to embody the questions asked by the poet Qu Yuan when he visited the shrines of former kings and ministers, and to concern legends depicted on the walls of these shrines.

17 i.e. it is not piercing the hide stretched as a target that counts. In this ancient rhymed saying Confucius saw a maxim which metaphorically resumed the whole way of the Ancient Sages, who ruled by Goodness, not by force. According to the *Zhou Li* (21.52) the local archery meeting was made the occasion for a general review of conduct, "points" in the competition being given for (1) not quarrelling; (2) correct deportment; (3) *zhu pi*（主皮）, explained as meaning "skill in archery"; (4) singing; (5) dancing.It is clear, then, that the *Zhou Li* does not give to *zhu* (主)the meaning "give chief place to"; it is, however, equally clear that in the *Lun Yu* passage *zhu* can only bear this meaning. Moreover, the

mention in *Lun Yu* of "strength" suggests that "piercing the hide" and not merely hitting the mark is what is meant.

18 *The Book of Songs*, No. 87, which begins by describing a lover's grief at being separated from his lady and ends by describing their joyful union. Confucius sees in it a general guide to conduct, whether in joy or affliction. The opening words are: "*Guan*（关）, *guan* cry the ospreys."

19 A disciple in whom Confucius was much disappointed.

20 Pun on *li* (栗) a chestnut-tree and *li* (栗) "to be in awe."

21 Guan Zhong, seventh century B.C., the statesman who built up the power of the Qi kingdom. Confucius regarded him as having merely increased the political prestige of his country without raising its moral status.

22 Each consisting of a wife and two "understudies" (bridesmaids); only a feudal lord was entitled to such an establishment.

23 A mound upon which to stand pledge-cups.

24 The *maestro*, music-master, who was always a blind man.

25 To improvise.

26 On the borders of the State of Wei.

27 Sages appear at regular intervals. One is now due.

28 A rattle, used to arouse the populace in times of night-danger, and in general by heralds and town-criers.

29 This dance(at any rate according to the later Confucian theory)mimed the peaceful accession of the legendary Emperor Shun; the War Dance mimed the accession by conquest of the Emperor Wu, who overthrew the Yin.

BOOK Ⅳ

1 A justification of the maxim, "When right does not prevail in a kingdom, then leave it," and of Confucius's own prolonged travels.

2 It is the will not the way that is wanting.

3 i.e. a set of qualities which includes virtues.

4 As opposed to physical compulsion. The Zhu Xi interpretation is "The gentleman thinks of *de*, the small man of material comfort; the gentleman, of punishments (i.e. justice); the small man of favours." In his conversations (section on *Lun Yu* in *Zhu Zi Quan Shu*) he records that Yin Shun (1071-1142) construed the sentence as I have done; and Huang Kan (sixth century) notes this rendering as an alternative one. The absence of any "then," "in that case" in the second and fourth clauses makes the sentence obscure, and I fancy that *ze* ("then" 则) has been suppressed in order to admit of an interpretation such as Zhu Xi's, by people who unlike Confucius, believed in government by penalties. Zhu Xi's interpretation of *huai tu*（怀土）is hopelessly forced.

5 They *an tu*(安土), "are content with the soil," and prepared to defend it.

6 "Within yourself scrutinize yourself ." *Er*(尔) is the second person singular pronoun, not the conjunction?

7 Particularly in order that if they die he may be able to come back and perform the rites of mourning.

8 If he knows that they are not so old as one might think.

9 If he realizes that they are very old.

10 Whenever one individual or one country substitutes *de* for physical compulsion, other individuals or other countries inevitably follow suit.

11 Cf. 12. 23. The character that I have translated "repeated scold-

ing" means literally "to enumerate."Hence to "enumerate people's faults," to "tick off ."It is taken in this sense here by Yu Yue (died 1906). The *Ji Jie* gives it the meaning "quick," "hasty." Cf. *Liezi*, 2.8: "Anyone who is good at swimming can quickly learning," and *Zhuangzi*, 19.4. But Zheng Xuan, the great Han dynasty commentator, explains it as meaning "enumerating one's own services." Finally, the current explanation gives it the meaning "numerously," "repeatedly." Comparison with 12.23 seems to show that this last explanation is right.

BOOK Ⅴ

1 The commentators identify Nan Rong with Nangong Kuo, son of Meng Xi, head of the powerful Meng Family. This is, however, no ground for this identification, nor any reason to suppose that Confucius ever formed so exalted a family connection.

2 According to later tradition Confucius's elder brother was a cripple and for this reason his duties devolved on Confucius.

3 For this saying, set in the context of a longer anecdote, see *Kongzi Jia Yu*, XIX and *Shuo Yuan*, Ⅶ. A work called *Fuzi* (i.e. sayings of Master Fu) was current until the first century A.D., and the stories about Fu's ideal governorship which are found in works of the third century B.C. and onwards may be extracts from *Fuzi*. See G. Haloun, *Asia Major*, Ⅷ, fasc. 3, pp.437 *seq*. But there is no reason to suppose that any of these stories supplies us with the original context of this saying in the *Analects*.

4 A man of particular capacities, but lacking the general state of electness known as *ren* (Goodness).

5 i.e. the highest sort of vessel.

6 What Confucius proposes is, of course, to go and settle among the barbarians. Cf. 3. 5 and 9. 13. A certain idealization of the "noble savage" is to be found fairly often in early Chinese literature; cf. the eulogy of the barbarians put into the mouth of a Chinese whose ancestors had settled among them, *Shi Ji*, V and the maxim "When the Emperor no longer functions, learning must be sought among the Four Barbarians," north, west, east, and south ("Zhao Gong," seventeenth year, *Zuo Zhuan*).

7 See above, 2. 6.

8 The disciple Ran Qiu.

9 The disciple Gongxi Hua.

10 Ran Qiu is known to history as a faithful henchman of the Lu dictator. Gongxi Hua's ambition was to perfect himself in the etiquette of State ceremonies. See 11. 25.

11 See 3.21.

12 Impervious to outside influences, intimidations, etc.

13 See Terms, p.311.

14. *Zhang*("insignia" 章) means literally "emblems"(usually representations of birds, beasts or plants) figuring on banners or dresses to show the rank of the owner. Hence metaphorically, the outward manifestations of an inner virtue.

15 As it is before it has been embellished with "culture."

16 i.e.why was he accorded this posthumous title? see Terms, p.311. He was a statesman of the Wei State who died between 484 and 480 B.C. He figures in the chronicles as a disloyal and self-seeking minister.

17 Minister in the Zheng State, died 522 B. C.

18 Or "was." The Qi minister Yanzi, famous for his wise counsels, died in 500 B.C.

19 Minister of Lu in the seventh century B.C.

20 The country of Cai was famous for its tortoises.

21. Such decoration was proper only to the Emperor's ancestral temple and palace.

22. i.e. his knowledge of ritual. For a tortoise kept on a special terrace and smeared daily with the blood of four bulls.

23 Middle of the seventh century B.C.

24 In 548 B.C. The Duke of Qi had seduced his wife.

25 Another Qi minister.

26 A minister of Wei (seventh century B.C.), famous for his blind devotion to his prince, whose enemies had incarcerated him in a deep dungeon. Here Ning managed to feed his prince through a tube.

27 About 492 B.C.?

28 Legendary brothers, almost always bracketed together in this way. The "old ills" were the misdeeds of the last Yin ruler. When he was attacked by the Zhou tribe, the brothers refused to take up arms against their sovereign, despite his great wickedness. Their lack of *yuan* ("rancour"怨) was a classical theme; cf. 7.14. This was shown by their attitude after each in turn had resigned his rights of accession to the rulership of the small State to which they belonged. Having proposed this act of "cession" (*rang*让), they carried it out loyally and uncomplainingly.

29 Weisheng Gao is the legendary paragon of truthfulness. Confucius adopts the same formula as the rhyme:

The Germans in Greek
Are sadly to seek.
All except Hermann;
And Hermann is a German.

How rare, how almost non-existent a quality uprightness must be, Confucius bitterly says, if even into the legend of the most upright of all men there has crept an instance of falsity!

30 When later Confucians were attempting to make Confucius in some way responsible (either as author or editor) for the whole of early Chinese literature, they turned Zuo Qiuming into a disciple of Confucius and credited him with the authorship (under the Master's direction) of the *Zuo Zhuan* chronicle. Nothing further is known about him.

31 i.e. self-improvement in the most general sense. Not book-learning.

BOOK Ⅵ

1 The disciple Ran Yong.

2 Trying him as a ruler.

3 i.e. too lax to "set with his face to the south."

4 A merely nominal amount. Confucius disapproved of her being given any at all.

5 A good deal more; but still not a great deal.

6 Ten times (?) more than a measure. Ran entirely disregards Confucius's advice.

7 i.e. Gongxi Hua. He ought to have left behind sufficient provision for his mother.

8 i.e. one unsuitable for sacrifice.

9 In sacrificing to the hills and streams. The implication is that Ran Yong was of humble origin. This, says Confucius, ought not to prejudice us against him.

10 On the strength of sayings such as this, the Taoists claimed Yan Hui as an exponent of *zuo wang*("sitting with blank mind" 坐忘), the Chinese equivalent of *yoga*.

11 Became head of the actual administration of Lu in 492 B.C.

12 *Da* (达) means "to put through," "penetrate." So (1) to "put oneself through," to turn one's *de* to account, to get on in the world, to progress; to get one's meaning or one's doctrines through, i.e. to "put them across," (2) to get through, penetrate, i.e. understand.

13 i.e. the government. He would not serve a usurper.

14 The great stronghold of the Ji Family.

15 i.e. I shall take refuge in the neighbouring land of Qi, where I cannot be got at. He was faithful to the legitimate ruler, the Duke of Lu.

16 Literally, a split bamboo-sectionful.

17 Metaphor of marking boundary-lines of estates or the like.

18 A word of very uncertain meaning. Perhaps "unwarlikeness." From the Han dynasty onwards the word *ru*, which is of very uncertain origin, was applied to those who devoted themselves to the study of the *Songs*, the *Books*, the ritual treatises, etc., and hence to followers of Confucius in general. It seems, however, to have originally been a contemptuous nickname given by the warlike people of Qi to their more pacific neighbours in Lu. Cf. "Ai Gong," 21st year, *Zuo Zhuan*. But since the word occurs only this once in the *Analects*, without adequate context, it is impossible to know for certain what meaning the compilers attached to it. The meaning of the saying may be "The unwarlikeness of gentlemen means a preference for *de*(moral force), that of inferior people is mere cowardice."

19 i.e. strictly follows our Way. There is probably some further point in this story, that is lost to us owing to our knowing so little about Tantai Mieming.

20 At a battle with Qi outside the Lu capital in 484 B.C. To belittle his own achievements(the opposite of boasting) is the duty of a gallant gentle-

man. So a modern airman who had stayed behind to fight a rear action might say, "I was in a funk all the time, but I couldn't get away; my engine was missing fire."

21 The *zhu*("priest" 祝) recited invocations addressed to the ancestors. Both Tuo and Chao flourished about 500 B.C.

22 Though it is the obvious and only legitimate way out of all our difficulties.

23 i.e. when nature prevails over culture.

24 The Way.

25 That belong to a higher stage of learning.

26 When the Spirits of hills and streams do not receive their proper share of ritual and sacrifice they do not "keep their distance," but "possess" human beings, causing madness, sickness, pestilence, etc.

27 This saying, in the form in which it now occurs, is completely Taoistic, save that the word Good (Goodness) has been substituted for "Tao." Taoism, it is true, drew its vocabulary and ideas partly from a stock common to all early Chinese thought. But nowhere else in the *Analects* is it suggested that anyone save the *sheng* ("Divine Sage" 神) can achieve his ends by inactivity, and as this passage stands it is impossible not to give it a more general application. But comparison with other sayings in the *Analects* and elsewhere suggests that this saying originally had a very different form. In 15.32, it is *shou* "keeping what one has gained" (守) [and not *shou* ("longevity"寿)] which is the consequence of Goodness, but cannot result from wisdom alone. Moreover, in the *Gu-liang Zhuan* we twice get the saying "The wise man schemes (*lü* 履)··· the Good man keeps"("secures," *shou*守) what the scheming has achieved. Both passages are concerned with politics, not with the moral life of the individual, and mean that State successes gained by cleverness will not

be permanent; only the State that is based on Goodness can have any permanence.As it stands, the saying runs very awkwardly. It is first said that the Good man delights (*le* 乐) in mountains and then that it is the wise man who "delights"; whereas the Good man is long-lived(*shou*寿) as opposed to "delighting"(*le*). I cannot help believing that the original sense of the last two phrases was: "The wise ruler schemes; but the Good ruler alone can give permanent effect to schemes," as in the *Guliang Zhuan*.The Good "stay still," because their effects are achieved by *de* ("moral force") not by *li* ("physical force"力). The dictum easily passes into the vocabulary of full-blown, systematic quietism.Bao Xian, in the first century, takes the whole saying as referring to the ruler. But it is usually taken to refer to the individual in general, and is interpreted in a completely Taoist sense: All exercise of the emotions destroys the soul and leads to early death.

28 A particular sort of bronze goblet was called *gu*（觚）, which is written "horn" beside "gourd," though the object in question is not shaped like a gourd and is not a drinking-horn. The saying is, of course, a metaphorical way of lamenting over the political state of China, "ruled over" by an Emperor who had no temporal power and local sovereigns whose rights had been usurped by their ministers.

29 The gentleman (like jade) can be broken, but not bent.

30 i.e. deceived as to facts; but cannot be enticed into wrong conduct.

31 The wicked concubine of Duke Ling of Wei.

32 "Made a solemn declaration," literally "arrowed it." Here metaphorical; but probably the character "arrow" has its ideogrammatic sense and is not a phonetic substitute. For the use of a bundle of arrows in oath-taking, see H. Maspero (Mé langes chinois et bouddhiques, Ⅲ, p.270). *Le Serment dans la procédure judiciaire*··· The bundle of arrows is a

symbol of the unbreakable, in contrast with a single arrow, that can easily be snapped. Cf. the memorial inscription of the Mongol leader Menggu (13th century) by Yao Sui (A.D. 1238-1314): He broke an arrow and swore saying: "May every act in which I am not utterly faithful to the Khan be snapped like this!" We see here that it is against his acts and not against himself that the speaker invokes destruction. Confucius's *yan zhi*（厌之） is generally translated "crush (reject, forsake) me." But the text says "it" not "me," following a formula similar to that of the Mongol oath. There is no evidence that *yan*（厌）can mean "reject." Nor is there any suggestion in the text that improper conduct had taken place between Nanzi and Confucius, but only that his seeing her at all, as a means of obtaining influence at the Wei Court, was improper.

33 Confucius's Way was essentially one of moderation: "To exceed is as bad as to fall short." See Terms, p.308. It is upon this passage that the whole Confucian philosophy of compromise, of "too much is as bad as too little," is built. What *zhong yong*（中庸）meant to start with is very doubtful. To the compilers of the *Analects*, I do not think it meant anything different from *zhong dao*（Tao）（中道）, the Middle Way. But the interpretation "middle and usual," i.e. "traditional," is a quite possible one.A Confucian treatise of very mixed content, strongly tinged with Taoism, deals in several passages with the power of *zhong yong*, and bears these two words as its title. (It is known in Europe as the *Doctrine of the Mean*.) The material that this treatise contains is partly, at any rate, as old as the first half of the third century; but the unification of China is referred to, and the actual compilation of the work must be as late as the end of the third century B.C.Is there not, however, some connection between this passage and *Song* 142, which recounts the virtues of Zhong Shanfu? The 6th verse says: "Moral force (*de*) is light as a hair; but

among the people there are few that can lift it"(i.e. that can use it).I suspect that in its original form the saying was parallel to that about Taibo in 8.1, and ran: "How transcendent was the *de* of Zhong Shanfu (Minister of King Xuan of Zhou). That among the people there are few (who know how to use *de*) is an old story!" in allusion to *Song* 142, verse 6.

34 *Jiu yi*（久矣）constantly has an idiomatic sense of this sort, and does not mean simply "a long while."

35 See Introduction, p. 289.

36 For *fang*（方）, "direction," cf. 11. 25.

BOOK Ⅶ

1 The Chinese Nestor. It is the special business of old men to transmit traditions.

2 For the idiom *he you*（何有）, "there is no further trouble about," see above, 4. 13.

3 The passage in inverted commas consists of two rhymed couplets, and is probably traditional.

4 See Introduction, p. 289.

5 Music, archery and the like.

6 As in modern Chinese school-fees are called "the bundle of dried flesh," it would not occur to the average reader that *shu xiu*（束脩）in this passage could possibly mean anything but "a bundle of dried flesh," brought as a humble present to the teacher. This, however, was not the view of many outstanding commentators. Zheng Xuan (died A.D. 200) says it means "fourteen years old": the Master accepted any pupil who had attained to years of discretion. The alternatives arise in this way: *shu*（束）= to tie, tie one's belt; *xiu*(脩)= "to put right," "to cure"; hence to

"cure" meat, so that "tied cured" means "a bundle of dried flesh" or one who has "tied his belt and put himself to rights," i.e. has donned the garb of manhood. There is, however, no trace of this idiom till Han times; whereas "dried flesh," as a humble form of offering, occurs in texts which have every chance of being pre-Han. I therefore think that Huang Kan (sixth century) was right in championing the "dried flesh" theory against the view of Zheng Xuan.

7 i.e. the whole army.

8 Cf. *The Book of Songs*, No. 295, verse 6. The reply is clearly intended as a snub to the impulsive Zilu. The song is one which I omit in my translation.

9 i.e. the most menial."Gentleman," *shi*（士）, in such contexts is used with a slightly ironical intention, as one might say in French, *le monsieur qui*···

10 The study of the Ancients.

11 A special sacrifice was held before the departure of military expeditions, and the sacrificial meat was distributed among the soldiers. The populace flocked to the Ancestral Shrines, wailing to the Ancestors for assistance. Sickness was exorcized by sacrifices to hills and streams.

12 See 3. 25.

13 i.e. did not notice what he was eating.

14 The older commentators take "this" to mean the land of Qi, i.e. "I did not expect to find such music here in Qi." This may be right.

15 When Duke Ling died in the summer of 493 B.C., the throne passed to his grandson, his son having previously abdicated his rights to the accession. Soon, however, the son went back on his word and attempted to oust the grandson from the throne.

16 See above, 5. 22. The contrast is between Boyi and Shuqi on the

one hand (they are always spoken of as though they were to all intents and purposes a single person) and Duke Ling's son on the other. The two "good men of old " harboured no rancour after their act of cession; whereas Ling's son became discontented with his lot. Zigong sounds Confucius indirectly upon his attitude, because the Master was at this time living in Wei and would have been loath to make an open pronouncement on the question.

17 Whereas in daily life he used the Lu dialect. Similarly the Swiss, for example, use their own dialect in daily life, but Hochdeutsch in church services or in reciting a poem by Schiller. There is not much doubt that *ya* ("refined," "standard," "correct" as applied to speech 雅) is etymologically the same word as the ethnic term Xia, the common name of the Chinese, as opposed to the barbarians. To avoid the implication that Confucius sometimes spoke in his native dialect, Cheng Hao in the eleventh century interpreted *ya* as meaning not "standard," but "standardly," i.e. frequently. Hence Legge's "His frequent themes were···" But Zheng Xuan interprets the passage exactly as I have done.

18 An adventurer, known originally as Shen Zhuliang; first mentioned in 523 and still alive in 475. The title "Duke of She"was one which he had invented for himself.

19 According to the traditional chronology Confucius was sixty-two at the time when this was said.

20 Disorders of nature; such as snow in summer, owls hooting by day, or the like.

21 Minister of War in Song.

22 Familiar name of Confucius. There is no evidence that Confucius is here disclaiming the possession of an esoteric doctrine.

23 See Introduction, p. 289.

24 An impotent cipher pretending to be a Duke, powerless tools of adventurers.

25 See Terms, p.307. For "fowling," see *The Book of Songs*, p. 36.

26 As I do.

27 The higher being innate knowledge, which Confucius disclaims above, 7. 19. He thus (ironically) places himself at two removes from the hypothetical people who can dispense with knowledge, the three stages being: (1) those who do not need knowledge; (2) those who have innate knowledge; (3) those who accumulate it by hard work.

28 Unknown. Probably one of the places Confucius passed through during his travels.

29 The "capping" of boys marked their initiation into manhood.

30 A suppliant of any kind (whether asking a Master for teaching or Heaven for good crops) purifies himself by fasting and abstinence in order to enhance the power of his prayer.

31 Later regarded as a disciple of Confucius.

32 Duke Zhao, reigned from 541 to 510 B.C.

33 This is, of course, ironical. It would have been improper for Confucius to criticize his own late sovereign.

34 i.e. is there any ancient authority for such a rite?

35 What justifies me in the eyes of Heaven is the life I have led. There is no need for any rite now. In a fragment of one of the lost books of *Zhuangzi* there is a parallel story in which Zilu wants to take the omens about Confucius's chance of recovery, and Confucius says, "My omen-taking was done long ago!"

36 Cf. 3. 4. The lavishness of the Ji Family became presumption when it led them to have eight rows of dancers (3.1) and thereby infringe upon a ducal prerogative.

BOOK Ⅷ

1 Taibo was the eldest son of King Dan, legendary ancestor of the Zhou sovereigns. He renounced the throne in favour of his youngest brother.

2 Compare 17. 8.

3 The Pelliot Ms. supplies these words, which have dropped out of the current version.

4 While a man was dying four people held his hands and feet, "one for each limb"(*Li Ji*, XXII). After death, the hands and feet were freed(see supplement to the *Hou Han Shu*, Part III , fol. 1). Zeng says that he has got through safely, his moral course is run; there is no need to hold his hands and feet, which was done "in case the dying man should in his death-struggle get into some 'non-ritual' attitude." He interprets the *Song* 295 as describing the heavy responsibilities of the man who has "taken Goodness for his load"; see below, 8. 7. The passage quoted from the *Li Ji* refers, it must be admitted, to the death of an emperor, not a private person.Trussing up of various kinds and the placing of heavy weights on the body occur in many parts of the world, in some cases before death, in some cases after it. Where such practices take place after death, they are explained by anthropologists as being due to fear of the dead returning to life. Where they occur before death this explanation obviously does not hold good. The question is complicated by the fact that in China (and probably elsewhere?) many practices originally belonging to the period preceding death were in less primitive days delayed until death had actually taken place; see De Groot, *The Religious Systems of China*, I, p.9.

5 Son of Meng Wu (see 2. 6). He appears to have been still alive in

430 B.C.

6 Cf. our belief concerning "swan-songs."

7 It has been suggested that the friend in question was Yan Hui.

8 Literally, an orphan of six feet (i.e. four of our feet).

9 Literally, the command of a hundred leagues.

10 i.e. the Way.

11 i.e. of obtaining a paid appointment.

12 See 3. 20. For Zhi, see 18. 9.

13 In old days (see 17. 16) people at any rate had the merits of their faults.

14 For the legendary rulers Yao, Shun and Yu, see Introduction, p. 289.

15 i.e. Yao's *de*.

16 So that it remained a *yin de*（隐德）, "secret prestige." Cf. above, 8. 1.

17 The Warrior King, founder of the Zhou dynasty.

18 His mother, and his nine brothers? King Wu's statement that he had "ten ministers" is found in several passages of old literature; e.g. "Duke Xiang," 28th year, *Zuo Zhuan*.

19 i.e. the accession of Shun.

20 i.e. for "the right material," for an abundance of good ministers. Yet even then there were only five.

21 And by this act of cession (*rang*) building up the *de* required for his subsequent campaign.

22 To ancestors, and spirits of hill, stream, etc.

23 For Yu, see Introduction, p. 290.

BOOK Ⅸ

1 The commentators take the villager's "vastly learned," etc. not as

irony but as praise; for to achieve a reputation in any one line is unworthy of a *jun zi*（君子）. This seems to make Confucius's comment unintelligible. I take the villager to be a boorish, ignorant man who does not know that a true gentleman ought not to be known as a specialist in any one line.

2 For wear at the ancestral sacrifice; made of threads twisted from a very thin yarn, very costly to manufacture.

3 A border town held at various times by Zheng, Wei, Song and Lu. The people of Kuang are supposed to have mistaken Confucius for the adventurer Yang Huo (see 17.1) who had formerly created a disturbance in Kuang. The mistake was made more natural by the fact that Confucius's carriage was being driven by a man who had previously been associated with Yang Huo.

4 Gentlemen do not stoop to practical accomplishments; much less the Sage.

5 But the wickedness of the world prevented it.

6 The arrival of this magical bird and the sudden revelation of a magical chart were portents that heralded the rise of a Saviour Sage. See Terms, p.320.

7 Heaven does not intend to let me play a Sage's part.

8 A sign of respect.

9 Goodness.

10 Literally, "overtoppingly," like a mountain-top or the top of a tree.

11 The question at issue is, of course, whether a man of talent should try to obtain office. Confucius declares that he himself is only too anxious to "sell his jewel"(i.e. accept office), should any opportunity present itself.

12 The words of the Court pieces (*ya*雅) are contained in the second

and third parts, the Recitations (*song* 颂) in the last of the four great divisions of the *Book of Songs*.

13 Another instance of the idiomatic *he you*.

14 This surely refers to Yan Hui's early death.

15 Name of a collection of moral sayings?

16 Name of another collection of moral sayings, on the "choice" and "promotion" of the virtuous?

17 Confucius quotes these two lines from *Songs*, No.67.

18 Pun on two senses of *zang*（臧） (1) excellent; (2)treasure, to treasure up, to store.

19 i.e. with whom one cannot collaborate in office. Cf. 10.3 and 16. 13.

20. When one pulls it to pluck the blossom. Cf. *Songs*, 268. 1. Image of things that are torn apart after a momentary union. Evidently a verse from some song not included in our *Book of Songs*.

21 Men fail to attain to Goodness because they do not care for it sufficiently, not because Goodness "is far away." I think the old interpretation, which treats 29 and 30 as one paragraph, is definitely wrong.

BOOK X

1 The place where the ruler takes up his stand when seeing off important guests?

2 Symbol of the ruler's feudal investitute; the *gui*（圭）.

3 On a level with his forehead.

4 Here the compilers have forgotten to alter *jun zi* (gentleman) to Kongzi (Confucius).

5 Usually translated "purple." But the term is applied to the coats of

horses and cannot mean anything that we should call purple. These colours were reserved for times of fasting and mourning.

6 To do otherwise, would be like going out into the town in one's shirt-sleeves.

7 To give him freedom of movement .

8 Which are lucky talismans; or (in a more sophisticated vein of explanation) symbolic ornaments indicating his rank. Those of an ordinary gentleman were of jade.

9 i.e. "plain" articles must be worn, approximately to those worn by the mourner.

10 *Ming yi*(明衣), the "spirit robe" used during the period of purification.

11 All the above refers to periods of preparation for sacrifice.

12 For the Nuo (expulsion rite) see *Zhou Li*, ch. 48 and 54. The exorcist accompanied by four "Madmen" (see *The Book of Songs*, p.222) "wearing over their heads a bear's skin with four eyes of yellow metal (copper or gold?), clad in a black coat and red skirt, grasping halberd and raising shield, leads all the house-servants and performs the Nuo of the season, searching the house and driving out noxious influences."In many parts of Europe the whole household still visits every corner of the house and outbuildings on New Year's Eve, banging forks on dish-covers and so on, in order to drive out the Old Year.The *Ji Jie* says that Confucius stood on the eastern steps of the ancestral shrine during this ceremony "in order to reassure the ancestral spirits" of the house, who might otherwise have taken flight along with the "noxious influences." In Tang times the Nuo was stylized as a Court dance.

13 The place occupied by one who is presiding over a ceremony.

14 Head of the all-powerful Ji Family.

15 i.e. with his face to the North, where lies the land of the Dead.

16 Or "when he sees."

17 Traditionally explained as meaning "census tablets."

18 Does not look about promiscuously.

19 Pointing is considered maleficent, unlucky, rude, as the case may be, in many parts of the world.

20 Is circumspect in choosing a new State in which to settle.

21 This quatrain (if such it is intended to be) resembles in content the songs by means of which the people commented on current political events. It is natural to interpret it as referring to the circumspect conduct of Confucius when the Ji Family (through the agency of Zilu) invited him to return to Lu. One makes an offering to birds or animals whose behaviour suggests that they are sent by Heaven as omens or portents. For an anecdote of Zilu and a pheasant, see *Lü Shi Chun Qiu*, 44.1.

BOOK XI

1 This classification of the disciples is not put into the mouth of Confucius, as is clear from the form in which the names are given.

2 Min Ziqian's mother died when he was a child and his father married again. One day when he was driving his father's carriage he let the reins slip. His father found that he was wearing such thin gloves that his hands were numbed with cold. On going home he looked at the gloves worn by the two children born to him by his second wife and found that they were thick and warm. He said to his wife, "I married you solely in order to have someone to look after my motherless children. Now I can see that you have been imposing upon me. Leave my home at once!" Ziqian said, "If my step-mother remains, one child will be imperfectly

clad; but if she goes, several children will be cold." His father said no more about it. (Fragment of lost portions of *Shuo Yuan*.)

3 The Song in question is No. 271; see verse 5: A flaw in a white jade sceptre may be polished away; but a flaw in words cannot be repaired. "Gave him his brother's daughter," cf. 5. 1.

4 *Guo* (the word translated "enclosure" 椁) meant, as may be seen most clearly from the paragraph on "Inspecting the *guo* and grave-figures" in *Yi Li*, Ⅻ, a protection for the coffin made by laying beams longways and crossways, like the framework at the top of a well. In later times *guo* meant an "outer coffin," a "shell." In Japan the term "stone *guo*" has been applied to the *allées couvertes* of Japanese megalithic structures.

5 Confucius thus apologizes for putting his son on a level with Yan Hui.

6 The name means "carp-fish." Later tradition makes him die later than Yan Hui.

7 It was the *shi* ("knights," "gentlemen," those who fought in chariots and not afoot) who ranked after the Great Officers, and it is possible that Confucius ranked as "leader of the *shi*." See Terms, p.305.

8 Failed to assert my right to bury him in the way I thought suitable.

9 Zilu. For his death in 480 B.C. during the accession struggles in Wei, see "Ai Gong," 15th year, *Zuo Zhuan*. Confucius may well have said this on hearing of Zilu's death. The words are usually regarded as a prophecy.

10 The point of the remark is very uncertain. Duke Zhao, who fled from Lu in 517, had used this building as a basis for operations against his enemies, the Ji Family. It is probable, therefore, that the remark of Min Ziqian was applauded by Confucius for its loyalist, pro-dynastic tendency.

11 i.e. Zizhang or Zixia.

12 i.e. Ran Qiu. The form in which the name is given suggests that these words were spoken by Confucius or a disciple and are not a statement of the compiler's.

13 Gao Chai, associated with Zilu in the Wei accession troubles.

14 Master Zeng.

15 Zizhang. The meaning of the epithet *pi*（辟）is very uncertain. Zhu Xi's "it means that he was expert in ritual attitudes and deportment, but lacked sincerity" is not a philological gloss on *pi*, but an application to this passage of what is said about Zizhang in 19.16.

16 Tradition represents Zilu as a converted swashbuckler.

17 To Goodness. The rest of the paragraph runs very awkwardly and is probably corrupt.

18 Of the Ancients.

19 Brother of the head of the Ji Family.

20 See 6. 7.

21 The Millet is in early texts always closely associated with the Holy Ground and not treated as the object of a separate cult. It was interpreted as symbolizing the fruits of the soil in general. It was no doubt a sheaf of millet (if grain had been meant another word would have been used) and may have been the Last Sheaf, kept over from the previous harvest. "Last Sheaf" ceremonies are common in India, Indo-China and Indonesia.

22 In which the "stupid" (see 11. 17) Chai was not proficient.

23 The pertness of Zilu's remark consists of the fact that he throws in the Master's teeth a favourite Confucian maxim.

24 For *fang*, "direction," cf. 6. 28. Courage, it will be remembered, is the lowest of the three virtues. Next comes wisdom; next Goodness.

25 Which are the perquisites of the upper classes as opposed to the common people.

26 Scrupulously defined as "Audiences" by the later ritualists, because in theory they were presided over by the Son of Heaven (the king of Zhou).

27 i.e. Zeng Xi; he was the father of Master Zeng.

28 Or "I fear my choice will seem inferior to that of…"

29 A technical name for the clothes worn at the ceremony?

30 *Rang*, "giving up," "ceding to others."

31 i.e. it is impossible to conceive of Gongxi Hua functioning on such an occasion except as the ruler of a kingdom; so that, in effect, all three were asking for kingdoms.

BOOK XII

1 A formula of thanks for instruction.

2 i.e. ruling by Goodness, not by force.

3 i.e. in handling public affairs.

4 A native of Song; brother of Huan Tui, 7. 22.

5 Here again Confucius is evasive about the meaning of Goodness. He first puns on *ren*(讱), "chary," and *ren*, "Goodness"; and then in his second reply answers as though his first reply had meant "Goodness is a thing one ought to be chary of talking about." The implication is that the questioner had not yet reached a stage at which the mysteries of *ren* could be revealed to him.

6 This may merely mean that his brother Huan Tui, being an enemy of Confucius, could no longer be regarded by Niu as a brother. When Niu died in 481 B.C. he left behind him at least three brothers.

7 That bound the universe.

8 A statesman of Wei.

9 The man of good birth is potentially capable of "patterning his coat" with culture, and thus distinguishing himself from the common herd. But good birth alone, though essential as a basis for culture, is not enough to make a gentleman in the Confucian sense.

10 All the people.

11 "If right prevails in a country, then serve it; if right does not prevail, then seek service elsewhere."

12 Couplet from *Song* 105.3, in which a lady says: I came all this long way to marry you, and you do not give me enough to eat. I shall go back to my country and home. Your thoughts are occupied with a new mate. If it is true that it is not because of her riches, then it is simply for the sake of a change. The last phrase ("only for a change") is susceptible of other interpretations. But it is clearly thus that Confucius understands it, and he uses this story of a man who got a wife from a far country, and then promptly neglected her in favour of someone taken up "simply for a change," as an example of "being in two minds," "not knowing one's own mind."

13 Died 490 B.C. The last of a long line of powerful and successful dukes. The closing years of his reign were clouded by the intrigues of the Chen Family, which menaced the security of the dynasty (the prince was no longer a prince; ministers, i.e. the leaders of the Chen faction, were no longer content to be ministers); and by succession-squabbles among his sons (the father no longer had the authority of a father; the sons were not content to be sons).

14 Figure of speech denoting utter insecurity. Legend makes Duke Jing haunted by the fear of death.

15 This is a rhetorical way of saying that if Ji Kang did not accumulate valuables, he would not be robbed. But coupled with this meaning is the suggestion that the ruler's moral force operates directly on the people, as a magic, not merely as an example.

16 *Da*, able to turn his *de* to account. See 6. 6.

17 *Lü yi xia ren* （虑以下人）. Cf. "Xuan Gong," 12th year, *Zuo Zhuan*, "A people whose prince knows how to defer to others (*neng yi xia ren* 能以下人) may be treated as reliable." *Lü*（虑）sometimes means "in general," "on the whole." (See Wang Niansun, *Du Shu Za Zhi,* 8.4 and Yu Yue, H.P. 1392, fol.7.) I doubt if that is the sense here.

18 See above, para. 10. Here all three phrases rhyme; the phrases supplied by Confucius also rhyme, and are presumably quotations from a didactic poem.

19 A rhyming triplet. Not knowing the full context either of the poem which the disciple quotes or of the one which Confucius utilizes in his reply, we cannot hope to understand the exact force of this passage.

20 This applies only to the second answer.

21 See above, 2. 19.

BOOK XIII

1 So that your time may not be taken up with petty preliminaries.

2 The whole of this highly elaborate, literary paragraph bears the stamp of comparatively late date. See Introduction, p. 293. The links in chain-arguments of this kind are always rhetorical rather than logical; and it would be a waste of time to seek for a causal sequence. Later Confucian literature supplies many examples of such rhetorical "chains."For *gou* ("chance" 苟) see *Han Shi Wai Zhuan*, III. fol. 1 and IV. fol. 1 verso.

Also "Zhao Gong," 18th year, *Zuo Zhuan*. It is used when things are done "somehow or other," in a "hit or miss" offhand fashion, when everything is "left to chance." In hypothetical clauses it means "if by any chance," "if somehow or other." It applies wherever a result is achieved by mere accident and not as the result of *de* ("virtue," moral power). Cf. 8. 8.

3 Bear false witness in lawsuits.

4 Confucius took the traditional view that it is for common people to work with their hands, for gentlemen to work with their *de*. Fan Chi had evidently been influenced by views similar to those of Xu Xing (*Mencius*, 3.1) who held that it was unfair to live by the labour of others and maintained that "the wise man should plough side by side with the common people." There is a parallel passage in *Mozi* ("Lu Wen," Pian 49), where "a low fellow, from the south of Lu, called Wu Lü," reproaches Mozi with preaching justice, while all the time living on the labour of others. Mozi's reply amounts practically to saying that he is promoting justice more by teaching it to others than he would be by practising it himself.

5 Besides delivering his message, he must be able to give an answer of his own to particular enquiries relative to this message.

6 On the rise of the Zhou dynasty to power, Lu was given to the fourth and Wei to the seventh son of King Wen. The saying expresses, one may suppose, the disillusionment of Confucius on finding that things in Wei were no better than in Lu. In early times, however, it was understood as a commendation of Wei.

7 Flourished about 558 B.C.

8 My household rites.

9 See Terms, p.320.

10 The play on *zheng*（正）"to straighten, put right" and *zheng*（政）

"to govern" makes this passage impossible to translate satisfactorily.

11 From the Court of the Ji Family, who had usurped the Duke's powers.

12 i.e. have no official post.

13 The stop should come after *ruo shi*（若是）.

14 i.e. about the tokens of good government.

15 A town in Lu.

16 For *da*, see 6. 6.

17 A legendary paragon of honesty.

18 For *keng keng*（硁硁）, see 14. 42.

19 "Mere thimblefuls," as we should say.

20 Than the timid and conscientious.

21 Play on *heng*（恒）(1) a rite for stabilizing, perpetuating the power of good omens and auspicious actions. It seems clear that *heng* was the name of a ritual. Cf. *Zhou Li*, ch. 50: "If a great calamity befalls the land, then send for *wu* (*shamans* 巫) and perform the *wu heng* (shamanistic *heng* ceremony)." The explanations given by Zheng Xuan and other *Zhou Li* commentators are forced and unconvincing. *Mozi* (XXXII. Forke's translation. p.371) quotes from a "book of the former kings": "to perform the *heng* dance in the palace is called yielding to the influence of shamans." To dance *heng* "continually" (which is the usual interpretation) makes poor sense. I would also suggest that the words "ill, *heng*, not die" in the *Book of Changes*, section16, mean "if anyone is ill, perform the *heng* rite and he will not die." The saying of the "men of the south" (i.e. of Chu?) is also quoted in Section 32 of the *Changes*;(2)steadfast, in the moral sense.

22 For "*shaman* or witch-doctor" the *Li Ji* (33, fol.3) has "diviner by the yarrow stalks."

23 “Accommodating” (*tong* 同) means ready to sacrifice principles to agreement. Cf. the common phrase *gou tong*（苟同）, “to agree somehow or other,” i.e. at all costs.

24 Or “wooden,” i.e. simple.

25 i.e. followers of the Way. The “instruction” is, of course, in virtue, not in the use of arms.

BOOK XIV

1 With regard to accepting rewards. It will be remembered that it was Yuan Si(see above, 6.3) who was rebuked for refusing a salary. The omission of his surname has led to the supposition that he was the compiler of this chapter.

2 See Terms, p.305.

3 Son of Meng Yi; see 2. 5.

4 A legendary hero. His name is cognate to the word for rainbow.

5 Shook his enemies out of it, at the great battle in which he destroyed the Zhenxun clan.

6 Yi was slain by his minister Zhuo of Han. Zhuo's son Ao was in turn slain by Shao Kang.

7 For Great Yu drained the land and so made it suitable for agriculture. Hou Ji, from whom the Zhou people were descended, was [as his name implies; *ji*（稷）=millet] the patron deity of agriculture.

8 As opposed to physical strength such as that displayed by Yi and Ao.

9 As a father loves a son or a prince his people.

10 Flourished in the middle of the sixth century B.C.

11 The word is often used in a bad sense. Kindliness is often a feeble

amends for neglect of duty. Thus Zichan took people across the rivers in his own carriage; but he ought to have mended the bridges.

12 A famous minister of the Chu State; assassinated in 479 B.C. According to the accounts of him in the *Zuo Zhuan* he did and said much of which Confucius would certainly have approved. The exclamation with which his name is here received is, however, certainly one of disapprobation. The story that he prejudiced his prince against Confucius was probably merely invented to explain this passage.

13 A stock expression, merely meaning "in humble circumstances."

14 So great was Guan Zhong's prestige. This is the tenor of many stories about Guan Zhong. He struck with an arrow the man who was afterwards to become Duke Huan of Qi; yet the Duke forgave him and made him Prime Minister. He broke all the sumptuary laws; yet if never occurred to the people of Qi to regard him as "presumptuous."

15 As the head of the Bo Family managed to do.

16 Let alone in a great State like Lu. Meng Gongchuo was a Lu politician who flourished about 548 B.C. The Zhao and Wei were noble families in Jin.

17 Middle of the sixth century; grandson of Zang Wenzhong, 5. 17.

18 The paragon of legendary prowess.

19 Presumably a retainer of Gongshu Wen.

20 Spoken of as "very aged" in 504 B.C., and apparently dead in 497 B.C, the year (according to the traditional chronology) of Confucius's first visit to Wei, Gongshu Wen's native place. See "Ding Gong," 6th year and 13th year, *Zuo Zhuan*.

21 Took rewards.

22 In 550 Zang Wuzhong, accused of plotting a revolt, was obliged to go into exile. On his way he seized the fief of Fang, and then sent word to

the Duke offering to proceed into exile and relinquish Fang, on condition that he should be allowed to hand the fief over to his brother Zang Wei. The request was granted.("Duke Xiang," 23rd year, *Zuo Zhuan*.) The later commentators fail to realize that "Wei" is a proper name and unsuccessfully attempt to turn it into *wei*（为）, "to do." Translators have followed suit.

23 The usual interpretation, "Wen was crafty and not upright, Huan was upright and not crafty" is, as Wang Niansun long ago observed (*Jing Yi Shu Wen*, on this passage), nonsensical. The story of Wen (Double Ears, as he was called) is known to us chiefly through a heroic legend embodied in *Guo Yu*, Ⅸ and Ⅹ. The commentators try to discover a lack of ritual correctness in the story of his being visited by the Divine King (Tian-wang, i.e. the ruler of Zhou). But this requires some ingenuity. We only know a legend that praises him; we must suppose Confucius to have known one which denigrated him.Of Duke Huan's failure in emergencies no convincing example is cited. For this sense of *jue*（谲）, see Liu Baonan's *Lun Yu Zheng Yi*.

24 Both Guan Zhong and Shao Hu were supporting Prince Jiu's claim to the dukedom. Prince Xiao Bai (afterwards to become Duke Huan)murdered his brother Prince Jiu and seized the ducal throne; whereupon Guan Zhong, the great opportunist, transferred his allegiance to the murderer.

25 i.e. Guan Zhong's.

26 As the barbarians do. Duke Huan stemmed the great invasion of the Di tribes.

27 As a historical event; not at the time when it happened.

28 The head of the Ji Family.

29 Known posthumously as Kong Wen.

30 Goodness.

31 As became a suppliant. The assassination took place in 481 B.C.

32 A famous Wei minister. See below, 15.6.

33 Or "is trying to lessen his offence." Qu Boyu may have promised to get Confucius a post in Wei and failed to do so. The message may mean that he is still trying, but has not yet succeeded arranging anything.

34 Zeng illustrates Confucius's saying by quoting an old maxim, which also figures, in practically identical form, in the first appendix ("Xiang") of the *Book of Changes*, section 52. In my paper on the *Book of Changes* (Bulletin of the Museum of Far Eastern Antiquities, No.5), I quote this saying as though it occurred in the text of the *Book* itself, an error which I take this opportunity of correcting.

35 Is precisely how you yourself behave. Usually taken as referring to Confucius's disclaimer("I myself have met with success in none," etc. and meaning, "So you yourself say; but we know that is only due to your modesty, and do not take your words literally)."

36 Usually taken as meaning "who does not anticipate deceit… and, yet immediately perceives it when it occurs." There are two objections to this rendering:(1) the *yi*（抑）of *bu xin*（不信）, *yi*… usually means "or," not "but"; (2) *xian jue*（先觉）normally means to perceive beforehand, not "to perceive immediately," and the text says nothing about "when it has occurred," or the like.

37 Familiar name of Confucius, the form of address is discourteous. It is surmised that Weisheng Mu was a recluse.

38 It is no use going on and on trying to convert a prince. After a time one must give it up, and try elsewhere.

39 A famous horse of ancient times. A rhymed couplet.

40 It originally meant "Let the ruler meet discontent among his sub-

jects with *de* and not with violence."Confucius here uses it in a much more general sense.

41 No ruler recognizes my merits and employs me.

42 The self-training consisting in the study of antiquity.

43 A retainer of the Ji Family, friendly with Zigong.

44 Ji Kang's.

45 This continues the theme of the last paragraph. If *Tao* (the Way) does not prevail, it is better to flee altogether from the men of one's generation, rather than to go round "perching first here, then there" as Confucius himself had unsuccessfully done, or to wait till the expression of the ruler's face betrays that he is meditating some enormity; or worst of all, to wait till his words actually reveal his intention.

46 i.e. inventors, "culture-heroes," originators of fire, agriculture, metallurgy, boats, carriages, the potter's wheel, the loom. Their names are variously given.

47 On the frontiers of Lu and Qi? Both this and the next paragraph belong to popular legend rather than to the traditions of the school.

48 In *Song* 54. The meaning here is, "Take the world as you find it."

49 *Guo*(果) here means "*en effet*," not "effective," "resolute."

50 i.e. in mourning for his father. Gao Zong's traditional date is 1324-1266B.C.

51 i.e. carries on immemorial usages and customs.

52 Other gentlemen.

53 Whereas he ought to have been standing when his teacher arrived and only to have sat down when told to do so.

54 i.e. taking advantage of his visits to the house of Confucius.

BOOK XV

1 As though by a flood.

2 Familiar name of Zigong.

3 Familiar name of Zilu.

4 *Wu wei*(无为), the phrase applied by the Taoists to the immobility of self-hypnosis.

5 In your place at Court.

6 Having failed to persuade Duke Ling of Wei to use the services of Qu Boyu, the recorder Yu gave directions that when he (the recorder) died his body should not receive the honours due to a minister, as a posthumous protest against the Duke Ling's offences.

7 Qu Boyu left Wei owing to the tyrannical conduct of Duke Xian in 559 B.C. No tense is expressed in the first clause. I say "is" because in 14.26, Qu Boyu appears to be still alive. It is, however, not very probable that he was, as legend asserts, still alive when Confucius visited Wei in 495 B.C.

8 His jewel; i.e. his talents.

9 About the Way.

10 The written forms of *zhi* (志) and *ren* are here half-punningly insisted upon.

11 It was believed that in the Xia dynasty the year began in the spring.

12 Which were less ornate than those of Zhou, say the commentators. But this is a mere guess.

13 Which had some resemblance to our scholastic mortar-board.

14 The words to these tunes are in the seventh book of the *Songs*. But it was probably to the character of the music not to that of the words

that Confucius objected. The tunes of Zheng and Wei are often referred to as "new music" or the "common music of the world." Towards classical music, the "music of the former Kings" (*Mencius*, 1. 2) ordinary as opposed to serious-minded people had the same feelings as they have towards our own classical music to-day. "How is it," the Prince of Wei asked Zixia, "that when I sit listening to old music, dressed in my full ceremonial gear, I am all the time in terror of dropping off asleep; whereas when I listen to the tunes of Zheng and Wei, I never feel the least tired?"(*Li Ji*, XIX , fol.5).

15 To lead into the Way.

16 Which contradicts the saying before. As both sayings completely lack context, it would be a waste of time to try to reconcile the contradiction.

17 This is a proverbial saying, capable of many interpretations. To the Taoists it meant "Seek Tao in yourself (through the practice of quietism) and not in the outside world."

18 Xia,Yin and Zhou.

19 When in doubt; instead of trusting to his imagination.

20 Another instance of diffidence, parallel to "leaving blanks." The current interpretation is "lent it to others to drive." This gives a sense totally unconnected with what goes before. Moreover, *jie ren*(借人) occurs elsewhere in the sense "to avail oneself of the services of others," but never is the sense "to lend to others." *Jie*(借) in the sense "to lend" is very rare in early texts, while in the sense "to borrow" it is very common.

21 Without effort on his part. Play on "Way" and "road." "A man can widen a road …", etc.

22 Whereas one should never condemn one who is amending his faults.

23 This paragraph reads at first sight as though it were the record of a personal experience. In reality it is meant in a much more general way.

24 This paragraph with its highly literary, somewhat empty elaboration, and its placing of ritual on a pinnacle far above Goodness, is certainly one of the later additions to the book. For the chain-like rhetorical development, cf. 13. 3.

25 The usual interpretation is "It is impossible for us to recognize a gentleman when he is merely employed in small matters." But I do not see how such a sense can be forced out of the text as it stands. For the undesirability of a gentleman's having miscellaneous accomplishments, cf. 9.6.

26 A symbolic "treading upon fire" is still used in China as a rite of purification. According to the *Lun Heng* (Pian 45) a processional wading along the river was part of the rain-making ceremony. Confucius says that Goodness (on the part of the ruler) is a greater and safer purifier than even water or fire.

27 Between us and the Sages. Any of us could turn into a Yao or Shun, if we trained ourselves as they did.

28 *Ci*（辞）means pleas, messages, excuses for being unable to attend to one's duties, etc.

29 Music-masters were blind.

BOOK XVI

1 A small independent State within the borders of Lu.

2 Who were in the service of the Ji Family.

3 The Zhou Emperors.

4 An ancient sage.

5 Military metaphor, here applied to politics.

6 i.e. it is the fault of the person in charge of these things.

7 The chief castle of the Ji Family.

8 For the ideas underlying this passage, see Terms, p.311.

9 His own lack of *de* and the fact that he has bad advisers.

10 The *ming*（命）of a State is the charge whereby the Emperor appoints its feudal lord.

11 People not belonging to the Imperial family.

12 Surrendered by the Duke to the Three Families.

13 The heads of the Ji Family. The first three paragraphs of this book seem to form a connected unity. It was under Ji Kang (succeeded in 492 B.C.) that Zilu and Ran Qiu were colleagues. If we take paragraph 3 as having been spoken subsequent to 492 B.C., the five powerless Dukes must be Cheng, Xiang, Zhao, Ding and Ai; and the four Ministers, Ji Wu, Ji Ping, Ji Huan and Ji Kang. But it would be a mistake to try to fit into too strict a chronology sayings that may be purely legendary. For the late date of Book XVI, see Introduction, p.296.

14 The Three Families, Ji, Meng and Shu.

15 This is clearly the same formula as 8. 1(end), where, however, it is used in praise and not, as here, in condemnation.

16 i.e. are not Boyi and Shuqi, examples of people who dwelt in seclusion to fulfil their aims, by deeds of righteousness extended the influence of the Way?

17 Confucius's son; see 11. 7.

18 *Zi*（子）here means "son" and not "you, my master."

19 As a sign of respect.

20 On public occasions.

21 There is a definite ritual severance between father and son. A father may not carry his son in his arms. A son may not, when sacrifice is being made to his deceased father, act as the "medium" into whom the spirit of the deceased passes. See *Li Ji*, I, fol. 5.

22 This paragraph is a passage on etiquette from some old handbook

of ritual, and was probably inserted here merely because it was found along with the manuscript of this *pian* ("chapter"篇). It will be noticed that although the words *ren* ("person" 人) and *jun* ("prince" 君), here applied to a lady, are not exclusively masculine, they are chiefly and prevailingly applied to men rather than to women. For example, in 8.20, Confucius says that King Wu had not really "ten *ren*" to help him; for one of them was a woman. *Xiao tong* ("little boy"小童) means a pageboy, and is an exclusively masculine term. Thus it may be said that the sovereign's wife may not be referred to (either by himself or anyone else) by any term that is feminine in implication and must in referring to herself use a term that is definitely masculine.This is in obedience to the general principle that a sovereign must be spoken of as though he were free from ordinary human needs and desires. It will also be noted that the sovereign speaks of himself as the "lonely one." This he does under all circumstances, and not only in reference to his wife. Thus his city is "the lonely one's city," etc. In China he was "lonely" in the sense that his father whose throne he had inherited, was necessarily dead. But a king is often technically motherless as well as fatherless. For at his accession he must either, as in some parts of the world, marry his mother, and so lose her as a mother; or else "never set eyes on his mother." Or again, his mother has been ritually sacrificed during the funeral ceremony of his father. It is possible that the expression "the lonely one" goes back in China to times when the king was technically motherless as well as fatherless.

BOOK XVII

1 The person who seized power in Lu in 505 B.C.

2 i.e. his talents.

3 The form of assent Confucius uses implies reluctance. This story, like those in Books XVIII and XIII, certainly originated in non-Confucian circles and comes from the same sort of source as the Confucius Anecdotes in the Taoist works *Zhuangzi* and *Liezi*.

4 This proverbial saying has wide possibilities of application. It here presumably means that Goodness is a matter of training and application and not an inborn quality.

5 Where Ziyou was in command. See 6. 12.

6 A saying of proverbial type meaning, in effect, that in teaching music to the inhabitants of this small town Ziyou is "casting pearls before swine." The proverb may well have had a second, balancing clause, here alluded to, but not expressed; such as, "To teach commoners one does not use a zithern."

7 Warden of Mi, the chief stronghold of the Ji Family. He revolted in 502, but in 498 he fled to Qi and later to Wu where he is said to have plotted, in a spirit of petty revenge, against his native State of Lu.

8 Confucius believes that Gongshan intends to restore the Duke to his rightful powers.

9 Create a second Golden Age, comparable to the early days of the Zhou dynasty.

10 This is almost certainly a quotation from some text of the *Shu Jing*. Cf. 20. 1, where most of it reappears.

11 A Jin officer.

12 A town in Wei, captured by the Jin(in 490?).

13 Till it is dry and can be used as a vessel.

14 Play on two senses of *shi*（食）(1) to eat; (2) to get a salary, an official post.

15 i.e. learning the Way of the ancients.

16 i.e. keeping regrettable pacts and promises to the detriment of *yi* ("what is right under the circumstances" 义).

17 The tendency to fling oneself into any revolutions or upheavals that are going on in the world around one.

18 i.e. the "correct names," the names in the ancient Court dialect used in ritual, as opposed to the local names.

19 The first two books of the *Songs*.

20 What follows is a paradox, for we expect to hear that the people have improved; whereas it turns out that the "lost parts" were redeeming features.

21 By command of Heaven.

22 Of whom practically nothing is known. He had evidently disgraced himself.

23 For parents. Three years is often interpreted as meaning "into the third year," i.e. 25 months.

24 The mourning for parents entailed complete suspension of all ordinary activities.

25 A traditional saying.

26 *Ren* is here used in its later sense, "possessing human feelings," "kind." This chapter, it will be remembered (see Introduction, p.293), shows many signs of late date.

27 The whole object of this paragraph is to claim Confucius as a supporter of the three years' mourning. This custom was certainly far from being "universal," and was probably not ancient.

28 *Liu*(流) has been wrongly inserted here on the analogy of 19. 20.

29 This "said" has accidentally been transferred to the clause above.

BOOK XVIII

1 i.e. from the tyrant Zhou, last sovereign of the Yin dynasty. The lord of Wei was his step-brother. Ther lord of Ji and Bi Gan were his uncles.

2 A comparatively humble post. Its occupant was chiefly concerned with criminal cases.

3 As pointed out in the Introduction, Book XVIII is wholly legendary in content. The Confucius who ranked above the head of the Meng Family is already well on the way towards apotheosis.

4 In order to weaken the power of the government. A common folk-lore theme.

5 The father of Ji Kang; died 492.

6 From his carriage.

7 Or should do; for he claims to be a Sage.

8 Cf. 14.20.

9 Who would not know how to choose the right seed for sowing. The five kinds of grain are rice, two kinds of millet, wheat and pulse.

10 The palms pressed together in an attitude of respect.

11 Brother of Taibo, 8. 1.

12 Confucius seems here to be commenting on some text which is unknown to us.

13 This whole paragraph is certainly corrupt. Liuxia Hui hung on to office despite every rebuff, and cannot be counted as a "lost subject." After the name of Yiyi some phrase must have followed meaning "those who concealed their discontent," or the like.

14 Or "at the second course."

15 i.e. to the north of.

16 To an island.

17 Cf. 13. 25.

18 A sign that a country had reached the maximum of plenty and fertility was that one woman should bear four pairs of twins.

BOOK XIX

1 Saying for example that *de* has its uses, but that the ultimate appeal must always be to physical compulsion.

2 i.e. tolerates.

3 Literally, what becomes of that [*qi*(其) in such usages corresponds to the Latin *iste*] "keeping others at a distance" of yours?

4 Such as agriculture, medicine, etc. The idea that specialized knowledge is incompatible with true gentility prevailed in England till well towards the close of the nineteenth century.

5 Cf. 2. 18, 7. 15, 13. 18 and 15. 21.

6 i.e. all the different sorts of…

7 In matters such as loyalty, keeping promises, obedience to parents, the laws which govern his conduct are absolute. In lesser matters he is allowed a certain latitude. Several early writers attribute the saying to Confucius himself.

8 Died in 550 B.C.

9 Meng Xian, died in 554 B.C.

10 Meng Wu, who succeeded to the headship of the clan in 481 B.C., usually explained as meaning Meng Yi, predecessor of Meng Wu. But in his time (if we are to follow the traditional chronology) Master Zeng would have been too young to be consulted. It must be remembered, however, that the Confucian legend was not built up by people who had

chronological tables open in front of them.

11 A post involving the judging of criminal cases.

12 Unknown.

13 So called to distinguish him from a number of Gongsun Chaos in other countries.

14 i.e. Confucius.

15 The usual interpretation:"It is still here among men," implies a very abrupt construction.

16 Flourished c. 500 B.C.

BOOK XX

1 *Tian zhi li shu*（天之历数）was no doubt understood in a quasi-abstract sense by the compilers of the *Analects*: "Heaven's succession," i.e. the succession accorded by Heaven. It is possible, however, that in its original setting, as a formula used in the accession-rites of kings, it had a much more concrete sense: "The calendar and counting-sticks of Heaven"(i.e. of the Ancestors).There is a hiatus after "his charge to Yu." In other Chinese works (e.g. in the forged portions of the *Shu Jing*, in *Mozi* and in the *Guo Yu*) many of the sentences strung together in this paragraph will be found utilized for a different purpose and interpreted with a different meaning. A discussion of all these parallels belongs rather to the textual criticism of the *Shu Jing* than to a study of the *Analects*, and I shall not attempt it here.The Gu version treated 20. 2 and 3 as a separate book.

2 i.e. "sooner shall the sea run dry, than this gift···" For *yong zhong*（永终）, cf. *Shu Jing*, *Metal Casket*, 10.

3 Founder of the Yin dynasty, when informing the Supreme Ancestor of his (Tang's) accession. Lü was his personal name.

4 The Xia, whom Tang had defeated.

5 This "scape-goat" formula is constantly referred to in early Chinese literature.

6 i.e. those who distinguished themselves in the campaign against Yin. The speaker is presumably King Wu.

7 "He who is broad" down to "undertakes" occurs also in 17. 6.

8 For these enumerations, cf. 16. 4-8.

9 i.e. cannot get beneath the surface-meaning and understand the state of mind that the words really imply.

原版译者引言

TRANSLATOR'S INTRODUCTION

THOUGHT grows out of environment. Ideally speaking the translator of such a book as the *Analects* ought to furnish a complete analysis of early Chinese society, of the processes which were at work within it and of the outside forces to which it reacted. Unfortunately our knowledge of the period is far too incomplete for any such synthesis to be possible. The literary documents are scanty and of uncertain date; scientific archaeology in China has suffered constant setbacks and is still in its infancy. All that I have attempted in the following pages is to arrange such information as is accessible under a series of disconnected headings, in a convenient order, but without pretence of unity or logical sequence.

CONFUCIUS

The Confucius of whom I shall speak here is the Confucius of the *Analects*.[1] One could construct half a dozen other Confuciuses by tapping the legend at different stages of its evolution. We should see the Master becoming no longer a moral teacher but a "wise man" according to the popular conception of wisdom that existed in non-Confucian circles

1 I omit the obviously legendary material in Book XVIII, and the ritual portrait in Book X. Also a few passages akin to Book XIV (such as 14.34, 41, 42, and 17.1)in that they clearly emanate from circles hostile to Confucius.

in China and in our own Middle Ages, an answerer of grotesque conundrums, a prophet, a magician even. We should see the disappointed itinerant tutor of the *Analects* turning into a successful statesman and diplomatist, employed not only in his own country but in neighbouring States as well.[1]

But I shall act here on the principle recently advocated by that great scholar Gu Jiegang, the principle of "one Confucius at a time." Not that we can regard the Confucius of the *Analects* as wholly historical; still less, that we must dismiss as fiction all data about the Master that do not happen to occur in this book. But in the first place the biographical facts deducible from the *Analects* are those which are most relevant to an understanding of the book itself; and secondly, the picture of Confucius given in the *Analects*, besides being the earliest that we possess, differs from that of all other books in that it contains no elements that bear patently and obviously the stamp of folk-lore or hagiography. What then was Confucius? It appears from the *Analects* that he was a private person who trained the sons of gentlemen in the virtues proper to a member of the ruling classes. It is clear, however, that he was not content with this position and longed for a more public one, either in his own State or in some other, which would give him the opportunity to put into practice the Way which he regarded as that of the Former Kings, the Way of Goodness, long ago discarded by the rulers of the world in favour of a Way of violence and aggression. There is not the slightest indication that he ever obtained such a position. Twice, however, he speaks of himself as "following after" the Great Officers of Court. Those who ranked next to the Great Officers (*dai fu* 大夫) were the Knights(*shi* 士), and if

1 The legend of Confucius's worldly success, transferred to the West, has continued its growth on European soil. Meyer's *Konversationslexicon*(1896) goes so far as to say that he was "received with the highest honours at every Court" in China.

Confucius ranked immediately after the Great Officers(as he seems to suggest) he must at the time have been *shi-shi*(士师)[1], Leader of the Knights, which was not politically speaking a position of any importance. Discontented with the slow progress of his doctrines in the land of Lu, Confucius travelled from State to State,[2] seeking for a ruler who would give the Way its chance. The only disciples actually mentioned as accompanying him are Ran Qiu,Zilu, and his favourite disciple Yan Hui. The States and towns which they visited(Qi, Wei, Chen, Cai and Kuang)all lay within the modern provinces of Shandong and Henan. The strangers evidently met with a hostile reception, and had occasionally to endure severe privation. Several of the disciples were in the service of Ji Kang, the dictator of Lu;and it may have been owing to their good offices that Confucius was at last encouraged to return to his native State.

Concerning his private life, we learn from the *Analects* that he had been brought up in humble circumstances.[3]Of his marriage nothing is said;but two children are mentioned, a daughter[4] and a son whom the Master outlived. [5]An older brother is mentioned, but Confucius seems to have acted as head of the family, and this is explained by later tradition as due to the fact that the elder brother was a cripple.

Confucius speaks of himself in one place(2.4) as being over seventy.

---

1 The original function of the *shi-shi* was to "keep the Knights in order"; cf. *Mencius* 1.2,6.2. In practice he acted under the orders of the Minister of Justice and functioned as a sort of policemagistrate. In the second stage of its development the Confucian legend represents the Master as achieving the position of Minister of Justice, an idea which may well have grown out of his having in fact been Leader of the Knights.

2 This mobility was typical of Chinese society. Not only moralists, but warriors, craftsmen and even peasants moved from State to State, if they thought that by doing so they could improve their chances of success.

3 9.6. But the saying from which we learn this was a disputed one, and an alternative version of it is given immediately afterwards, "But Lao says the Master said…"etc. This alternative version refers to lack of official employment,but not to poverty. **4** 5.1. **5** 11.7.

As to the exact dates of his birth and death the *Analects* tell us nothing. It can be inferred, however, from references to contemporary persons and events, that the time of his main activity was the end of the sixth and the first twenty years or so of the fifth century.[1]

After his apotheosis in the Han dynasty Confucius was credited with the omniscience and moral infallibility of the Divine Sage. This view of him appears, indeed, to have been current even during his lifetime;for we find him at pains to disclaim any such attributes.[2] Nor would he allow himself to be regarded as Good, [3] a disclaimer that is natural enough, seeing that he accords this title only to a few legendary heroes of the remote past. Even in the social virtues which formed the basis of his teaching he claimed no preeminence. There was not, he said, a hamlet of ten houses but could produce men as loyal and dependable as himself. He denied (though one disciple at least seems to have had the opposite impression) that he possessed any unusual stock of knowledge;[4] still less would he admit that such knowledge as he possessed was innate or inspired. [5] What he regarded as exceptional in himself was his love of "learning," that is to say, of self-improvement, and his unflagging patience in insisting upon the moral principles that had (in his view) guided the godlike rulers of the remote past. His task, then, like that of the English trainer of *jun zi* ("gentlemen's sons") in the great Public Schools, was not so much to impart knowledge as to inculcate moral principles, form character, hand down unaltered and intact a great tradition of the past. [6] He speaks of himself as a veritable Peng Sou(i.e. Nestor) in his

---

1 I will not here enter into the difficult question of how the dates (551-479 B.C.) later accepted as official were first arrived at. Cf. Maspero, *La Chine Antique*, p.455.

2 7.33. **3** *Ibid.* **4** 15.2. **5** 7.19. **6** 7.1.

devoted reliance upon "antiquity"; and if we want further to define what he meant by this reliance on the past, we find it, I think, in Mencius's saying:Follow the rules of the Former Kings, and it is impossible that you should go wrong.[1]

What then was this antiquity, who were the great figures of the past whom Confucius regarded as the sole source of wisdom?

THE ANCIENTS

Were we to take them in the order of their importance to him, I think we should have to begin with the founders and expanders of the Zhou dynasty; for in his eyes the cultures of the two preceding dynasties found their climax and fulfilment in that of the early Zhou sovereigns.[2] Above all, we should have to deal first with Dan, Duke of Zhou, who had not only a particular importance in the Lu State, but also a peculiar significance for Confucius himself.[3] But it is more convenient to take them in their "chronological" order, that is to say, in the order in which the mythology of Confucius's day arranged them. We must begin then with the *sheng*, the Divine Sages.[4] These were mythological figures, historicized as rulers of human "dynasties"; but still endowed with divine characteristics and powers. The *Analects* mention three of them, Yao, Shun and Yu the Great;but they occupy a very restricted place in the book[5]. Yao and Shun are twice[6] mentioned in the stock phrase (if a man were to do this), then "even Yao and Shun could not criticize him"; meaning that

---

1 *Mencius*, 4.1. **2** 3.14. **3** 7.5.

4 See *The Way and Its Power*,p.91. Mencius and later writers use the term *sheng* in a much wider sense, applying it even to a comparatively recent person such as Liuxia Hui.

5 I except Book XX , which has not necessarily anything to do with the beliefs of Confucius. Yu is legendary;but the Xia dynasty is probably not wholly mythological. **6** 6.28;14.45.

such a man would himself be to all intents and purposes a *sheng*. Yao appears otherwise only in the eulogy of 8.19, where he is exalted as the equal of God.[1] The eulogy of Shun which follows tells us that with only five servants to help him he kept order "everywhere under Heaven." Elsewhere[2] he is said to have ruled by *wu wei* (non-activity无为), through the mere fact of sitting in a majestic attitude "with his face turned to the South." We have here the conception,familiar to us in Africa and elsewhere, of the divine king whose magic power regulates everything in the land. It is one which is common to all early Chinese thought, particularly in the various branches of Quietism that developed in the fourth century B.C. The *sheng*, however, only "rules by nonactivity" in the sense that his divine essence (*ling* 灵) assures the fecundity of his people and the fertility of the soil. We find Shun assisted in his task by "five servants,"[3] who are clearly conceived of as performing the active functions of government.

Yao and Shun are not mentioned in the *Book of Songs*, and there is reason to suppose that their cult did not form part of the Zhou tradition. The third Divine Sage, Yu the Great, generally [4] associated in Chinese legend with a Deluge Myth akin to that of the Near East, figures in the *Analects* not as the subduer of the Flood but as patron of agriculture. He drains and ditches the land [5] and tills the fields, [6] his name being coupled with that of the harvest-god Hou Ji. Yu the Great is "historicized" as founder of the Xia dynasty, whose "times" (i.e. calendar of agricultural operations) Confucius recommends, in answer to a question about the

1 *Tian* (天): literally, "Heaven." **2** 15.4.

3 8.20.One of them was presumably Gao Yao, mentioned in 12.22.

4 But not in the *Songs*, where he generally appears as a Creator connected indeed with irrigation, only once as a flood-subduer.

5 8.21. **6** 14.6.

ideal State.[1]

Tang, the founder of the Shang-Yin dynasty which preceded the Zhou, is only once mentioned. It was supposed in Confucius's day that the remnants of the Shang-Yin people had settled in Song and that the Song State perpetuated the traditions of the fallen dynasty. But Confucius himself doubted whether Yin culture could really be reconstructed by evidence supplied from Song.[2]

THE DISCIPLES

Later tradition credits Confucius with seventy-two [3] disciples;but the compilers are hard put to it to bring the number up to anything like so imposing a total. In the *Analects* some twenty people figure, who might possibly be regarded as disciples, in so far as they are represented as addressing questions to Confucius. But far fewer appear as definite "frequenters of his gate." The most important of them, in the history of Confucianism, is Master Zeng, who is credited in the *Analects* with twelve sayings of his own. The Master Zeng of Book Ⅷ is, however, a very different person from the Master Zeng of Book Ⅰ, the latter resembling far more closely the Zeng of later tradition, and of the *Zengzi* fragments. Humanly the most distinctive of the disciples are Yan Hui and Zilu, who are perfect examples of the contrasted types of character that psychologists call introvert and extravert. Both of them died before Confucius, and were thus unable to influence the subsequent development of the

---

1 15.10.

2 3.9. Systematic excavation at Anyang, the site of one of the Yin capitals, has put us in possession of far more information about Yin culture than Confucius was able to obtain.

3 Seventy-two is a sacred number, connected with the quintuple division of the year of 360 days. Cf.11.25.

school. Zilu played a considerable part in contemporary history and is mentioned in the chronicles from 498 down to the time of his death in 480. Two other disciples are well known to history, Ran Qiu appears as a lieutenant of the usurping Ji Family from 484 till 472;and Zigong figures largely in inter-State diplomacy from 495 till 468.

The name of Master You, who figures so prominently in Book Ⅰ, only to disappear almost completely in the remaining Books, happens by chance to occur in the *Zuo Zhuan* chronicle under the year 487. But he was evidently not a person of high social status;for he served as a foot-soldier.

It is clear that after the Master's death,Zixia, like Master Zeng, founded a school of his own; for his disciples are spoken of in Book XIX. To him, too, are attributed about a dozen sayings. Two other disciples, Zizhang and Ziyou, are also obviously regarded by the compilers of the *Analects* as being of special importance;for they, too, are credited with sayings of their own.

THE ANALECTS[1]

There is not much doubt that *Lun Yu* (*Analects*, to use the English equivalent that Legge's translation has made so familiar) means"Selected Sayings." *Lun*（论）, as a term connected with the editing of documents, occurs indeed in *Analects*, 14.9. The contents of the book itself make it clear that the compilation took place long after the Master's death. Several of the disciples already have schools of their own, and the death of Master Zeng, which certainly happened well into the second

1 This section might well be omitted by readers without special knowledge of Chinese literature.

half of the fifth century, is recorded in Book VIII. It is clear, too, that the different Books are of very different date and proceed from very different sources. I should hazard the guess that Books III – IX represent the oldest stratum. Books X and XX (first part) certainly have no intrinsic connexion with the rest. The former is a compilation of maxims from works on ritual;the latter consists of stray sentences from works of the *Shu Jing* type. Book XIX consists entirely of sayings by disciples. The contents of XVIII and of parts of XIV and XVII are not Confucian in their origin, but have filtered into the book from the outside world, and from a world hostile to Confucius. Book XVI is generally and rightly regarded as late. It contains nothing characteristic of the milieu that produced Books III – IX , and it would not be difficult to compile a much longer book of just the same character by stringing together precepts from works such as the *Zuo Zhuan* and *Guo Yu*. Only in one passage of the *Analects* do we find any reference to ideas the development of which we should be inclined to place later than the ordinarily accepted[1] date of the book, namely, the middle of the fourth century. I refer to the disquisition on "correcting names" in 13.3. In *Mencius* (early third century B.C.) there is not a trace of the "language crisis,"[2] and we have no reason to suppose that the whole sequence of ideas embodied in this passage could possibly be earlier in date than the end of the fourth century. That the writer of the passage realized its incompatibility with the doctrines of Confucius—the insistence on punishments is wholly unConfucian—is naïvely betrayed in the introductory paragraphs. Zilu is made to express

---

1 I mean accepted by scholars as the date of the material contained in the book. The date of its compilation may well be later.

2 See *The Way and Its Power*, p.59. *Mencius*, 6.2. VI is unintelligible, and has in any case never been interpreted as relevant.

the greatest astonishment that Confucius should regard the reform of language as the first duty of a ruler and tells him impatiently that his remark is quite beside the point.

We may, of course, be wrong in thinking that the whole complex of ideas connected with "reforming language in order to adjust penalties" dates from as late as the end of the fourth century. There may be special reasons why we find no echo of such ideas in *Mencius*. Or again, the compilation of the *Analects* may be much later than we suppose; but this alternative involves linguistic difficulties. It may, on the other hand, be a better solution to regard this passage as an interpolation on the part of Xunzi or his school, for whom the absence of any reference in the sayings of Confucius to what they themselves taught as a fundamental doctrine must certainly have been inconvenient.

It is curious that only one pre-Han text shows definite evidence of familiarity with the *Analects*. The "Fang Ji" (part of the *Li Ji*;supposed to be an extract from the *Zi Si Zi*) quotes *Analects*, 2.11, and names the *Lun Yu* as its source. The "Fang Ji" also quotes books of the *Shu Jing* which were unknown in Han times, not being found either in the official collection or among the books rediscovered but uninterpreted. It is therefore certainly a pre-Han work. There are, apart from this, many cases in which pre-Han authors,such as Xunzi, Lü Buwei, Han Fei, use maxims or anecdotes that are also used in the *Analects*. But there is nothing to show that the writer is quoting the book as we know it now. Mencius, it is clear, used a quite different collection of sayings, which contained, indeed, a certain number of those which occur in the *Analects*, often differently worded and allotted to quite different contexts;but he quotes at least three times as many sayings that do not occur in the *Analects* at all.

It would be rash, however, to conclude that the *Analects* were not known or did not exist in the days of Mencius and Xunzi.We possess only a very small fragment of early Confucian literature. Could we read all the works that are listed in the *Han Shu* bibliography, we should very likely discover that some particular school of Confucianism based its teaching on the *Analects*, just as Mencius based his on another collection of sayings. The *Doctrine of the Mean* and the *Great Learning*, works of very uncertain date but certainly pre-Han, both use sayings from the *Analects*, which may well be actual quotations.

The history of the text from *c*. 150 B.C.[1] till the time (second century A.D.) when at the hands of Zheng Xuan the book received something like its present form I must leave to others to write. The task is one which involves great difficulties. The data are supplied not by scientific bibliographers but by careless repeaters of legend and anecdote. Some of the relevant texts (e.g. *Lun Heng*, Pian 81) are hopelessly corrupt;the real dates of supposedly early Han works which show knowledge of the *Analects* are impossible to ascertain. At every turn, in such studies, we are forced to rely, without any means of checking their statements, upon writers who clearly took no pains to control their facts.

This much, however, is certain: during the period 100 B.C. to 100 A.D. two versions were currently used, the Lu version (upon which our modern version is chiefly based) and the Qi version[2] , which had two extra chapters. Much later (second century A.D.?) a third version came into general use. This was the Gu Wen (ancient script) text collated by

---

1 It is quoted by name in the *Han Shi Wai Zhuan*, which presumably dates from the middle of the second century.

2 Now lost,save for a few fragments.

Zheng Xuan when he made his famous edition. We know some twenty-seven instances in which the Gu version differed from the Lu,and in all but two of these instances the version we use to-day follows Gu not Lu. I state these facts merely that the reader may know roughly what is meant when in the course of this book I mention Gu and Lu readings. The real origin of the Gu version remains very uncertain and a discussion of the question, bound up as it is with the history of the other Gu Wen texts, would lead us too far afield.

A last question remains to be answered. How far can we regard any of the sayings in the *Analects* as actual words of Confucius? In searching for such authentic sayings we must use certain precautions. Obviously, we shall not find them in Book X [1], nor in Book XX [2]. Books XVI - XVII clearly do not emanate from a source at all near to the earliest Confucianism. Book XVIII is, indeed, full of anti-Confucian stories, of just the same sort that we find in Taoist works, naïvely accepted by the compilers; Book XIV has a considerable element of the same description(34,41,42). The story of the meeting with Yang Huo(17.1) is of just the same kind. We shall have to remember that in ancient Chinese literature sayings are often attributed to a variety of people;(indifferently, for example, to Master Zeng and Confucius, or to Confucius and Yanzi) and bear in mind that such sayings were probably more or less proverbial. We certainly must not forget that Confucius describes himself as a transmitter, not an originator, and that the presence of rhyme or archaic formulae, or of proverbial shape in the sayings often definitely stamps them as inherited from the past. Bearing all these facts in mind I think we are

1 Which is simply a collection of traditional ritual maxims.

2 Which, apart from the few sayings appended at the end, is a collection of sentences from texts of the *Shu Jing* type.

justified in supposing that the book does not contain many authentic sayings, and may possibly contain none at all. As I have already pointed out, I use the term "Confucius"throughout this book in a conventional sense, simply meaning the particular early Confucians whose ideas are embodied in the sayings.

Supposing, however, someone should succeed in proving that some particular saying was really uttered by the Master, it would still remain to be proved that the context in which the remark occurred in the *Analects* was really the original one;and the context of a remark profoundly affects its meaning. In later literature, particularly the *Li Ji*(Book of Rites) and *Shi Ji* (Historical Records), we find a good many of Confucius's more cryptic remarks given contexts, put into settings of an explanatory description, and it has been suggested that in such cases we have the original form and intention of the sayings, which in the *Analects* have for some reason become divorced from their proper surroundings. That this should be so is against all the canons of textual history. Always, in similar cases, we find that the contexts have been invented as glosses upon the original *logia*. In the oldest strata of the Synoptic Gospels isolated sayings occur which in the more recent strata are furnished, often very arbitrarily, with an explanatory setting. It is a process that we can see at work over and over again in Buddhist hagiography. I have therefore seldom called attention to these manipulations of the text by the later Confucian schools, and have been content to leave the isolated *logia* as I found them.

名词解释　TERMS

REN(仁)

This word in the earliest Chinese means freemen, men of the tribe, as opposed to *min*(民),"subjects," "the common people."[1] The same word, written with a slight modification, means "good" in the most general sense of the word, that is to say, "possessing the qualities of one's tribe." For no more sweeping form of praise can be given by the men of a tribe than to say that someone is a "true member" of that tribe. The same is true of modern nations;an Englishman can give no higher praise than to say that another is a true Englishman. In the *Book of Songs* the phrase "handsome and good"(*ren*)occurs more than once as a description of a perfectly satisfactory lover. *Ren* , "members of the tribe" show a forbearance towards one another that they do not show to aliens, and just as the Latin *gens*, "clan," gave rise to our own word "gentle," so *ren* in Chinese came to mean "kind," "gentle," "humane." Finally, when the old distinction between *ren* and *min*, freemen and subjects , was forgotten and *ren* became a general word for "human being , " the adjective *ren* came to be understood in the sense "human" as opposed to "animal," and to be applied to conduct worthy of a man, as distinct from the behaviour of mere beasts.

---

1 See the *Way and Its Power*, p. 148.

Of this last sense (human, not brutal) there is not a trace in the *Analects*. Of the sense "kind," "tender-hearted" there are only two examples[1], out of some sixty instances in which the word occurs. Confucius's use of the term, a use peculiar to this one book, stands in close relation to the primitive meaning. *Ren*, in the *Analects*, means "good" in an extremely wide and general sense. "In its direction"[2] lie unselfishness and an ability to measure other people's feelings by one's own. The good man is "in private life, courteous; in public life, diligent; in relationships, loyal." [3] Goodness (on the part of a ruler) is complete submission to ritual. [4] The Good do not grieve [5] and will necessarily be brave.[6] At the same time, it cannot be said that *ren* in the *Analects* simply means "good" in a wide and general sense. It is, on the contrary, the name of a quality so rare and peculiar that one "cannot but be chary in speaking of it."[7] It is a sublime moral attitude, a transcendental perfection attained to by legendary heroes such as Boyi, but not by any living or historic person. This, however, is far from being understood by the disciples, who suggest as examples of goodness not only Ziwen (seventh century B.C.),Chen Wen (sixth century), Guan Zhong (seventh century), but even contemporaries and associates such as Zilu, Ran Qiu, Gongxi Hua, Ran Yong. All such claims the Master abruptly dismisses. Indeed so unwilling is he to accord the title *ren* that he will not even allow it to a hypothetical person who "compassed the salvation of the whole State."[8] Such a one would be a Divine Sage (*sheng*), a demi-god; whereas *ren* is the display of human qualities at their highest. It appears indeed that *ren* is a mystic entity not merely analogous to but in certain sayings practically identical with the Tao of

1 12.22 and 17.21. **2** 6.28. **3** 13.19.
4 12.1. **5** 9.28. **6** 14.5.
7 12.3. **8** 6.28.

the Quietists. Like Tao, it is contrasted with "knowledge." Knowledge is active and frets itself away; Goodness is passive and therefore eternal as the hills[1]. Confucius can point the way to Goodness, can tell "the workman how to sharpen his tools,"[2] can speak even of things "that are near to Goodness." But it is only once, in a chapter bearing every sign of lateness, [3] that anything approaching a definition of Goodness is given.

In view of this repeated refusal to accept any but remote [4]mythological figures as examples of *ren*, to accept [5] or give a definition of Goodness, there is surely nothing surprising in the statement of Book IX (opening sentence) that "the Master rarely discoursed upon Goodness."[6]

It seems to me that "good" is the only possible translation of the term *ren* as it occurs in the *Analects*. No other word is sufficiently general to cover the whole range of meaning;indeed terms such as "humane," "altruistic", "benevolent" are in almost every instance inappropriate, often ludicrously so. But there is another word, *shan*（善）, which though it wholly lacks the mystical and transcendental implications of *ren*, cannot conveniently be translated by any other word but "good." For that reason I shall henceforward translate *ren* by Good(Goodness, etc.) with a capital;and *shan* by good, with a small g.

Unlike *ren, Tao* has not in the *Analects* a technical or peculiar meaning, but is used there in just the same sense as in early Chinese works in

---

1 6.21. For the capital G, see below.

2 15.9.

3 XVII.

4 Boyi , Shuqi, Bi Gan, Weizi and Jizi is the complete list.All of them belonged, according to legend, to the end of the Yin dynasty. The last three occur in Book XVIII, which emanated from non-Confucian circles.

5 Cf.14.2.

6 A vast mass of discussion has centred round this passage. Cf.*Journal of the American Oriental Society*, December 1933 and March 1934.

general. *Tao* means literally a road, a path, a way. Hence, the way in which anything is done, the way in which, for example, a kingdom is ruled;a method, a principle, a doctrine. It usually has a good meaning. Thus "when *Tao* (the Way) prevails under Heaven" means when a good method of government prevails in the world;or rather "when the good method prevails," for Confucius "believed in the ancients," that is to say, he believed that the one infallible method of rule had been practised by certain rulers of old, and that statecraft consisted in rediscovering this method. But there seem to have been other "Ways," for Confucius[1] speaks of "this Way" and "my Way." Moreover, in one passage [2] he is asked about *shan ren zhi dao* (Tao)（善仁之道）, "the Way of the good people," and replies(according to my interpretation) disapprovingly that "those who do not tread in the tracks (of the ancients)" cannot hope to "enter into the sanctum." "Good people" is a term often applied in Chinese to those who share one's views. Thus Quietists called other Quietists "good people." The "good people" here intended evidently sought guidance from some source other than the example of the ancients, and they may well have been Quietists.

But we are also told that Confucius did not discourse about the Will of Heaven [3] or about "prodigies" and "disorders" (of Nature). [4] We have only to read other early books to see that the world at large attached extreme importance to the Will of Heaven as manifested by portents such as rainbows, comets, eclipses; and to monstrosities such as two-headed calves and the like. It may be that the doctrine of those who sought guidance from such signs rather than from the records of the

---

1 It would be pedantic always to say "the early Confucians" or the compilers of the *Analects*; though that is , strictly speaking, what I mean when I say "Confucius."

2 11.19. **3** 5.12. **4** 7.20.

Former Kings came to be known as the "Way of the good people." In general, however, the word *Tao* in the *Analects* means one thing only, the Way of the ancients as it could be reconstructed from the stories told about the founders of the Zhou dynasty and the demi-gods who had preceded them.

The aspect of Confucius's Way upon which Western writers have chiefly insisted is his attitude towards the supernatural. It has been rightly emphasized that he was concerned above all with the duties of man to man and that he "did not talk about spirits."[1] From a false interpretation of two passages (6. 20 and 11.11) the quite wrong inference has, however, been drawn that his attitude towards the spirit-world was, if not sceptical, at least agnostic. In the first passage a disciple asks about wisdom. The wisdom here meant is, of course, that of the ruler or member of the ruling classes, and the point at issue is one frequently debated in early Chinese literature: which should come first, the claims of the people or those of the spirit-world? In concrete terms, should the security of the whole State, which depends ultimately on the goodwill of the Spirits of grain, soil, rivers and hills, be first assured by lavish offerings and sacrifices, even if such a course involves such heavy taxation as to impose great hardship on the common people? Or should the claims of the people to what it is "right and proper"(*yi* 义) for them to have be satisfied before public expenditure is lavished upon the protecting spirits? The reply of Confucius is that the claims of the people should come first;but that the spirits must be accorded an attention sufficient to "keep them at a distance," that is to say, prevent them from manifesting their ill-will by attacking human beings; for just as we regard sickness as due to the onslaught of microbes, the

1 7.20.

Chinese regarded it as due to demoniacal "possession."

The same question concerning the priority in budget-making of human and ghostly claims is discussed in the second passage. Zilu asks about "the service of spirits," meaning, as has generally been recognized, the outlay of public expenditure on sacrifice and other ceremonies of placation. The Master's reply is, "How can there be any proper service of spirits until living men have been properly served?" Zilu then "asked about the dead. " A much debated question was whether the dead are conscious;and it was suggested that if they are not, it must clearly be useless to sacrifice at any rate to that portion of the spirit-world which consists of the spirits of the dead, as opposed to those of hills, streams, the soil, etc. Confucius does not wish to commit himself to any statement about, for example, the consciousness or unconsciousness of the dead, and adroitly turns the question by replying, "Until a man knows about the living[1], how can he know the dead?" All that is meant by the reply (which is a rhetorical one and must not be analysed too logically) is that for the *jun zi* questions about the existence led by the dead are of secondary importance as compared to those connected with the handling of living men.

There is not, as Western writers have often supposed, any allusion to an abstract metaphysical problem concerning the ultimate nature of life.Nor are the two passages discussed above in any way isolated or exceptional. They are, on the contrary, characteristic of the general diversion of interest from the dead to the living, from the spirit-world to that of everyday life, which marks the break-up of the old Zhou culture, founded upon divination and sacrifice.[2]

---

1 Or "knows about life."

2 Cf.*The Way and Its Power*, pp. 24 seq.

DE(德）[1]

This word corresponds closely to the Latin *virtus*. It means, just as *virtus* often does, the specific quality or "virtue" latent in anything. It never(except by some accident of context) has in early Chinese the meaning of virtue as opposed to vice, but rather the meaning of "virtue" in such expressions as "in virtue of" or "the virtue of this drug." In individuals it is a force or power closely akin to what we call character and frequently contrasted with *li*（力）, "physical force." To translate it by "virtue," as has often been done,can only end by misleading the reader, who even if forewarned will be certain to interpret the word in its ordinary sense (virtue as opposed to vice) and not in the much rarer sense corresponding to the Latin *virtus*. For this reason I have generally rendered *de* by the term "moral force," particularly where it is contrasted with *li*, "physical force." We cannot, however, speak of a horse's *de* as its "moral force." Here "character" is the only possible equivalent; and in the case of human beings the term "prestige" often comes close to what is meant by *de*.

SHI（士）

This word is often translated "scholar";but this is only a derived, metaphorical sense and the whole force of many passages in the *Analects* is lost if we do not understand that the term is a military one and means "knight". A *shi* was a person entitled to go to battle in a war-chariot, in contrast with the common soldiers who followed on foot. Confucius, by a metaphor similar to those embodied in the phraseology of the Salvation Army, calls the stout-hearted defenders of his Way "Knights";and

---

1 Cf. *The Book of Songs*, p.346.

hence in later Chinese the term came to be applied to upholders of Confucianism and finally to scholars and literary people in general. The burden of most of the references to *shi* in the *Analects* is that the Knight of the Way needs just the same qualities of endurance and resolution as the Soldier Knight. A saying such as "A knight whose thoughts are set on home is not worthy of the name of knight" [1] refers in the first instance to real knights, and is only applied by metaphor to the spiritual warriors of Confucius's "army." If like Legge we translate "the scholar who cherishes his love of comfort…", we lose the whole point. As we shall see later, Confucius was himself a knight in the literal sense, and it is probable, as we have seen, that in his later years he was senior knight, "leader of the knights," responsible for their discipline.

JUN ZI（君子）

Jun is the most general term for "ruler," and a *jun zi* is a "son of a ruler." The term was applied to descendants of the ruling house in any State, and so came to mean "gentleman," "member of the upper classes." But the gentleman is bound by a particular code of morals and manners; so that the word *jun zi* implies not merely superiority of birth but also superiority of character and behaviour. Finally the requisite of birth is waived. If an ox is of one colour and thus fit for sacrifice, what does it matter that its sire was brindled? [2] He who follows the Way of the *jun zi* is a *jun zi*; he who follows the way of "small" (i.e.common) people is common. And what is the Way of the Gentleman? With the detailed code of his manners I shall deal presently, when discussing Book X. As to his deportment in general, it is defined for us by the disciple Zeng[3] in terms that

---

1 14.3. **2** 6.4. **3** 13.4.

exactly correspond to the traditional Western conception of a gentleman:we recognize him by the fact that his movements are free from any brusqueness or violence, that his expression is one of complete openness and sincerity, that his speech is free from any low and vulgar or as we should say "Cockney" tinge.

As regards his conduct, he must be extremely careful to make friends only with people of his own sort.[1] But he need never be lonely;for so long as he behaves as a gentleman should, he will be welcomed by his "brothers"(i.e. by other gentlemen) "everywhere within the Four Seas."[2] The whole world is his club. The alliances of "small people"are directed against others, are hostile and destructive in intent;but those of the gentlemen exist only for mutual satisfaction. He has no politics, but sides with the Right wherever he finds it.[3]

He must not lay himself open to the accusation of "talking too much";[4] still less must he boast [5] or push himself forward or in any way display his superiority, except in matters of sport, [6]and even here he is restrained by the complicated dictates of fair play, by the elaborate etiquette which constitutes the "rules of the game." Nor must he exalt himself by the indirect method of denigrating other people, a method characteristic of "small men."[7]

His education, like that given till recently at gentlemen's schools in England, consists chiefly of moral training;he learns in order to build up his *de* (character). To learn anything of actual utility, to have practical accomplishments, is contrary to the Way of the *jun zi* [8] and will lead to his merely becoming a "tool,"[9] an instrument dedicated to one humdrum

---

1 1.8. **2** 12.5. **3** 4.10. **4** 17.17.

5 14.29. Here,as in other points, the Chinese code has a particular affinity with ours. "Swank" in all its forms is far more severely condemned by the English gentleman than by the patrician, for example, of Latin countries. **6** 3.7.

7 12.16. **8** 9.6. **9** 2.12.

purpose.Such a general, moral education will produce a Knight of the Way ready to face all emergencies "without fret or fear." [1] His head will not be turned by success, nor his temper soured by adversity.[2] Success, however, is a theme seldom dealt with in the *Analects*; for it is well known that the Way "does not prevail in the world," and the merits of the true *jun zi* are not such as the world is likely to recognize or reward. "Lack of recognition" is, indeed, one of Confucius's most frequent topics, and to feel no resentment (*yuan*) when repeatedly cashiered or neglected is the *jun zi's* highest virtue.

Moderation in conduct and opinion is a well-known hallmark of the true gentleman: "The *jun zi* avoids the absolute, avoids the extreme."[3] Mencius tells us that "Confucius was one who abstained from extremes."[4] "To exceed is as bad as not to reach."[5] This conception of virtue as a middle way between two extremes is one which we have no difficulty in understanding;for it is familiar to us as part of our popular heritage from Greek philosophy. It is, however, one which rapidly disappears so soon as purely magical, non-social virtues are held in esteem. The reputation of an Indian ascetic, for example, is in proportion to the "excessiveness" of his behaviour; and a society which admired St. Simeon on his pillar would not easily have understood either the *μηδὲν ἄγαν* of the Classical Greeks or the "middle conduct"(*zhong xing* 中行) inculcated by Confucius.

That good lies between two extremes has been very generally accepted by those who have tried to view the world rationally. As a political principle it was the foundation of nineteenth-century Liberalism and in

---

1 12.4. **2** 1.1.

3 *Han Fei*, 33.(Roll 12); adapted in *Dao De Jing*, XXIX. **4** *Mencius*, 4.2.

5 *Analects*, 11.15.Cf.13.21.I leave out of account the famous dictum (6.27) about the Golden Mean (*zhong yong*); for the original meaning of the passage is far from clear.

particular of English Liberalism. In many cases the doctrine is one which can hardly be disputed. Thus "softness" (unwillingness to inflict pain or take life) carried to its logical conclusion involves extinction; and so, with equal sureness, does "hardness" (indifference to the infliction of death and suffering). Unfortunately it is extremes and not compromises that most easily become associated with strong emotional impulse. The downfall of Liberalism has been due to the failure to associate the Middle Way with any strong trend of emotion. The success of Confucianism, its triumph over "all the hundred schools" from the second century B.C. onwards, was due in a large measure to the fact that it contrived to endow compromise with an emotional glamour.

As regards the translation of the term *jun zi* I see no alternative but to use the word "gentleman," though the effect is occasionally somewhat absurd in English. One needs a word which primarily signifies superiority of birth, but also implies moral superiority. Neither Legge's "superior man," nor Soothill's various equivalents ("man of the higher type," "wise man," etc.) fulfil this condition. The late Sir Reginald Johnston proposed "the princely man"; but this seems to me (I may be peculiar in my interpretation) to suggest lavish expenditure rather than superiority of birth or morals.[1]

XIAO（孝）

This word seems originally to have meant piety towards the spirits of ancestors or dead parents.[2] In the *Analects* it still frequently has this meaning; but it is also applied to filial conduct towards living parents, and

---

1 This was written before Sir Reginald Johnston in his *Confucianism and Modern China* adopted "gentleman" as the most exact equivalent to *jun zi*.

2 In the *Book of Songs xiao* refers almost exclusively to piety towards the dead. Out of twelve instances nine can only be taken in this sense; the other three are non-committal.

this is its usual meaning in current Chinese. In this change of meaning we may see, I think, another example of that general transference of interest from the dead to the living which marked the break-up of the old Zhou civilization. There is, however, reason to believe that filial piety played a relatively small part in the teaching of the earliest Confucians. By far the larger number of references to it in the *Analects* occur in Books Ⅰ and Ⅱ which do not, I think, belong to the earliest strata of the work. But it seems clear that during the fourth century B.C. a place of extreme importance had already been allotted by the Confucians to *xiao* in its extended sense of piety towards living parents. For it was with reference to this virtue that the followers of Confucius came into conflict with those of Mozi, who taught that affection and solicitude ought to be equally extended to all mankind and not reserved in a special degree for parents or relations. Towards the end of the third century B.C. *xiao* became, at any rate in certain Confucian schools, the summit of all virtues, and in the *Canon of Filial Piety* which may have existed [1] in some form in the third century, but did not, I think, reach its present form till at least a century later , *xiao* is surrounded by the mysterious halo that attends the term *ren* in the *Analects*.

But it seems that the compilers of the *Canon of Filial Piety* were hard put to it to get their material. For in one place [2] they have reproduced a panegyric upon the potency of ritual observance, preserved in the *Zuo Zhuan* chronicle, [3] and by altering the word *li* ("ritual" 礼) to *xiao* they have turned it into a eulogy of filial piety.

---

1 The allusion to the *Canon of Filial Piety* in *Lü Shi Chun Qiu* is probably an intrusion of commentary into text.

2 Paragraph 7.

3 "Zhao Gong," 25th year.

WEN（文）[1]

The original meaning of the word *wen* is criss-cross lines, markings, pattern. It also means a written character, an ideogram. This, however, is scarcely a separate meaning from that of pattern, for in early China certain patterns served equally as ideograms, both being conventionalizations of pictures. Thus the character for "eye" also figures as a decoration on Zhou bronzes. *Wen*, again, means what is decorated as opposed to what is plain, ornament as opposed to structure, and hence the things that vary and beautify human life, as opposed to life's concrete needs. In particular, *wen* denotes the arts of peace(music, dancing, literature) as opposed to those of war. The arts of peace, however, everything that we should call culture, have a *de* that is useful for offensive purposes. They attract the inhabitants of neighbouring countries; and it must be remembered the States of ancient China were just as anxious to attract immigration as modern European States are to repel it. For vast areas still remained to be opened up for agriculture;there was room for everyone, and fresh inhabitants meant fresh recruits for the army. "If the distant do not submit, cultivate the power of *wen* to bring them to you."[2] It is clear then that *wen* means something very like our own word culture and served many of the same purposes. The prestige(*de*) of culture is to-day used by us for military purposes. During the War, for example, efforts were made by both sides to win over neutrals by displays of culture, [3] such as the sending of theatrical companies, pictures and the like. The power of *wen* is also used, as in ancient China, to attract immigrants, but only those of

---

1 Cf. *The Book of Songs*, p.346.

2 16.1.

3 "Just as military preparations must not be revealed, so too culture must not be concealed." *Guo Yu*, ch. 2.

the temporary kind called tourists.

For Confucius the *wen* (culture) *par excellence* was that established by the founders of the Zhou dynasty. To gather up the fragments of this culture and pass them on to posterity was the sacred mission entrusted to him by Heaven. [1] His native State, Lu, was generally regarded as the main depository of Zhou culture; [2] but we find him, on a visit to Qi, ready to admit the superiority of a musical performance there to anything of the kind he had known in Lu,[3] and it was only "after his return from Wei"[4] that the correct ritual use of the ancestral hymns and Court songs was properly established.

The term *wen* is, however, often used in the *Analects* in a narrower sense than that of civilization or culture. We have seen that one of its primary senses is that of "a written character," and it occurs once[5] in the *Analects* with this meaning. *Wen xue* (letter-study 文学) is the ordinary Chinese term for literature or literary pursuits, and it already has this meaning in the *Analects*. Moreover, when we are told that one in whom "substance preponderates over ornament"(*wen*) will degenerate into a mere savage;while one in whom ornament prevails over substance degenerates into a mere scribe, it is obvious that the *wen* in question is literature and not culture in general.

The earlier English translators were embarrassed by the term *wen,* because although they knew that it corresponded in a general way to our word "culture," they were entirely unfamiliar with the practical efficacies (*de*) with which the Chinese associated the word. Legge, indeed, in one passage translates *wen* "the Cause of truth ," not being able to convince himself that Confucius could have been interested in transmitting

---

1 9.5. **2** Cf. "Zhao Gong," 2nd year, *Zuo Zhuan*.
3 7.13. **4** 9.14. **5** 15.25.

anything so frivolous as a mere "culture."

TIAN（天）

Apart from cases where Heaven (*tian*) merely means "the sky" [for example, in the common phrase *tian xia*（天下）, "that which is under heaven ," i.e. the whole world],[1] it clearly corresponds to our word Heaven and to the German *Himmel* in the sense of Providence, Nature, God. Heaven is the dispenser of life and death, wealth and rank (12. 5). The *jun zi* must learn to know the will (*ming* 命) of Heaven and submit to it patiently, a hard lesson that Confucius himself did not master till the age of fifty (2.4). Concerning "the ways of Heaven" he was unwilling to discourse (5.12); but its name lingered on his lips in certain ancient formulae, such as those of oath-taking and of submission to fate in times of affliction. His "Heaven has bereft me!" at the time of Yan Hui's death and his "It is (Heaven's) will that we should lose him," at the death-bed of Bo Niu, correspond to the Moslem *kismet* and to our own "God's will be done." Confucius is made sometimes to speak as though he regarded himself as under the special protection of Providence, just as he certainly regarded himself as charged with a peculiar mission as transmitter of the rapidly disappearing Zhou culture. [2] But I fancy that phrases such as "Heaven implanted *de* in me; what can such a one as Huan Tui do to me?" (7. 22) are, like "Heaven has bereft me," etc., pious formulae, signifying confidence in God's protection.

Tian then corresponds for the most part to our Heaven and, as with us, occurs chiefly in pious, traditional formulae. There is, however, at any

---

1 Or again in the "climbing to the sky" of 19. 25.

2 9.5.

rate one passage where the translation "Nature" would not be out of place: "Does Nature(*tian*) speak? No; but the four seasons are regulated by it; the crops grow by it" (17.19). The Chinese conception of Heaven is, then, a very familiar one. The only question that arises is why a word meaning "sky" should also have the connotations God, Providence, etc.? The problem is clearly one which cannot be attacked from the Chinese side alone.

The Sanskrit *deva*, the Greek *θεός*, the Latin *deus* — indeed, the words for "God" in most Indo-European languages — are sometimes alleged to be connected with roots meaning "sky." This is far from certain. It is only between Chinese and Germanic that we get a complete parallel in the use of *tian* "Heaven" (*Himmel*). Is the original meaning of *tian* "sky" and hence God, because God lives in the sky; or was it the other way round? To the term Heaven as used in the average early Chinese text exactly corresponds the term *shang di*（上帝）used constantly in the *Book of Songs*, and occasionally elsewhere. *Shang*（上） means upper, topmost, supreme; *di*(帝)means[1] "ancestor" in the sense in which the Ancestors sometimes figure in the religions of the South Seas or Africa. A *di* is not simply an ancestor, i.e. a grandfather, great-grandfather or the like. It is not a word of relationship, but means a royal ancestor, the deified spirit of a former king. The *di* dwells in the Court of Heaven; and it seems to me that *tian*, "Heaven," is used in Chinese as a collective term meaning "those who dwell in Heaven," just as the "House of Lords" frequently means those who sit in that House. [2]The older term *shang di,* found side by side with *tian* in the *Book of Songs* and used

1 i.e. in actual use. I am not concerned with the philosophic glosses of the early dictionaries and commentaries.

2 Cf. *The Way and Its Power*, p.21.

apparently in exactly the same sense, originally meant, I think, the Supreme Ancestor, in the sense of the first of the line of Royal Ancestors. But it is commonly taken in the sense "The *di* that is above," i.e. in the sky, and alternates with *tian di*（天帝）, "Heavenly *di.*" The fuller expressions "Supreme *di*" and "Heavenly *di*" do not occur in the *Analects*; but in the collection of ancient fragments which constitutes Book XX , the word *di* is used by itself in the sense of Heaven or God, in a very personal sense, for *di* is spoken of as having servants and a heart.

XIN(信)

This character is written *ren* ("man" 人) at the side of *yan* ("word" 言), and is generally translated "good faith," "faithfulness," "truth," etc. In early Chinese it almost always refers to keeping promises, fulfilling undertakings. It does not mean telling the truth; nor do all early peoples regard telling the truth as good in itself. What early Chinese literature, as also that of the Hebrews, condemns is "bearing false witness," i.e. telling lies that lead to harm. Other sorts of lie are ritually enjoined; for example, that of saying one is ill instead of bluntly refusing an invitation or declining to see a visitor. The necessity of this sort of lie is recognized by "society" in Europe; but not by the Church. Confucius once (17.20) told a lie of this kind, and Soothill wrote (in 1910) concerning it, "That such laxity on the part of China's noblest Exemplar has fostered that disregard for truth for which this nation is notorious, can hardly be denied."In this instance a man of the world would have understood Confucius better than a clergyman has done. In the passage concerned Confucius shows not "laxity," but on the contrary a strict attention to manners.

SI(思)

The mere fact that the physical sensations connected by the Chinese with "thinking" were evidently very different from our own, should warn us against believing that what they meant by *si* (the word ordinarily translated "think") was identical with what we mean by "to think." The Chinese located thought as going on in the middle of the body. We locate it in the head, and though this may be due to self-suggestion, we definitely connect it with sensations in the head and not in the belly.

There is evidence that in its origin the word *si* meant to observe outside things. A *si ting* was an observation-post in the market, from which the overseer could observe which stall-holders were cheating. [1] So it came to mean to fix the attention not only on something exterior but also on a mental image, as for example, that of a person from whom one is separated; hence "to be in love." This use occurs once in the *Analects* (9. 30): "It is not that I do not think of you…" There are nine other passages where *si* occurs, and in all but two the meaning implied is that of "directing one's attention ," or something very close to it. When one sees people who are better than oneself, one should turn one's attention to equalling them (4.17). One should not act till one has looked into the matter three times (5.19). When one sees a chance of gain, one should divert one's attention to whether it can be pursued without violation of what is right (14.13). [2] One should occupy one's attention with what belongs to one's own rank in society (14.28). There are "nine points" which should occupy a gentleman's attention (16.10). One should question searchingly and pay close attention to what one is told (19.6).

---

1 There is, of course, the possibility that *si* is here merely a phonetic substitute for some other character.

2 19.1, is practically a repetition of this.

It may be rather forced to use the word "attention" in some of these cases; but what I want to emphasize is that in each case we are dealing with a process that is only at a short remove from concrete observation. Never is there any suggestion of a long interior process of cogitation or ratiocination, in which a whole series of thoughts are evolved one out of the other, producing on the physical plane a headache and on the intellectual, an abstract theory. We must think of *si* rather as a fixing of the attention (located in the middle of the belly) on an impression recently imbibed from without and destined to be immediately re-exteriorized in action.

These considerations will help us to understand the two remaining passages in which *si*, "to think," is used. "If one learns but does not think, one is lost;if one thinks but does not learn, one is in danger"(2.15). "I once ate nothing all day and did not go to bed all night in order to think. It was no use. Far better, to learn"(15.30).

"Learning ," as I clearly show in my note on the passage, means copying the ancients. It may be objected that the meaning of both passages is evident, and that I am making a great fuss about nothing. They are, however, certainly open to misunderstanding. Zhu Xi (died A.D. 1200) paraphrases *si* as "seeking within the heart ," evoking a whole complex of ideas — the "good knowledge" of Mencius, the "inward power " of Laozi, the *bodhi* of the Zen Buddhists — which are entirely foreign to the *Analects*. Mencius, the Quietists, the Buddhists all believed that a well of wisdom lay buried deep in the human breast. But Confucius believed nothing of the kind, and all suggestions that *si* in these passages means some kind of *yoga*, seem to me utterly unfounded. Moreover, I think that the average European reader of the current translations, coming across the maxim "Learning without thought is useless" (Legge, Soothill), might easily imagine that "thought" meant a process of logical reasoning, a sustained interior argumentation, full of "therefores" and "becauses." There is, as a matter of fact, hardly a single example of these conjunctions in the *Analects*. The "all day and all night" of 15.30, is simply a way of saying "you may think (i.e. survey the matter in hand as the overseer surveys the market) till you are blue in the face. You are wasting time. It is much better to find out what the ancients did under similar circumstances." The theme of 2.15 is slightly different: Learning and turning over in your mind what you have learnt are equally important. Here again, however, the sort of "thought" that we write with a capital ,contrast with Action, and associate with a wrinkled brow, is not in the least what is meant.

WANG(王)

Zhou legend centres round its two first kings (*wang*),Wen and Wu. *Wen* in this name probably meant "mighty";[1] Wu means "warrior." But in Confucius's time *wen*, as we have seen, meant the arts of peace as opposed to those of war, and a theory had grown up that every great armed conquest was preceded by a period of cultural preparation, a building up of *de* (moral force) as distinct from the *li* (physical force) of the warrior, which unless backed by *wen* (culture) cannot prevail. King Wen, the first Zhou monarch, was naturally credited with the initial, cultural achievements and King Wu (the Warrior) with the military triumphs which established the Zhou hegemony.

To Confucius, however, it was neither Wen nor Wu, but Wu's brother Dan, Duke of Zhou, who was the real hero of the Zhou conquest. This point of view was a purely local one. The Duke of Zhou is barely mentioned in the *Book of Songs*[2]. But legend regarded him as the founder of the Ducal House

1 As it presumably does when it occurs as a stock epithet of "ancestor." *Wen*, "pattern" is probably quite a different word.

2 There are only two *Songs* (232 and 251) which mention him.

in Lu; and Confucius, as a professed Conservative and Legitimist, dwelt fondly on the memory of this local Ancestor and felt a profound discouragement when the Duke of Zhou no longer appeared to him in his dreams. [1]

The coming of Divine Sages and World Monarchs, in China as elsewhere, was heralded by portents. Confucius watched in vain for the appearance of such signs: "the phoenix does not arrive and the river gives forth no chart."[2] Birds have everywhere been regarded as intermediaries between Heaven and Earth. The sudden appearances and movements of birds were interpreted as ominous, in China as in the West. The sacred *feng* (phoenix 凤), half-bird, half-snake, acclaimed the holy kingship of Shun; it was a winged messenger, part man, part bird that heralded the coming of the western Saviour.

The legend of the river-omen existed in two forms, which were merely local variants of the same belief. The portent referred to in the *Analects* is the "River Chart,"[3] which is brought out of the river (usually understood to mean the Yellow River) by an animal that is a mixture of horse and dragon. The variant Legend concerns the "Writings from the Luo River," which are brought out of the Luo River (in Henan) by a Divine Tortoise. But the "River Chart" is also sometimes spoken of as being brought by the Tortoise;indeed, the confusion between the two legends lasts till the thirteenth century.

There are two explanations as to what the Chart and the Writings consisted of. One is, that they contained the divinatory diagrams of the *Book of Changes,* that is to say , the eight trigrams arrived at by arranging two symbols in every possible group of three. The other is, that they were magic arrangements of numbers. The two theories are closely related; for the process[4] of shuffling the forty-nine stalks in order to dis-

---

1 7.5. **2** 9.8. **3** *Tu*（图） means "plan," "plot," "scheme" ; it may be cognate to *tu*, "land," and mean originally "to plot out land."

4 Well described in Richard Wilhelm's book on the *Yi Jing*, which is about to appear in an English version.

cover which divinatory diagram concerned one, was bound up both with ideas of numerical symbolism and with the natural properties of numbers. At the beginning of the Song dynasty the theory was that the River Chart was the "magic square"

4 9 2

3 5 7

8 1 6

in which the columns, whether added horizontally, vertically or diagonally always come to fifteen. Many Song writers [1] are quite definite on this point. The River Chart with its nine chambers, they say, "has five for its centre, carries nine on its head , treads on one, has three at the left, and seven at the right, has two and four on top, and six and eight below."

But the magic square had behind it a long history. It was believed, certainly in the second century B.C. and probably much earlier, that the Nine chambers of the Ming Tang (the ruler's audience-hall) had in ancient times been an architectural embodiment of the magic square.[2] It would then, I think, be fairly safe to assume that Confucius regarded the River Chart as a magic arrangement of symbols or numbers, and that he very likely identified it with the "magic square" (492, 357, etc.) alluded to above.

WANG (王)AND BO(伯)

In the *Analects* and in subsequent Chinese literature we find the term *wang* (king) used in a very special sense, that of a Saviour King who, unlike the monarchs of the world around us, rules by *de*, by magico-moral

---

1 See *Tu Shu* encyclopaedia, 21.51, and charts on fols. 3.12 and 4.12.

2 *Da Dai Li Ji*, 67.

force alone. The coming of such a Saviour was looked forward to with Messianic fervour. Were a True King to come, says Confucius, in the space of a single generation Goodness would become universal. [1] With the Saviour King is always contrasted the *bo* (verb, *pa*, "to be a *bo*").The word originally means "elder," "senior," and in the early days of the Zhou dynasty when the various conquered domains were ruled by descendants of the conquering House it was applied to the senior among the feudal barons. After the central authority of the Zhou declined it was applied to any local ruler who succeeded in acquiring an ascendancy over the rest, with a view (in theory at any rate) to re-establishing the pontifical authority of the Zhou monarch. The greatest of the *bo* were Huan of Qi (middle of the seventh century) and Wen of Jin (second half of the seventh century). A *bo* acts by *li* (physical force) and not by *de*. His achievements cannot lead to the reign of universal Goodness. The material consequences of such a hegemony may be immense. The two great *bo* saved China from complete immersion by the barbarians:but for the efforts of Huan "we should be wearing our hair loose and folding our garments to the left."[2] But the *bo* is guided by opportunism alone, his Way is not that of the Former Kings, his achievements are in the political not in the moral sphere. His fellow barons may reluctantly yield to his superior strength;but he cannot inspire "everywhere under Heaven" that longing for spontaneous submission which overcame even the wild tribes of the west and north when the Saviour King Tang appeared: "when he advanced towards the East, the savages of the West were jealous; when he advanced towards the South, the barbarians of the North were jealous, saying, 'Why did he not advance upon us first?' Everywhere the people turned their gaze towards him, as men gaze towards a rainbow in days of drought."

1 13.12.
2 14.18.

译名对照表

Bilingual Table of Translated Nouns or Terms

本表收录人名、地名、书名等专有名词，按汉语拼音字母次序排列，所有名词均在后面的括号里注明所出现的页码。

A

哀公	Duke Ai	（16，26，52，128）
	Duke Ai of Lu	（160）
奡	Ao	（152）
奥	the Shrine	（24）

B

八佾	eight teams of dancers	（20）
百工	the hundred apprentices	（218）
百姓	the Hundred Families	（128）
拜下	obeisance	（88）
北辰	pole-star	（10）
裨谌	Bi Chen	（154）
佛肸	Bi Xi	（198）
比干	Bi Gan	（208）
鄙夫	low-down creatures	（202）
辟公	rulers and lords	（20）
笾豆	the ordering of ritual vessels	（80）
卞庄子	Zhuangzi of Bian	（156）
秉	bundle	（52）
伯达	Elder-brother Da	（214）

播鼗	the kettledrummer	(214)
伯牛	Ran Geng	(54)
伯氏	the head of the Bo Family	(154)
伯适	Elder-brother Shi	(214)
伯夷	Boyi	(48,68,192,212)
伯鱼	Boyu	(192,200)
帛	silk	(200)

C

蔡	Cai	(46,110,214)
柴	Chai	(116)
长府	the Long Treasury	(114)
长沮	Changju	(210)
朝服	Court dress	(104)
朝廷	Court	(100)
臣	minister	(130,144,212)
	servant	(222,228)
陈	Chen	(48,110,170)
晨门	the gate-keeper	(166)
陈成子	Chen Heng	(160)
陈亢	Ziqin	(192)
陈恒	Chen Heng	(160)
陈司败	the Minister of Crime in Chen	(74)
陈文子	Chen Wen	(46)
陈子禽	Ziqin	(226)
枨	Cheng	(44)
成人	the perfect man	(156)
赤	Chi	(42,52,120,122)
楚	Chu	(208,214)
川	streams	(54)
雌雉	hen-pheasant	(108)

赐	Ci	(8, 26, 44, 116, 162, 170)
	Zigong	(54)
崔子	Cui	(46)

D

达巷	Daxiang	(88)
大德	great moral	(220)
大伦	the Great Relationship	(212)
大人	great men	(190)
大夫	high officers	(224)
	Ministers	(188)
	State Ministers	(156, 186)
	the Great Officers	(112, 160)
箪	handful	(56)
祷	the Rite of Expiation	(74)
道	(the) Way	(2, 6, 8, 28, 32, 34, 36, 40, 42, 44, 48, 56, 58, 60, 64, 78, 80, 82, 98, 116, 118, 132, 150, 152, 160, 162, 164, 172, 178, 180, 182, 186, 188, 192, 196, 210, 212, 216, 218, 220, 222, 224)
德	*de*	(148)
	inner power	(164)
	inner qualities	(164)
	merit	(202)

	(the) moral force	(6,10,34,38,128,170,178,216)
	moral power	(60,64,78,86,94,152,174)
	(the) power	(64,70,210)
	true virtue	(202)
弟子	the disciples	(52)
帝	God	(228)
禘	the Ancestral Sacrifice	(24)
点	Dian	(120)
定公	Duke Ding	(26,144)
东里	Dongli	(154)
东蒙	Mount Dongmeng	(184)
东周	Zhou in the east	(198)

F

法度	the statutes and laws	(230)
法语	*Fa Yu*	(96)
樊须	Fan	(140)
樊迟	Fan Chi	(10, 58, 134, 140, 146)
反坫	cup-mounds	(28)
方	direction	(62)
方叔	Fang Shu	(214)
防	the fief of Fang	(156)
废官	disused offices	(230)
封人	the guardian of the frontier-mound	(28)
夫人	That person	(194)
夫子	employer	(184)
	(the) Master	(6, 36, 44, 60, 68, 90, 92, 120, 134,

		154, 156, 162, 164, 186, 196, 210, 212, 222, 224, 226)
桴	raft and float	(42)
釜	cauldron	(52)

G

干	Gan	(214)
干禄	the *Song* Ganlu	(14)
皋陶	Gao Yao	(134)
高宗	Gao Zong	(166)
公	the Duke	(130, 160)
公伯寮	Gongbo Liao	(164)
公绰	Meng Gongchuo	(156)
公门	the Palace Gate	(100)
公明贾	Gongming Jia	(156)
公卿	the Duke and his officers	(194)
公山弗扰	Gongshan Furao	(198)
公室	the Ducal House	(188)
公叔文子	Gongshu Wen	(156, 158)
公孙朝	Gongsun Chao	(224)
公西华	Gongxi Hua	(74, 116, 118)
公冶长	Gongye Chang	(40)
公子荆	grandee Jing	(142)
公子纠	Prince Jiu	(158)
恭	courteous	(6, 44)
	modesty	(226)
	obeisances	(18)
觚	horn-gourd	(60)
鼓	the big drummer	(214)
告朔	the announcement of each new moon	(26)

故旧	old dependents	(78)
寡小君	This lonely one's little prince	(194)
怪	prodigies	(70)
《关雎》	the *Ospreys*	(26,84)
管氏	Guan	(28)
管仲	Guan Zhong	(28,128,154,158)
圭	the tablet of jade	(102)
贵	rank	(32)

H

汉	the River Han	(214)
和	harmony	(6)
河	the River	(214)
后帝	sovereign God	(228)
瑚琏	sacrificial vase of jade	(40)
互乡	Hu village	(72)
桓公	Duke Huan	(158)
桓魋	Huan Tui	(70)
回	Yan Hui	(12)
	Hui	(12,42,54,56,94,110,112,116,118,124)
会同	the Straight Gown	(120)
慧	acts of clemency	(176)

J

击磬	the player of the stonechimes	(214)
箕子	the lord of Ji	(208)
棘子成	Ji Zicheng	(128,208)
季	the head of the Ji	(208)

季騧	Youngest-brother Gua	(214)
季桓子	Ji Huan	(208)
季康子	Ji Kang	(54,132)
	Kang of the Ji Family	(110)
季路	Zilu	(50,110,112)
季氏	the Head of the Ji Family	(20, 22, 114, 184, 208)
	the Ji Family	(20, 22, 54, 114, 138,208)
季随	Youngest-brother Sui	(214)
季孙	the Ji Family	(164,186)
季文子	Ji Wen	(48)
季子然	Ji Ziran	(118)
稷	Ji	(154)
骥	the horse Ji	(164)
稼	agriculture	(154)
	farming	(140)
简公	Duke Jian of Qi	(160)
贱	obscurity	(32)
绞	harshness	(78,200)
接舆	Jieyu	(208)
桀溺	Jieni	(210)
晋文公	Duke Wen of Jin	(158)
九夷	the Nine Wild Tribes of the East	(192)
莒父	Jufu	(144)
具臣	stop-gap ministers	(118)
君	his Highness	(74)
	lord and ruler	(84)
	prince	(4,20,26,38,106, 118, 128, 130, 144, 146, 156, 160, 166, 182,200,202,212)

	the ruler	(100,194)
	your Highness	(160)
君夫人	That person of the prince's	(194)
君子	(the) gentleman	(2, 4, 6, 8, 14, 22, 28, 32, 34, 38, 40, 44, 56, 60, 74, 78, 80, 90, 110, 120, 128, 130, 136, 138, 140, 160, 170, 172, 176, 180, 182, 188, 190, 192, 196, 198, 204, 206, 212, 214, 216, 218, 220, 224, 226,230,232)
	(the) true gentleman	(14, 72, 76, 80, 92, 116, 126, 148, 150, 154, 162, 168, 176, 184,220)

K

康子	Kang	(106,160)
孔丘	Kong Qiu	(210)
孔氏	Master Kong	(166)
孔文子	Kong Wen	(44)
孔子	Master Kong	(16, 20, 26, 70, 74, 84, 88, 110, 130, 132, 144, 146, 152, 160, 162, 164, 170, 184, 188, 190, 192, 196, 198, 204, 208, 210,230,232)

匡	Kuang	（88，118）
狂	the madman	（208）
狂狷	the impetuous and hasty	（148）
昆弟	brothers	（110）

L

劳	tiresome	（78）
牢	Lao	（90）
老	Comptroller	（156）
老彭	old Peng	（64）
诔	the Dirges	（74）
礼	（the） rites	（66，74，120，138，204，230，232）
	ritual	（6，8，10，12，16，18，20，22，24，26，28，30，36，60，78，82，88，92，110，122，124，126，130，140，156，158，168，176，180，186，188，192，200，206）
鲤	Li	（112）
力	feats of strength	（70）
	strength	（164）
历数	succession	（228）
量	measures	（230）
谅阴	the Shed of Constancy	（166）
缭	Liao	（214）
林放	Lin Fang	（20，22）
令尹	the Grand Minister	（46）
柳下惠	Liuxia Hui	（174，208，212）

鲁	Lu	(28, 40, 60, 94, 114,140,156,210)
鲁公	the Duke of Lu	(214)
辂	State-coach	(174)
履	Lü	(228)

M

蛮貊	barbarians	(170,220)
门人	disciples	(216)
孟	the head of the Meng	(208)
孟公绰	Meng Gongchuo	(156)
孟敬子	Meng Jing	(80)
孟氏	the Chief of the Meng Family	(222)
孟孙	Meng	(10)
孟武伯	Meng Wu	(12,42)
孟懿子	Meng Yi	(10)
孟之反	Meng Zhifan	(56)
孟庄子	Meng Zhuang	(222)
费	Mi	(54,118,184,198)
冕	hat	(174)
(师)冕	Mian	(182)
冕者	anyone in sacrificial garb	(108)
闵子	Min Ziqian	(114)
闵子骞	Min Ziqian	(54,110,114)
明衣	the Bright Robe	(102)

N

南宫适	Nangong Kuo	(152,154)
南容	Nan Rong	(40,110)
南子	Nanzi	(60)

宁武子	Ning Wu	(48)
輗	yoke-bar	(16)
傩	Expulsion Rite	(104)

P

陪臣	the retainers of great Houses	(188)
匹夫	the humblest peasant	(96)
	ordinary men	(158)
匹妇	ordinary women	(158)
骈邑	the fief of Pian	(154)
便辟	the obsequious	(188)
便佞	those who are clever at talk	(188)
瓢	gourdful	(156)
圃	gardening	(140)

Q

漆雕开	Qidiao Kai	(40)
齐	Qi	(46, 52, 60, 68, 208,214)
	the State of Qi	(22)
齐桓公	Duke Huan of Qi	(158)
齐景公	Duke Jing of Qi	(130,192,208)
齐衰	anyone in mourning	(108)
祇	the earth-spirits	(76)
杞	the State of Qi	(22)
秦	Qin	(214)
磬	the stone-chimes	(166)
丘	Qiu	(70)
求	Ran Qiu	(54,186)
	Qiu	(114, 116, 118,

		120,122,164,184)
蘧伯玉	Qu Boyu	(162,172)
权	weights	(230)
缺	Que	(214)
阙党	the village of Que	(168)

R

冉伯牛	Ran Geng	(110)
冉求	Ran Qiu	(56,118,156)
冉有	Ran Qiu	(22, 68, 110, 114, 116, 118, 142, 156, 184)
冉子	Master Ran	(52,144)
让	yielding	(36)
仁	(the) Good	(2, 4, 20, 32, 34, 40, 42, 46, 58, 60, 62, 82, 98, 124, 152, 158, 162, 172, 174, 196, 198, 202, 222)
	Goodness	(2, 32, 34, 54, 58, 62, 64, 68, 72, 78, 80, 88, 124, 132, 136, 142, 146, 150, 154, 158, 172, 180, 182, 198, 200, 218, 232)
仁人	the Good Man	(32,228)
儒	*ru*	(56)
孺悲	Ru Bei	(204)

S

塞门	a screen to mask his gate	(28)
三饭	leader of the band at the third meal	(214)
三归	three lots of wives	(28)
三军	the Three Hosts	(66)
	the Three Armies	(96)
丧	mourning-rites	(20)
瑟	zithern	(114)
善人	a faultless man	(72)
	the right sort of people	(142)
善柔	those who are good at accomodating their principles	(188)
(卜)商	Shang	(114)
商	Shang	(22)
上大夫	the Upper Ministers	(100)
《韶》	the Succession	(68)
	the Succession Dance	(30,174)
少连	Shaolian	(212)
少师	the Minor Musician	(214)
召忽	Shao Hu	(158)
《召南》	the *Shao Nan*	(200)
叶公	Duke of She	(70,144,146)
社	the Holy Ground	(26)
社稷	(the) Holy Ground and Millet	(118,184)
射	chariot-driving	(88)
申枨	Shen Cheng	(44)
参	Shen	(36,116)
神	the sky-spirits	(76)
圣	a Divine Sage	(62,74,90)
圣人	Divine Sage	(72,190,220)

师	the Chief Musician	(84)
	the Music-master	(182)
(颛孙)师	Shi	(114,116)
《诗》	the *Song*	(78)
	(the) *Songs*	(8, 10, 22, 68, 82, 192,200)
石门	the Stone Gates	(166)
时	the seasons	(174)
史鱼	the recorder Yu	(172)
士	Knight	(34,214,216)
	(the) true Knight of the Way	(80,150,152)
士师	Leader of the Knights	(208,222)
世叔	Shi Shu	(154)
首阳	Mount Shouyang	(192)
《书》	the *Books*	(16,68,166)
叔齐	Shuqi	(48,68,192,212)
叔孙武叔	Shusun Wushu	(224,226)
叔夏	Younger-brother Xia	(214)
叔夜	Younger-brother Ye	(214)
黍	a dish of millet	(212)
束脩	a bundle of dried flesh	(64)
恕	consideration	(36,178)
庶人	commoners	(188)
帅	commander-in-chief	(96)
舜	Shun	(62, 84, 134, 168, 170,228)
司马牛	Sima Niu	(124,126)
思	thoughts	(10)
四饭	leader of the band at the fourth meal	(214)
兕	wild buffalo	(184)
宋	the State of Song	(22)
宋朝	Prince Chao of Song	(56)

《颂》	Ancestral Recitations	(94)
粟	an allowance of grain	(52)
	a dish of millet	(130)
绥	the mounting-cord	(108)

T

大师	the Chief Musician	(214)
太庙	the Grand Temple	(24)
	the Ancestral Temple	(106)
太宰	the Grand Minister	(90)
泰伯	Taibo	(78)
泰山	Mount Tai	(22)
澹台灭明	Tantai Mieming	(56)
汤	Tang	(134)
唐	Tang	(84)
唐棣	the wild cherry	(98)
堂	the Audience Hall	(100)
滕	Teng	(156)
天	Heaven	(10, 24, 28, 36, 44, 54, 60, 78, 82, 84, 86, 88, 90, 92, 112, 124, 126, 134, 154, 164, 188, 198, 204, 210, 224, 226, 230)
天道	the ways of Heaven	(44)
天命	the will of Heaven	(190)
天子	(the) Son of Heaven	(20,186)
徒	follower	(210)

W

枉	the crooked	(16)

王孙贾	Wangsun Jia	(24,160)
王者	Kingly Man	(142)
微生高	Weisheng Gao	(48)
微生亩	Weisheng Mu	(164)
微子	the lord of Wei	(208)
卫	Wei	(94,140,142,166,224)
卫君	the Prince of Wei	(68,138)
卫灵公	Duke Ling of Wei	(160,170)
位	the Stance	(100)
魏	Wei	(156)
温	cordial	(6)
文	culture	(24, 88, 92, 128, 136)
	letters	(60,130)
	the polite arts	(4)
	Wen	(44,158,224)
文德	the prestige of his culture	(186)
文王	King Wen	(88)
文章	culture and the outward insignia of goodness	(44)
汶	Wen	(54)
巫马期	Wuma Qi	(74)
巫医	*shaman* or witch-doctor	(148)
吴	Wu	(74)
吴孟子	Wu Mengzi	(74)
武	Wu	(214,224)
	King Wu	(224)
《武》	the War Dance	(30)
武城	the castle of Wu	(56)
	the walled town of Wu	(196)
武王	King Wu	(84)

舞雩	the Rain Dance altars	(120,134)

X

葸	timidity	(78)
下大夫	the Under Ministers	(100)
夏	Xia	(16,22,26,174)
先生	elders	(12)
	people older than himself	(168)
先王	the Former Kings	(6,184)
贤	the true sage	(162)
宪	Yuan Si	(152)
乡党	native village	(100)
	village	(52)
乡人	fellow-villagers	(148)
乡原	the"honest villager"	(202)
襄	Xiang	(214)
巷	street	(56)
萧墙	the screenwall of his own gate	(186)
小德	little moral	(220)
小人	common people	(148,150)
	low walks of life	(200)
	no gentleman	(140)
	people of low birth	(206)
	the small man	(14, 76, 130, 132, 160, 170, 176, 180, 190,206,218)
小童	Little boy	(194)
小相	junior assistant	(120)
小子	(the) little ones	(48, 78, 114, 200, 202)

	scholars	(220)
孝	a good son	(6,38)
	filial piety	(222)
	the treatment of parents	(10,12)
信	good faith	(140)
	keeping promises	(200)
行	getting on with people	(170)
行人	the Receiver of Envoys	(154)
刑	chastisements	(10)
薛	Xue	(156)
学	educated man	(4)
	learning	(64)
僎	Xun	(158)
僎与	*Xun Yu*	(96)

Y

亚饭	the leader of the band at the second meal	(214)
《雅》	Court pieces	(94)
雅乐	Court music	(202)
言游	Yan You	(220)
颜回	Yan Hui	(52,110)
颜路	Yan Lu	(112)
颜渊	Yan Hui	(50, 66, 92, 94, 110, 112, 118, 124, 174)
晏平仲	Yan Pingzhong	(46)
阳	Yang	(214)
阳肤	Yang Fu	(222)
阳货	Yang Huo	(196)
尧	Yao	(62,84,168,228)

伊尹	Yi Yin	(136)
仪	Yi	(28)
夷狄	the barbarians of the East and North	(20,147)
夷逸	Yiyi	(212)
沂	the river Yi	(120)
艺	dexterity	(64)
	the arts	(156)
邑	hamlet	(50)
义	(the) Right	(34, 140, 190, 192, 206,216)
羿	Yi	(152)
逸民	subjects whose services were lost to the State	(212)
殷	Yin	(16, 18, 22, 26, 86, 174,208)
《雍》彻	the *Yong Song*	(20)
(冉)雍	Ran Yong	(40,124)
	Yong	(52)
勇	courage	(200,206)
由	You	(14, 42, 54, 92, 96, 114, 116, 118, 122, 130, 138, 170, 186, 198)
有若	Master You	(128)
有子	Master You	(2,6,8)
予	Yu	(204)
	Zai Yu	(44)
禹	Yu	(84,86,154,228)
庾	measure	(52)
虞	Yu	(84)
虞仲	Yuzhong	(212)
御	archery	(88)

原壤	Yuan Rang	(168)
原思	Yuan Si	(52)
轨	collar-bar	(16)

Z

宰	governor	(52,54)
	steward	(138)
	Warden	(42,56,118,144)
宰予	Zai Yu	(42)
宰我	Zai Yu	(26,60,110,204)
臧文仲	Zang Wenzhong	(46,174)
臧武仲	Zang Wuzhong	(156)
灶	the stove	(24)
曾皙	Zeng Xi	(118,120)
曾子	Master Zeng	(2, 6, 36, 78, 80, 136,162,222)
张	Zhang	(222)
章甫	the Emblematic Cap	(120)
丈人	old man	(212)
昭公	Duke Zhao of Lu	(74)
赵	Zhao	(156)
正	straightening	(132)
政	domestic policy	(222)
	government	(126, 132, 138, 140,142,144,148)
	policy	(6,84,162,188)
	public business	(130)
	regulations	(10)
	Ruling	(132)
郑声	the tunes of Zheng	(174,202)
朕	my person	(228)

知	knowledge	(14)
	wisdom	(58,200)
直	Uprightness	(200)
直道	the Straight Way	(178)
直躬	Upright Gong	(146)
挚	Zhi	(84,214)
中牟	Zhongmou	(198)
中行	a middle course	(148)
中庸	the Middle Use	(60)
忠	devotion	(26)
	loyalty	(36)
冢宰	the Prime Minister	(166)
仲弓	Ran Yong	(52, 54, 110, 124, 138)
仲忽	Middle-brother Hu	(214)
仲尼	Zhongni	(224,226)
仲叔圉	Zhongshu Yu	(160)
仲突	Middle-brother Tu	(214)
仲由	Zilu	(54,118,210)
周	Zhou	(18, 24, 26, 86, 174,214,228)
周公	the Duke of Zhou	(64,82,114,214)
《周南》	the *Zhou Nan*	(200)
周任	Zhou Ren	(184)
纣	Zhou	(224)
朱张	Zhuzhang	(212)
诸侯	(the) feudal princes	(122,158,186)
	the rulers of all the States	(158)
祝鮀	the priest Tuo	(56,160)
颛臾	Zhuanyu	(184,186)
子	the Master	(2, 4, 6, 8, 10, 12, 14, 16, 18, 20, 22,

		24, 26, 28, 30, 32, 34, 36, 38, 40, 42, 44, 46, 48, 50, 52, 54, 56, 58, 60, 64, 66, 68, 70, 72, 74, 76, 78, 82, 84, 86, 88, 90, 92, 94, 96, 98, 110, 112, 114, 116, 118, 122, 124, 126, 128, 130, 132, 134, 136, 138, 140, 142, 144, 146, 148, 150, 152, 154, 156, 158, 160, 162, 164, 166, 168, 170, 172, 174, 176, 178, 180, 182, 196, 198, 200, 202, 204, 206, 212, 222,230)
子产	Zichan	(44,154)
子服景伯	Zifu Jingbo	(164,224)
子羔	Gao Chai	(118)
子贡	Zigong	(6, 8, 14, 26, 40, 42, 44, 60, 68, 90, 92, 110, 114, 126, 128, 136, 146, 148, 158, 164, 172, 178, 202,206,224,226)
子华	Gongxi Hua	(52)
子贱	Zijian	(40)
子路	Zilu	(42,44,50,60,66, 70,74,92,98,108,

		114, 116, 118, 120, 130, 138, 150, 156, 158, 160, 164, 166, 168, 170, 184, 198, 206, 210, 212)
子禽	Ziqin	(6)
子桑伯子	Zisang Bozi	(52)
子文	Ziwen	(46)
子西	Zixi	(154)
子夏	Zixia	(4, 12, 22, 56, 110, 126, 134, 144, 216, 218, 220, 222)
子游	Ziyou	(12, 38, 56, 110, 196, 220, 222)
子羽	Ziyu	(154)
子张	Zizhang	(14, 16, 46, 116, 126, 128, 130, 132, 166, 170, 172, 182, 198, 216, 230, 232)
宗庙	the Ancestral Temple	(120, 122, 224)
宗族	one's relatives	(146)
鄹	Zou	(24)
俎豆	the ordering of ritual vessels	(170)
左丘明	Zuo Qiuming	(48)

图书在版编目(CIP)数据
论语：汉英对照／杨伯峻今译；
（英）韦利英译. －长沙：湖南人民出版社，1999.9
(大中华文库)
ISBN 7-5438-2088-9

Ⅰ.论… Ⅱ.①杨… ②韦… Ⅲ.论语-汉、英 Ⅳ.B222.22

中国版本图书馆CIP数据核字(1999)第42253号

责任编辑：阳 天 莫 艳
审 校：刘重德

大中华文库
论 语
韦利 英译
杨伯峻 今译

出版发行者：
湖南人民出版社
(湖南长沙银盆南路78号)
邮政编码410006
外文出版社
(中国北京百万庄大街24号)
邮政编码100037
http://www.flp.com.cn
制版、排版者：
湖南省新华印刷三厂（湖南新华精品印务有限公司）
印制者：
深圳当纳利旭日印刷有限公司
开本：960×640 1/16（精装） 印张：26 印数：1-3000
1999年第1版第1次印刷
(汉英)
ISBN 7-5438-2088-9/B·49
定价：48.00元